Challenging Kids to Live Courageously as God's Special Agents

Gospel Light's Kids@Time

AGENTS IN ACTION

This 13-Session Course Is Perfect for:
- Special Summer Programming
- Small and Large Groups
- Preschool and Elementary Children, Ages 3 to 12

Includes Agent Music CD

REPRODUCIBLE

Gospel Light

How to Make Clean Copies from This Book

You may make copies of portions of this book with a clean conscience if

However, it is ILLEGAL for you to make copies if

>> you (or someone in your organization) are the original purchaser;

>> you are using the copies you make for a noncommercial purpose (such as teaching or promoting your ministry) within your church or organization;

>> you follow the instructions provided in this book.

>> you are using the material to promote, advertise or sell a product or service other than for ministry fund-raising;

>> you are using the material in or on a product for sale; or

>> you or your organization are not the original purchaser of this book.

By following these guidelines you help us keep our products affordable.
Thank you,
Gospel Light

Permission to make photocopies of or to reproduce by any other mechanical or electronic means in whole or in part any designated* page, illustration or activity in this book is granted only to the original purchaser and is intended for noncommercial use within a church or other Christian organization. None of the material in this book, not even those pages with permission to photocopy, may be reproduced for any commercial promotion, advertising or sale of a product or service or to share with any other persons, churches or organizations. Sharing of the material in this book with other churches or organizations not owned or controlled by the original purchaser is also prohibited. All rights reserved.

* Do not make any copies from this book unless you adhere strictly to the guidelines found on this page. Only pages with the following notation can be legally reproduced:

© 2007 Gospel Light. Permission to photocopy granted. *Agents in Action*

Senior Managing Editor, Sheryl Haystead • **Contributing Writers,** Mary Davis, Heidi Shelton-Jenck, Alison Simpson • **Contributing Editors,** Debbie Barber, Gwen Cram, Vivian Donner, Janis Halverson, Heather Johnston, Veronica Neal, Kelly Palmer, Susan Wood • **Art Directors,** Lenndy Pollard, Christina Renée Sharp, Samantha A. Hsu • **Designer,** Christina Renée Sharp

Founder, Dr. Henrietta Mears • **Publisher,** William T. Greig • **Senior Consulting Publisher,** Dr. Elmer L. Towns • **Senior Consulting Editor,** Wesley Haystead, M.S.Ed. • **Senior Editor, Biblical and Theological Issues,** Bayard Taylor, M.Div.

Scripture quotations are taken from the *Holy Bible, New International Version®*. Copyright © 1973, 1978, 1984 by International Bible Society. Used by permission of Zondervan Publishing House. All rights reserved.

© 2007 Gospel Light, Ventura, CA 93006. All rights reserved. Printed in the U.S.A.

How to Use This Guide

If you are a teacher or a small-group leader, follow these simple steps to lead your class in an exploration of what it means to live courageously as God's disciples in real-life situations.

1. Read "*Agents in Action* Overview" on pages 9-10 and the "*Agents in Action* Scope and Sequence" on page 11 to get an understanding of the purpose and goals of this curriculum.

2. Look at "Advice and Answers for Schedule Planning" on pages 14-18, choose the schedule that best fits your situation and decide which centers you will include.

3. Read the teaching tips articles (pp. 34-42) for each center you will lead, taking note of the ways you can make each center an effective learning experience for the kids in your group.

If you are the children's director or coordinator of *Agents in Action*, follow the above steps and add a few more!

1. Pay special attention to "Getting and Keeping the Very Best Staff" on pages 19-21. Remember to start recruiting early—several months before *Agents in Action* begins.

2. Read "Outreach Ideas," "Partnering with Parents," "Decorating Ideas" and "Theme Ideas" on pages 26-33 for exciting ideas to motivate interest in Agents in Action, special ways to involve parents, eye-catching decorating ideas and more!

3. Photocopy the materials you need for each session and distribute to small-group leaders or teachers.

Combining preschoolers and elementary-age children in one small group of children? Get advice for effective teaching of mixed ages by reading "Teaching Preschoolers and Elementary Children Together" on pages 24-25.

© 2007 Gospel Light. Permission to photocopy granted. *Agents in Action*

Contents

How to Use This Guide 3

Coordinator Information 7

This section contains concise and practical information that can help you plan and lead the *Agents in Action* program

Agents in Action Overview 9

Agents in Action Scope and Sequence 11

Leading a Child to Christ 12

Advice and Answers for Schedule Planning 14

Getting and Keeping the Very Best Staff 19

Publicity Guidelines and Schedule 22

Teaching Preschoolers and Elementary Children Together 24

Outreach Ideas 26

Partnering with Parents 27

Decorating Ideas 29

Theme Ideas 33

Bible Story Center Tips 34

Art Center Tips 36

Game Center Tips 37

Coloring/Puzzle Center Tips 39

Worship Center Tips 40

Agents in Action Lessons 43

In this section are 13 lessons to help your students discover what it means to live courageously as God's disciples in real-life situations.

Lesson 1 Families 45

Lesson 2 Fighting 59

Lesson 3 Honesty 73

Lesson 4 Fear 87

Lesson 5 Future 101

Lesson 6 Temptation 115

Lesson 7 Bullies 129

Lesson 8 Choices 143

Lesson 9 Money 157

Lesson 10 Friends 171

Lesson 11 Evangelism 185

Lesson 12 Getting Even 199

Lesson 13 Trash Talk 213

Resources 227

This section includes helpful resources that you can customize for use in your church.

Certificates 229

Family Talk 231

Parent Letters 232

Patterns 234

Planning Page 238

Publicity Flyers 239

Puzzle Answers 242

Song Charts 246

Coordinator Information

This section contains concise and practical information that can help you plan and lead the *Agents in Action* program. Included in this section is an overview of the course, the scope and sequence, guidelines for recruiting, and publicity suggestions, as well as tips for each of the activity centers in this program.

Agents in Action Overview

Agents in Action welcomes you to a 13-lesson adventure for children ages 3-12. Daily missions for God as His special agents will challenge children to live courageously as His disciples.

The Purpose and Goals

The purpose of *Agents in Action* is to help children develop skills that will help them meet the challenges they face and the choices they will have to make in today's world. Even very young children can learn ways of showing love and obedience for God in everyday life. This course is designed to help both preschool- and elementary-age children identify the daily missions God gives His disciples.

Each session provides the opportunity to lead children in discovering 13 topics of study in which they can discover key attitudes and actions exhibited by God's disciples. As children study each lesson's Bible verse—all words of Jesus—they will begin to develop an understanding of how to live as God's disciples in the situations of everyday life (see p. 11 for a complete scope and sequence).

The stories include a variety of both Old and New Testament Bible characters that will lead children to discover key ways in which they can live as disciples for God. For example, children will travel with Ruth to her future in a new land and learn of God's promise to be with them, no matter what happens now or in the future. They will walk in the footsteps of Elisha to discover how to stand up to bullies. Children will be challenged to follow Jesus' example of unselfish attitudes and actions as they seek to get along with family members. They will catch the vision of Paul's efforts to spread the good news of the gospel. Woven throughout these lessons is the love God has for His children, and how that love is the motivation for the courageous and compassionate ways He wants us to live.

As children focus on the words of Jesus (simplified for preschoolers), they will be led to consider the ways in which they can follow His example. Each lesson's Bible verse gives children a truth on which the daily missions of special agents for God are founded. Children will learn such truths as the characteristics of peacemakers, the source of generosity with money and possessions, the benefit of treating others in the same way you would like to be treated and the security God's disciples have because of His awesome promises.

After participating in 13 *Agents in Action* sessions, your children will discover significant ways to live every day as special agents for God—His courageous disciples.

Special Features

>> Each Bible story offers creative storytelling techniques to involve children in an active way. In addition, a unique Special Agent Option gives the teacher of elementary-age children a hidden message or code to solve to help children discover the lesson's daily mission.

>> Because children learn in diverse ways, *Agents in Action* is filled with a variety of activities to appeal to kids' many learning styles. In each session, the children may participate in active games and creative art activities that will help them express what they are learning.

Overview continued...

>> The Worship Center provides ideas for worship and prayer as well as lively, kid-appealing games and songs.

>> In each lesson, Bonus Theme Ideas are suggested to help create even more special-agent excitement for your students and leaders—and to keep attendance and enthusiasm high. You'll find a variety of creative activities designed for special agents, decorating ideas, snacks, games and more!

>> Get a quick overview of each lesson's activities by referring to the Planning Page. This page can also function as a supply list for quickly collecting the materials your leaders and teachers need.

Best of all, you'll appreciate the flexibility of this course! Every church and every group of children is different. Whether you are a large church with separate groups for each age level or a small church that combines preschoolers and elementary-age children together in one group, you can use this curriculum to meet your needs. The activity and schedule choices provide you with the opportunity to customize the lesson to make a perfect fit for your church. You'll find the resources you need to involve children and build relationships with them. *Agents in Action* can help you make the difference between leading kids in fun activities and guiding them in life-changing lessons so that God's daily missions for His disciples can be accomplished in their lives.

The *Agent* Music CD offers fresh and fun music that will keep your kids singing all week long about what it means to live as God's special agents. Make a copy for every child to take home!

Agents in Action — Scope and Sequence

	Lesson Topic	Life Focus	Bible Story	Memory Verse	Early Childhood Adaptation
1	**Families**	My unselfish actions help me live like Jesus and get along with my family.	Abraham's Unselfish Action Genesis 13:1-18	"Whoever wants to become great among you must be your servant." Matthew 20:26	"Serve others."
2	**Fighting**	When I feel like fighting, I can stop and ask for God's help to know how to make peace.	Isaac Makes Peace Genesis 26:12-33	"Blessed are the peacemakers, for they will be called sons of God." Matthew 5:9	"Live in peace."
3	**Honesty**	Obeying God's command to be honest helps others trust me.	Jacob's Lies Lead to Trouble Genesis 27:1-26	"Do not steal, do not give false testimony." Matthew 19:18	"Be honest."
4	**Fear**	When I'm afraid or worried, I can trust in God to help me.	Gideon Needs Proof Judges 6—7	"Do not let your hearts be troubled. Trust in God; trust also in me." John 14:1	"Trust in God's care."
5	**Future**	God promises to be with me, no matter what happens now or in the future.	Ruth's Adventure Ruth	"I am with you always, to the very end of the age." Matthew 28:20	"God is always with you."
6	**Temptation**	I can pray to God for help in saying no to temptation and living in right ways.	David Resists Temptation 1 Samuel 24:1-22; 26	"Lead us not into temptation, but deliver us from the evil one." Matthew 6:13	"Help me to do what is right."
7	**Bullies**	Treating others kindly, even while protecting myself, helps me show God's love to others.	Elisha's Surprise 2 Kings 6:8-23	"I tell you: Love your enemies and pray for those who persecute you." Matthew 5:44	"Love others and pray for them."
8	**Choices**	God's Word can help me make right choices and build good habits.	Sow and Grow Mark 4:1-20	"If you love me, you will obey what I command." John 14:15	"Love God and obey His commands."
9	**Money**	I can be generous with my money and possessions to show my thankfulness for God's gifts to me.	Bigger, Better Barns Luke 12:13-21	"Freely you have received, freely give." Matthew 10:8	"Be glad to give to others."
10	**Friends**	Obeying God's command to treat others like I want to be treated will help me make and keep my friends.	Widows in Need Acts 6:1-7	"So in everything, do to others what you would have them do to you." Matthew 7:12	"Treat others the same way you want to be treated."
11	**Evangelism**	My actions and words can be a witness for Jesus, helping others see and understand what it means to be a Christian.	Lydia Hears Good News Acts 16:6-15	"Let your light shine before men, that they may see your good deeds and praise your Father in heaven." Matthew 5:16	"Your good actions help others learn about God."
12	**Getting Even**	Because God forgives me, I can show mercy and forgive others who have treated me wrongly.	Philemon's Choice Philemon	"Be merciful, just as your Father is merciful." Luke 6:36	"Be merciful."
13	**Trash Talk**	Remembering my love for Jesus helps me talk to others in ways that show His love to them.	Word Power James 3:2-12	"By this all men will know that you are my disciples, if you love one another." John 13:35	"Love Jesus and show His love to others."

© 2007 Gospel Light. Permission to photocopy granted. *Agents in Action*

Leading a Child to Christ

Many adult Christians look back to their childhood years as the time when they accepted Christ as Savior. As children mature, they will grow in their understanding of the difference between right and wrong. They will also develop a sense of their own need for forgiveness and feel a growing desire to have a personal relationship with God.

However, the younger the child is the more limited he or she will be in understanding abstract terms. Children of all ages are likely to be inconsistent in following through on their intentions and commitments. Therefore, they need thoughtful, patient guidance in coming to know Christ personally and continuing to grow in Him.

Pray

Ask God to prepare the students in your group to receive the good news about Jesus and to prepare you to communicate effectively with them.

Present the Good News

Use words and phrases that students understand. Avoid symbolism that will confuse these literal-minded thinkers. Remember that each child's learning will be at a different place on the spectrum of understanding. Discuss the following points slowly enough to allow time for thinking and comprehending:

a. God wants you to become His child. Do you know why God wants you in His family? (See 1 John 3:1.)

b. You and I and all the people in the world have done wrong things. The Bible word for doing wrong is "sin." What do you think should happen to us when we sin? (See Romans 6:23.)

c. God loves you so much, He sent His Son to die on the cross for your sins. Because Jesus never sinned, He is the only One who can take the punishment for your sins. On the third day after Jesus died, God brought Him back to life. (See 1 Corinthians 15:3-5; 1 John 4:14.)

d. Are you sorry for your sins? Tell God that you are. Do you believe Jesus died to take the punishment for your sins? If you tell God you are sorry for your sins and tell Him you do believe and accept Jesus' death to take away your sins, God forgives all your sin. (See 1 John 1:9.)

e. The Bible says that when you believe that Jesus is God's Son and that He is alive today, you receive God's gift of eternal life. This gift makes you a child of God. This means God is with you now and forever. (See John 3:16.)

Give students many opportunities to think about what it means to be a Christian; expose them to a variety of lessons and descriptions of the meaning of salvation to aid their understanding.

Talk Personally with the Student

Talking about salvation one-on-one creates the opportunity to ask and answer questions. Ask questions that move the student beyond simple yes or no answers or recitation of memorized information. Ask open-ended, what-do-you-think questions such as:

>> "Why do you think it's important to . . . ?"

>> "What are some things you really like about Jesus?"

>> "Why do you think that Jesus had to die because of wrong things you and I have done?"

>> "What difference do you think it makes for a person to be forgiven?"

When students use abstract terms or phrases they have learned previously, such as "accepting Christ into my heart," ask them to tell you what the term or phrase means in different words. Answers to these open-ended questions will help you discern how much the student does or does not understand.

Offer Opportunities Without Pressure

Children normally desire to please adults. This characteristic makes them vulnerable to being unintentionally manipulated by well-meaning adults. A good way to guard against coercing a student's response is to simply pause periodically and ask, "Would you like to hear more about this now or at another time?" Loving acceptance of the student, even when he or she is not fully interested in pursuing the matter, is crucial in building and maintaining positive attitudes toward becoming part of God's family.

Give Time to Think and Pray

There is great value in encouraging a student to think and pray about what you have said before making a response. Also allow moments for quiet thinking about questions you have asked.

Respect the Student's Response

Whether or not a student declares faith in Jesus Christ, there is a need for adults to accept the student's action. There is also a need to realize that a student's initial responses to Jesus are just the beginning of a lifelong process of growing in the faith.

Guide the Student in Further Growth

There are several important parts in the nurturing process.

a. Talk regularly about your relationship with God. As you talk about your relationship, the student will begin to feel that it's OK to talk about such things. Then you can comfortably ask the student to share his or her thoughts and feelings, and you can encourage the student to ask questions of you.

b. Prepare the student to deal with doubts. Emphasize that certainty about salvation is not dependent on our feelings or doing enough good deeds. Show the student places in God's Word that clearly declare that salvation comes by grace through faith. (See John 1:12; Ephesians 2:8-9; Hebrews 11:6; 1 John 5:11.)

c. Teach the student to confess all sins. This means agreeing with God that we really have sinned. Assure the student that confession always results in forgiveness. (See 1 John 1:9.)

The Preschool Child and Salvation

>> The young child is easily attracted to Jesus. Jesus is a warm, sympathetic person who obviously likes children, and children readily like Him. These early perceptions prepare the foundation for the child to receive Christ as Savior and to desire to follow His example in godly living. While some preschoolers may indeed pray to become a member of God's family, accepting Jesus as their Savior, expect wide variation in children's readiness for this important step. Allow the Holy Spirit room to work within His own timetable.

>> Talk simply. Phrases such as "born again" or "Jesus in my heart" are symbolic and far beyond a young child's understanding. Focus on how God makes people a part of His family.

>> Present the love of Jesus by both your actions and your words in order to lay a foundation for a child to receive Christ as Savior. Look for opportunities in every lesson to talk with a young child who wants to know more about Jesus.

Advice and Answers for Schedule Planning

Begin your planning for *Agents in Action* by choosing when you will schedule the program. This 13-lesson curriculum can be used effectively for second-hour programs, midweek programs, Sunday School or summertime Sunday-morning or weekday programs.

No matter when or where *Agents in Action* takes place, there are two main format options—Self-Contained Groups and the Learning Center Plan. Read the following descriptions and select the learning format that fits your needs:

Self-Contained Groups

If you are confined to a single room or have a small number of children, Self-Contained Groups may be your best option. In this format, groups of six to eight students are formed. Each group has a teacher who leads his or her group in the activities. (If the size of the group is larger, additional teachers or helpers are needed.)

The greatest benefit of Self-Contained Groups is that teachers are able to form meaningful relationships with the students because they remain together during the entire session.

Self-Contained Groups are often a good option for small churches.

Learning Center Plan

The Learning Center Plan offers an exciting recruiting and schedule variation for *Agents in Action*. In this plan, each teacher prepares and leads only one activity. Guides (adults, teenagers or even responsible seventh and eighth graders) lead groups of students to rotate among the centers (Bible Story, Art, Game, etc.). In other words, each teacher leads only one part of the lesson. Each teacher's responsibility for only one center simplifies teacher preparation and often improves teaching effectiveness, as well as making it easier to recruit teachers. The Learning Center Plan also keeps inexperienced teachers from feeling overwhelmed. Teachers who don't enjoy leading games or who are apprehensive about telling Bible stories can leave those tasks to others more skilled in those areas.

The Learning Center Plan is often a good option for medium or large churches.

What do students do and who leads them?

>> Students are placed in small permanent groups (six to eight children is the best size). As much as possible, form groups with children of similar ages.

>> Each group has at least one guide who leads the group to various centers. (Color code name tags for easy group identification.)

>> Each group, along with its guide(s), visits each center during each session. All groups participate at once in the Worship Center.

>> If you have large numbers of children, two groups may participate in one center at the same time.

If you want to combine preschool and elementary children in the same group, read "Teaching Preschoolers and Elementary Children Together" on pages 24-25.

What do teachers do?

>> Each teacher takes responsibility for one center, remaining at the center and instructing each group as it visits the center. (Note: If both preschool and elementary-age children visit the same center, teachers modify activities as shown in each lesson.)

>> During the Worship Center, teachers (and guides) sit with students and participate with them in the activities.

What are the centers?

>> One room or outside area is designated for each of the *Agents in Action* learning centers. Post a large sign to identify each center.

>> Decorate centers (see Decorating Ideas on pp. 29-32) and give centers fun, interesting names such as Daily Mission Headquarters for the Bible Story Center, Tech Lab for the Art Center, Special Agent Adventure for the Game Center, Training Ops for the Coloring/Puzzle Center or Real Time Cam Center for the Worship Center. Choose from the centers suggested in the following diagram:

(Optional: The Bonus Theme Ideas offered in each session can be used as an additional learning center.)

How do I plan the time schedule?

>> The centers in *Agents in Action* can be taught in any order, but each center should last the same amount of time. For example, in a one-hour program, groups would remain in each center for 15 minutes and groups would be able to participate in three centers. (Add 5 minutes to the first center each group attends to provide for a brief welcome time.)

>> Allow 5 minutes for groups to move from center to center, following a preestablished route.

If you have more than one hour for each session, additional centers may be added or the time in each center may be lengthened (generally it is best to limit the time in each center to a maximum of 25 minutes in order to keep student interest high). If you have less than one hour for each session, use the Bible Story Center and one or two other centers of your own choosing.

Use the chart below as an example of how to schedule groups. As the number of children in your program grows, add teachers or helpers to each center to maintain a ratio of one leader for every six to eight children. You may also add duplicate centers.

Sample One-Hour Schedule

	11:00-11:20	11:25-11:40	11:45-12:00
Group 1	Welcome and Bible Story Center	Game Center	Worship Center
Group 2	Welcome and Game Center	Bible Story Center	Worship Center

How do I make the Learning Center Plan run smoothly?

>> Predetermine the route each group will travel, including room and building entrances and exits. Ask guides to walk their routes in advance to become familiar with all locations.

>> Establish a signal for notifying groups when it's time to move to the next center.

>> Provide labeled tables or other areas where students may leave their projects and belongings during the session.

>> Provide color-coded name tags to identify each group.

Schedule Options

You can adapt the sample schedule on page 16 to the needs and interests of your church. Other centers can be added or substituted in order to meet the needs of younger or older students. In addition to the centers suggested in this course, many churches include centers for such things as snacks, recreational outdoor games (soccer, baseball, volleyball), children's choir and elective classes (cooking, woodworking, etc.).

When planning the schedule, remember to include a variety of activities in an order that will meet the needs of children. For example, if students have been sitting in the adult worship service before coming to *Agents in Action*, plan an active center at the beginning of the session. If students attend *Agents in Action* after being in Sunday School, provide a snack at the beginning of the session.

For help in planning each session's schedule, give each leader and teacher a copy of the planning page on page 238.

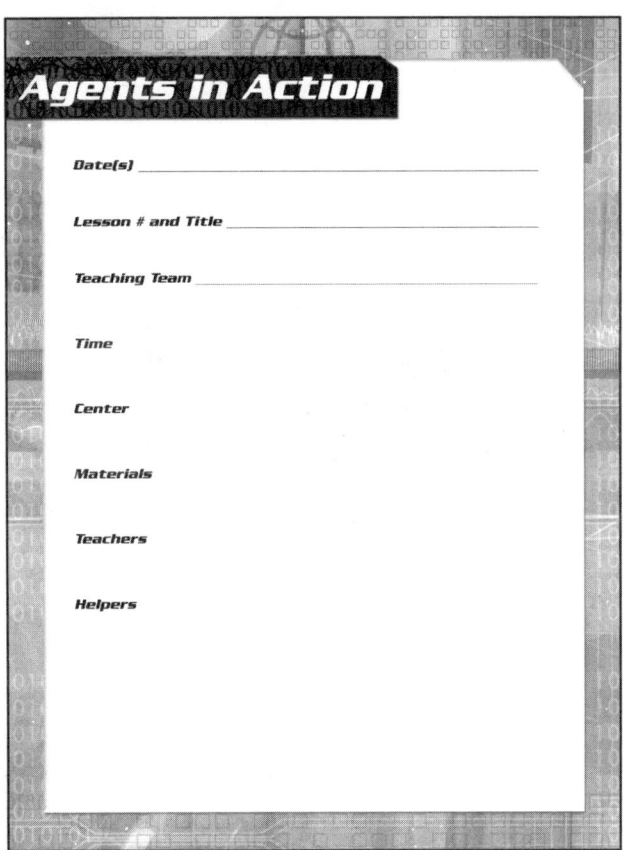

Option 1
(45-60 minutes)

Worship Center
15 minutes

Bible Story Center
15-20 minutes

Game or Art Center
15-20 minutes

Option 2
(60-75 minutes)

Worship Center
15 minutes

Bible Story Center
15-20 minutes

Game Center
15-20 minutes

Art Center
15-20 minutes

Option 3
(75-90 minutes)

Adult Worship Service
15 minutes

Game Center
15-20 minutes

Bible Story Center
15-20 minutes

Art Center
15-20 minutes

Worship Center
15 minutes

Option 4
(75-90 minutes)

Game Center
15-20 minutes

Bible Story Center
15-20 minutes

Art Center
15-20 minutes

Worship Center
15 minutes

Snack Time
15 minutes

Note: If you are teaching only preschoolers, plan your centers for a maximum of 15 minutes and consider adding additional centers. If you are teaching only elementary-age children, consider expanding your centers from 20 to 25 minutes.

Getting and Keeping the Very Best Staff

One of the most important elements in staffing a successful program is planning how you will recruit and organize your staff. However you do it, keep in mind that the best learning and the most fun take place when there is a teacher or helper for every six to eight children.

The optimum plan for staffing is to have the same teachers in place for the entire course. Both teachers and children benefit from regular interaction. Having long-term teachers creates a wonderful opportunity for spiritual growth in students as they build relationships with adults who are faithful in demonstrating God's love.

While it may be easier to recruit teachers to teach one session at a time, such short-term staffing creates other problems. Many churches have found that rotating teachers frequently not only makes learning and growth difficult for children, but it also creates a heavy workload in administration (distributing curriculum, orienting a constant stream of new teachers, etc.).

Here are some options if long-term commitment is difficult in your situation.

>> Ask teachers to teach for a shorter time period—four weeks at a time instead of 13 weeks.

>> Find two teams of teachers and helpers who will each teach for two weeks at a time. Then plan to rotate the two teams so that they alternate teaching two weeks at a time. During the course of the program, teachers and children become familiar with each other and can benefit from regular interaction.

>> If you must rotate some teachers, make sure that you have a number of consistent people who can greet and interact with children and parents on a weekly basis.

Recruiting Tips

Recruiting teachers and helpers is one of the key tasks to making *Agents in Action* an effective and fun learning experience for the children of your church and community. Keep the following tips in mind as you seek the volunteers and then match their talents to the tasks to be done:

>> Pray for guidance in finding the people God wants to serve in this ministry.

> If you are using *Agents in Action* with preschoolers, they will benefit greatly from consistent teachers. Young children need the security of familiar faces. This security creates a familiar and positive atmosphere, resulting in fewer separation and/or discipline problems and more positive learning!

>> Start early—at least three months before the *Agents in Action* program begins!

>> Keep all the leaders of all your children's ministries aware of and praying about staffing needs.

>> Develop a written job description for each staff position.

>> Make a list of potential teachers and helpers. Consider a wide variety of sources for volunteers: church membership list, new members' classes, suggestions from adult teachers or leaders, lists of previous and current teachers and survey forms. Get recommendations from present teachers. Don't overlook singles, senior citizens, youth and collegians. Some churches ask parents to teach during the summer months, giving school-year teachers a break. Be sure to follow your church's established procedures for screening volunteers.

>> Look for team members with interests and abilities in specific areas. For example, the teaching team for 24 children might consist of three adults: one who prepares and leads the Bible Story Center each week, one who prepares and guides the Game Center and a third who prepares and leads the Worship Center. While each team member has the primary responsibility to lead only one center, all team members are involved throughout the session as helpers.

>> Recruit a separate team of teachers and leaders for each center. Each team might consist of two or more adults who enjoy teaching together, or consider asking a family with teenagers to work together to form a teaching team.

>> Prayerfully prioritize your prospect list. Determine which job description best fits each person's strengths and gifts.

>> Personally contact the prospects. Sending a personal letter or a flyer (see p. 21) to each prospect or calling the prospect are good first steps. Follow up to answer any questions or to see if the prospect has made a decision. Show the prospect the *Agents in Action* manual and *Agent* Music CD. Ask the prospective volunteer what he or she would most enjoy doing as a leader or teacher in *Agents in Action*.

>> Provide new volunteers with all the needed materials, forms, helpful hints and training that will help them to succeed. For all teachers and helpers, you may want to schedule one or more training meetings at which you distribute curriculum, review the schedule and procedures, sing the songs together, etc.

>> During the volunteer's time of service, make sure the volunteer knows who will be available to answer questions or lend a helping hand. Look for specific actions and services contributed by the volunteer and offer your thanks!

>> Plan a thank-you brunch or dinner for teachers and their families. Even if they don't attend, they'll be grateful for your appreciation!

Recruiting Announcements

The team members who will be your *Agents in Action* teachers and helpers will appreciate clear, concise information about the program—and a little added inspiration couldn't hurt! Here are some attention-grabbing recruiting announcements.

Calling All... Agents in Action!

Your mission is to join in on all the action of kids who are discovering how to live as God's disciples every day. We're now taking applications for leaders and teachers who can show God's love to kids, use their imaginations and have fun uncovering the daily missions of special agents for God.

Agents in Action starts on

_____

and continues through _____

at _____

Accomplish the Mission!

_____ _____
(date)   (date)

_____
(times)

Come join a team of special agents on a 13-week discovery of our daily missions for God!

Agents in Action has fresh new songs, fun games, worship activities and great Bible stories that will give kids new ways to learn what it means to live courageously as God's disciples. But that's not all! You'll keep kids coming back for more through awesome art projects, tasty snacks, wacky games and more!

Act now to ensure your spot as an agent in this 13-week adventure!

Publicity Guidelines and Schedule

Well-planned publicity is critical to the success of any event, so take time to carefully schedule each part of your publicity plan. Publicity ideas are endless (bulletin-board displays, banners, coloring poster contests, parent letters, etc.), but be sure to include these basics: church bulletin and newsletter announcements, posters and flyers. Here is a suggested schedule:

12 Weeks Before:
- Determine the exact dates on which each publicity piece will be released.
- Assign publicity tasks.

8 Weeks Before:
- Print a teaser announcement in your church bulletin and/or newsletter.

6 Weeks Before:
- Display posters in well-traveled areas at your church facility and in your community.

4 Weeks Before:
- Print information about *Agents in Action* in your church newsletter and mail flyers to children.
- Print announcements in your church bulletin on a weekly basis.

1 to 3 Weeks Before:
- Continue bulletin announcements.
- Make verbal announcements during church worship services.

Publicity Ideas

Posters and Flyers

Use the posters and flyers on pages 239-241 to get the attention of children and families and invite them to participate in *Agents in Action*. You may also use the art on pages 234-237 to make your own posters and flyers, telling information about *Agents in Action*. Display the posters in a variety of locations around your church.

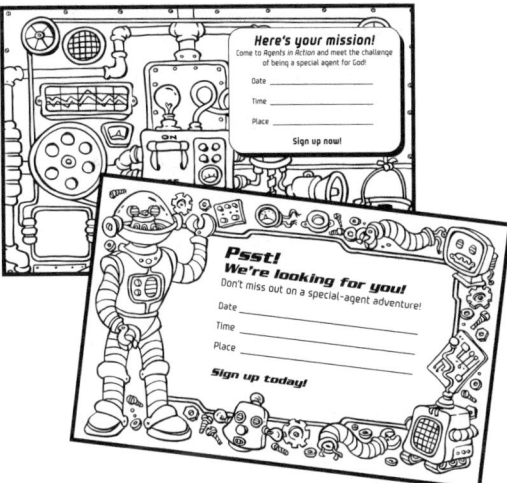

Church Website

Add information about *Agents in Action* to your church's website. Consider adding an online registration feature and a course outline and schedule that will help parents become familiar with the course. Create interest in *Agents in Action* by adding a photo of several kids and teachers dressed in theme-related clothing (bright T-shirt, black jacket, sunglasses, etc.).

Information Booth

Decorate a booth or table in the church lobby from which to recruit teachers and helpers and preregister children. Decorate the booth or table with a special-agent motif (see "Decorating Ideas" on pp. 29-32). Prepare promotional flyers, registration forms and volunteer sign-up sheets for use at the booth.

Kickoff Event

Prepare for and publicize the upcoming *Agents in Action* course with a kickoff event. Schedule the kickoff event two to three weeks before *Agents in Action* begins. Invite children and their parents to discover what the fun is all about. Publicize the event by distributing flyers to families in your church and community. Transform your church parking lot or a large multipurpose room into a special-agent mission command center. Set up three or four fun special-agent games or activities and offer a snack or two. Choose ideas from the Bonus Theme Ideas suggested in each lesson. Place a registration booth near the center of all the action so it is convenient for parents to register their children. Display flyers and posters at the booth.

>> Each activity needs at least one adult or older teenager to be in charge. Encourage all adult and teen helpers to dress in theme-related clothing.

>> Consider asking individual families in your church to sponsor activities. Each family would be responsible for purchasing supplies, setting up the activity and leading the activity during the event. In addition to having people who lead activities, have several helpers greet parents and encourage children to try an activity that is lacking participation.

>> Each activity needs a designated area. In most situations, the activities can be set up outside, preferably on a lawn. One simple way to mark each area is with stakes in each corner. Then tie a rope from stake to stake, marking the boundaries of the area. If using a parking lot, draw boundaries for each area with chalk. Each activity area needs a large sign identifying the activity. Awnings and tents may also be used to create your marketplace. Restrooms need to be open and clearly marked.

Teaching Preschoolers and Elementary Children Together

Whenever possible, it's recommended that you group preschool- and elementary-age children separately for *Agents in Action*. Teaching is most effective when children are grouped with others at similar developmental levels. While there is some benefit in mixing children of various ages together, it is difficult to prevent the older children from feeling that the activities are "baby" stuff because the younger kids are also involved. Even among children of similar ages, you are likely to find a variety of skills and abilities.

However, if there aren't enough children to form separate groups for preschool- and elementary-age children, you may need to combine children of both age levels together. The tips and ideas in *Agents in Action* will help you combine children from a wide variety of ages and still provide effective teaching.

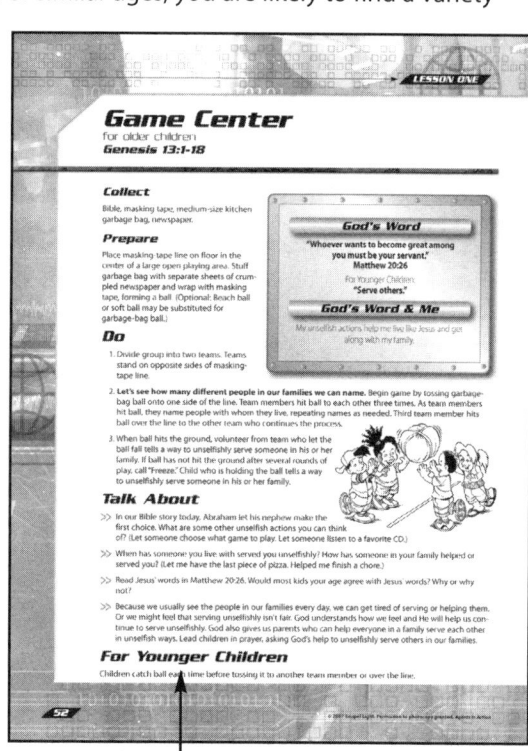

Game and Art Center Tips

>> Use the games and art activity ideas suggested for the age level of the majority of children in your class. If needed, modify the games and art activities as suggested in each lesson for either older (elementary) or younger (preschool) children. The modifications use the same or similar materials so that you don't have to collect and prepare an entirely new set of materials. If you are using this material with younger preschoolers, additional modification to the games and art activities may be needed, depending on the skill level of the children in your class.

>> Use the Bible memory verse that corresponds to the age of the majority of children in the group. However, in individual conversations with children, use the age-appropriate Bible memory verse, suggestions and discussion questions found in the lesson.

>> Have the older children help lead the games or have younger children cheer on their teams as the older children play.

Bible Story Center Tips

>> Even if children of varying ages are combined for art and game activities, consider keeping the Bible Story Center as a center through which small groups of children of similar ages rotate. Then the leader of the center can tailor the story to each particular group, ensuring that all children are taught the Bible story on their own level.

>> If you have primarily elementary-age children, use the Bible Story Center Option for Older Children. However, provide for preschoolers the lesson's coloring page as a way to involve them and extend their interest in the story.

>> If you have mostly preschoolers, use the Bible Story Center Option for Younger Children. Invite elementary-age children to participate by acting out the story or drawing Bible story murals.

Worship Center Tips

>> While preschoolers are not likely to feel comfortable volunteering for the fun team games and other activities, they will still enjoy cheering for their teams.

>> Make sure that the teachers and helpers of the preschoolers sit among the children to provide security and attention.

>> Set aside space for preschoolers to sit at the front of the Worship Center area so that they are able to see.

>> Make a copy of the *Agent* Music CD for each child to take home. Familiarity with the songs will help preschoolers feel comfortable in the large-group setting. Although pre-schoolers may not be able to remember all the words of a song, they will easily catch on to and sing the song's chorus and can still participate by doing the song's motions and/or by clapping or by playing rhythm instruments such as maracas. If a song doesn't include motions or clapping, add them.

Outreach Ideas

Because *Agents in Action* is packed with loads of exciting hands-on learning activities, you won't want any student to miss it! And because this program is also a great place for unchurched kids to learn about God in a relaxed, inviting atmosphere, you'll want to publicize it—even beyond your church! Here are ideas to help you not only plan to invite children to participate in *Agents in Action* but also to follow up on visitors.

Invitation Ideas

>> Keep accurate enrollment records for your ongoing children's programs. Several weeks prior to the beginning of *Agents in Action*, send flyers (see pp. 239-241) or make phone calls to children who have either stopped attending your church or who have visited recently.

>> Offer a small prize to any child who brings a friend to attend *Agents in Action*. (Note: Adapt one of the flyers on pp. 239-241 for use as an invitation children can give to friends.) Each week be prepared to welcome visitors by having a greeter(s) who can help visitors find the appropriate classrooms, make name tags available, and record contact information on registration forms. Consider recognizing visitors each session during the Worship Center. (Note: Prepare enough name tags so that visitors have same tags as other children.)

>> Plan with the adult ministry coordinator to offer a parenting or other special-interest class at the same time children will be participating in *Agents in Action*.

>> Make a large outdoor banner or paint a large sign and hang it in a visible place outside your church.

>> Mount flyers in businesses frequented by children and their families (grocery stores, laundromats, etc.) and on community bulletin boards.

Follow-Up

>> Invite parents to attend a special celebration as part of the final *Agents in Action* session (see invitation on p. 233). Children sing songs for their parents, families may tour classrooms and everyone enjoys a snack or potluck meal. Encourage teachers and leaders to make a special effort to introduce themselves to parents and look for natural opportunities to build friendships, answer questions about the church, etc.

>> During the 13 weeks of *Agents in Action*, encourage teachers and leaders to contact their students, including absentees, visitors or irregular attendees. Provide already-stamped postcards, prepared mailing labels, and address and phone lists.

>> Take one or more photos of children during *Agents in Action* and ask leaders and teachers to personally deliver photos to children's homes at the end of the program. (Obtain parent permission for use of photos.)

>> Make an *Agents in Action* Memory CD with lots of photos showing the variety of activities in which children participated. Send each CD to children who attended and include an invitation to other upcoming church programs.

>> Pray for the teachers, leaders and helpers and remind them to pray for the children in their groups, asking God to bring to their minds appropriate ways to keep in touch with the children and to nurture them in Christ.

Partnering with Parents

In Deuteronomy 6:7, God commanded parents to teach their children about Him "when you sit at home and when you walk along the road, when you lie down and when you get up." The most important learning in life takes place not in churches, schools or scout troops but in families. The hours and days parents and children spend together are the prime opportunities for building long-lasting spiritual foundations!

Choose one or more of the following ideas for ways you can help parents in their awesome responsibility of spiritually teaching their children:

>> Send home the Parent Letter (p. 232) to each parent at the beginning of the program and include a copy of the *Agents in Action* Scope and Sequence so that parents are aware of the content and goals of this course.

>> Offer a free or low-cost kid-friendly Bible to parents when they register their children for *Agents in Action*. Especially if your program will attract visitors or unchurched children, it's wise not to assume that every family will have a kid-friendly Bible.

>> Consider giving each parent a copy of the first page of each session. As parents read the devotional, they will develop an understanding not only of how they can model and demonstrate the focus of the session but also how they can talk with their children about the session's Bible truth.

>> If you don't use the Coloring Page or Puzzle Page in each session, send them home with children each week. Include an introductory letter with the first lesson's Coloring or Puzzle Page, explaining that these pages can provide an opportunity for parent and child to talk about the way in which Bible people came to know more about Jesus and how to be His followers.

>> Give parents of elementary-age children a copy of the Family Talk page (p. 231) and the *Agents in Action* Scope and Sequence page (p. 11). Encourage parents to use these with their children each week to read and study either the session's Bible story references or the Bible Memory Verse.

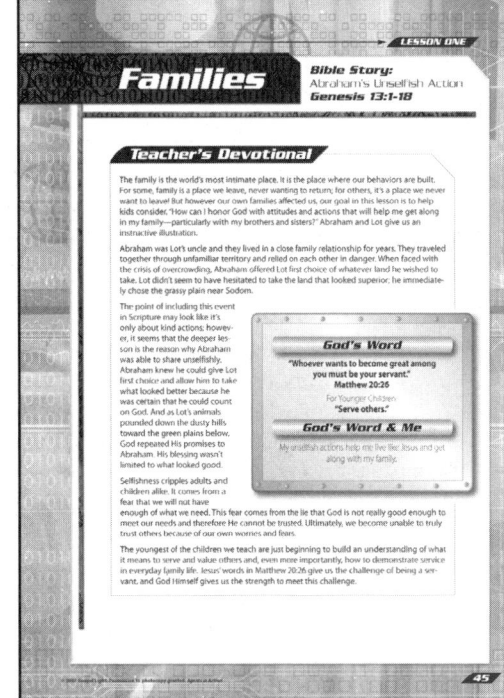

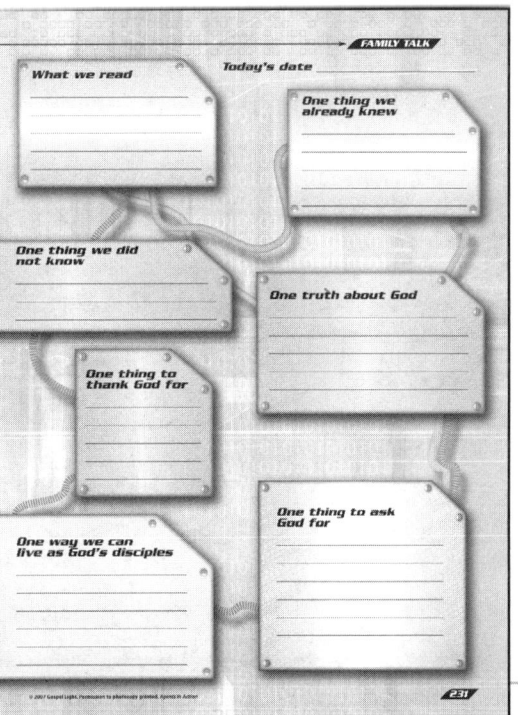

>> Make a copy of the *Agent* Music CD for families to listen to at home or in the car.

>> Ask parents to support *Agents in Action* by providing a special snack or by preparing the materials for an art activity or game. Invite the parent to join in on the fun! (See invitation on p. 233.) Observing the way in which teachers and leaders talk with children about the session's Bible content will model for parents effective ways of spiritual education. (Note: You may want to invite each parent to schedule a session when they will observe a full class session with his or her child.)

>> For the length of *Agents in Action*, invite parents to attend a parent support/prayer group that meets together twice a month or weekly to pray for their children, their teachers and each other. Enlist several parents to serve as hosts for this group. Hosts call parents to invite them to participate, arrange meeting space (homes, if possible), provide snacks, etc.

>> Establish a group Bible memory verse contest in which all parents and children work together to memorize a certain number of the memory verses from *Agents in Action*. If the goal is met, promise a party at which children create and eat snacks and play fun games (see Bonus Theme Ideas in each lesson). Using the patterns on pages 234-237, make a fun poster on which to record the number of verses memorized (large sheet of paper to which each parent and each child who can say a verse adds a mini-cell phone cutout, or a large sheet of poster to which each parent and each child who can say a verse adds a handprint). (Avoid identifying individual memory efforts.) Display the poster in a central area and have several people serve as Bible memory listeners. During arrival or dismissal, parents and children repeat verses.

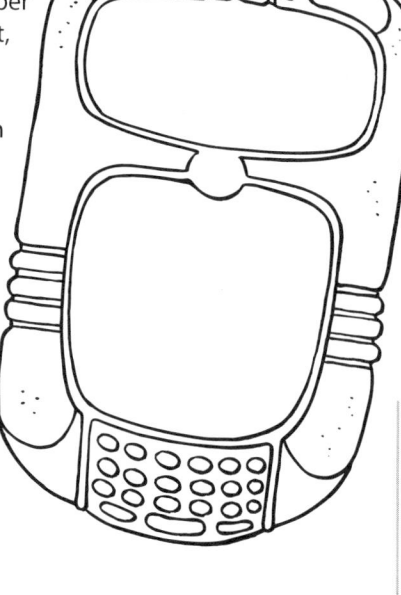

>> Plan Family Days several times throughout the course as suggested on the Bonus Theme Ideas pages in various lessons.

Decorating Ideas

No matter where you choose to hold your program, decorating the rooms where the action will take place can add fun and excitement to the proceedings! Children and teachers both will enjoy spending time in a theme-related atmosphere. A few simple decorations can transform an ordinary classroom into part of *Agents in Action*. Use a variety of real items and/or painted backdrops. Use the art patterns on pages 234-237 to help you create the perfect atmosphere for both fun and learning. Recruit people who love to plan and prepare for a party as your decorating team.

Before the program begins, invite your congregation to loan or donate theme-related items. Include any or all of the following: discarded cell phones, cameras, walkie talkies, head phones, binoculars, CD players, computers, toy robots, black jackets, hats, sunglasses and fake mustaches.

If you cannot leave decorations on the walls from week to week, consider simply attaching painted backdrops to rolling bulletin boards to be brought in during the sessions. You may also make murals on large sheets of butcher paper. Roll up murals after each session.

Create a Place

Name and label one or more rooms, especially if you are using a center method with this course. Places such as Daily Mission Headquarters, Tech Lab, Special Agent Adventure, Training Ops or Real Time Cam Center can create enthusiasm for this course. Decorate each room (or outdoor location) appropriately. Here are three ideas (see sketches on pages 30-32):

>> Daily Mission Headquarters

Create a room with all the eye-catching sights of a hi-tech command center. A large painted scene of a command center will add color and provide an interesting focal point. Talk with someone in your church or community who is familiar with painting backdrop scenes, and determine which material would work best for your backdrop (paper, fabric, cardboard, muslin and wood react differently to various kinds of paints). Make your backdrop at least 8x10 feet (2.4x3 m).

Photocopy the Headquarters Pattern (see p. 31) onto a transparency. Use a transparency projector to enlarge the design onto your backdrop material and trace the design with pen or pencil. Paint background colors first, adding details after the background has dried.

To really give your backdrop a hi-tech look, poke or drill holes in the backdrop and from the back, insert different colors of Christmas lights to make the control panels sparkle with real lights and color. Poke or drill holes in the starry sky and insert white twinkle lights to make the stars twinkle. (Optional: Place a table in front of the backdrop. On the table, set up one or more computer monitors with chairs. Set out several discarded tech items such as cell phones or head phones.)

If using as a classroom, cover tables with black butcher paper, and set out metallic or gel-ink pens for students to decorate tables. Play instrumental track from *Agent* Music CD in the background as children enter and exit this area.

>> Tech Lab

Play games or create art projects in a Tech Lab (see p. 32) where the many unusual gadgets used by special agents are created. Enlarge the Invention Diagram Patterns (see p. 234) onto butcher paper and attach them to the walls.

On tables and shelves, set out plenty of tinkering items such as small tools (screwdrivers, mallets, pliers, etc.), discarded appliance parts (springs, gears, bolts, hoses, wires, etc.), ordinary objects to transform into gadgets (radios, shoes, sunglasses, cell phones, etc.) and science equipment (telescope, microscope, beakers, etc.). Add a few science toys and novelties (Hoberman spheres, dippy birds, plasma lamps, lava lamps, gyroscopes) to your display. Complete the room with rope lights or Christmas lights.

>> Real Time Cam Center

Decorate a room or large area as a Real Time Cam Center (see below), where special agents monitor Earth activities to determine where agents are needed to carry out daily missions. Enlarge the pattern below onto butcher paper, paint and attach to one wall. Enlarge the various Earth-Cam Patterns (see p. 235) onto poster board or butcher paper, paint and attach to other walls of the room. (Optional: Cut out the center of each pattern. Use the patterns to frame posters or photographs of various locations on Earth [Statue of Liberty, Eiffel Tower, North Pole, desert, jungle, etc.]. At the bottom of each pattern, print the location shown on the monitor.)

Set real or paper clocks to display times in various cities around the world, and attach to the wall. Place a paper sign over each clock to indicate which city it is showing.

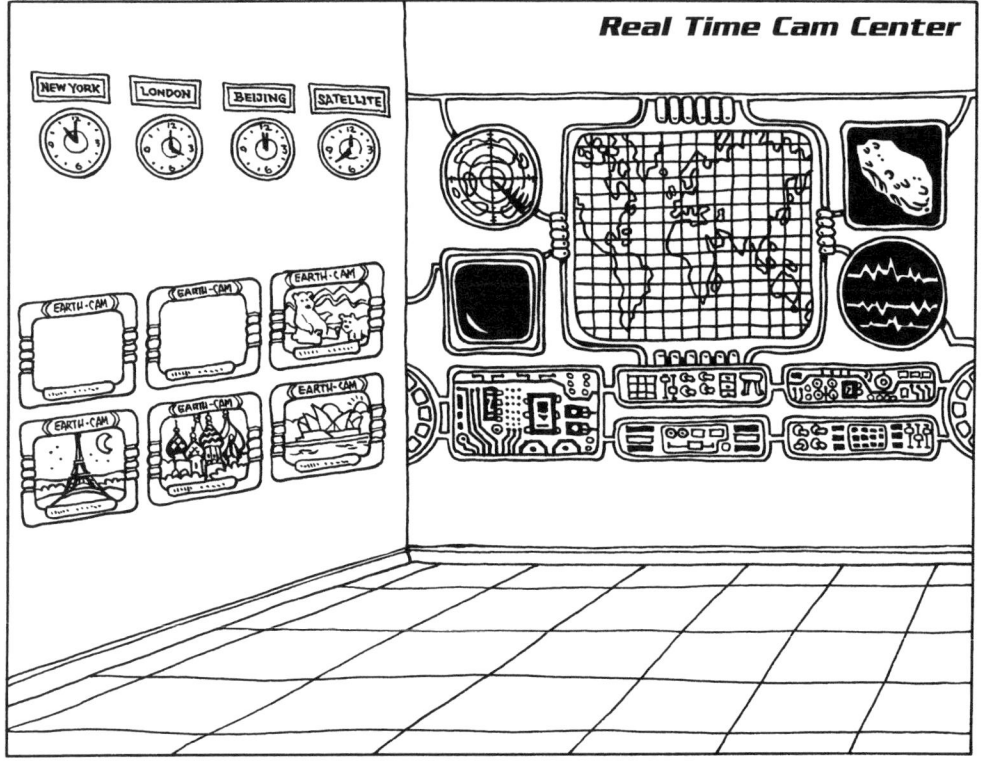

Daily Mission Headquarters

Tech Lab

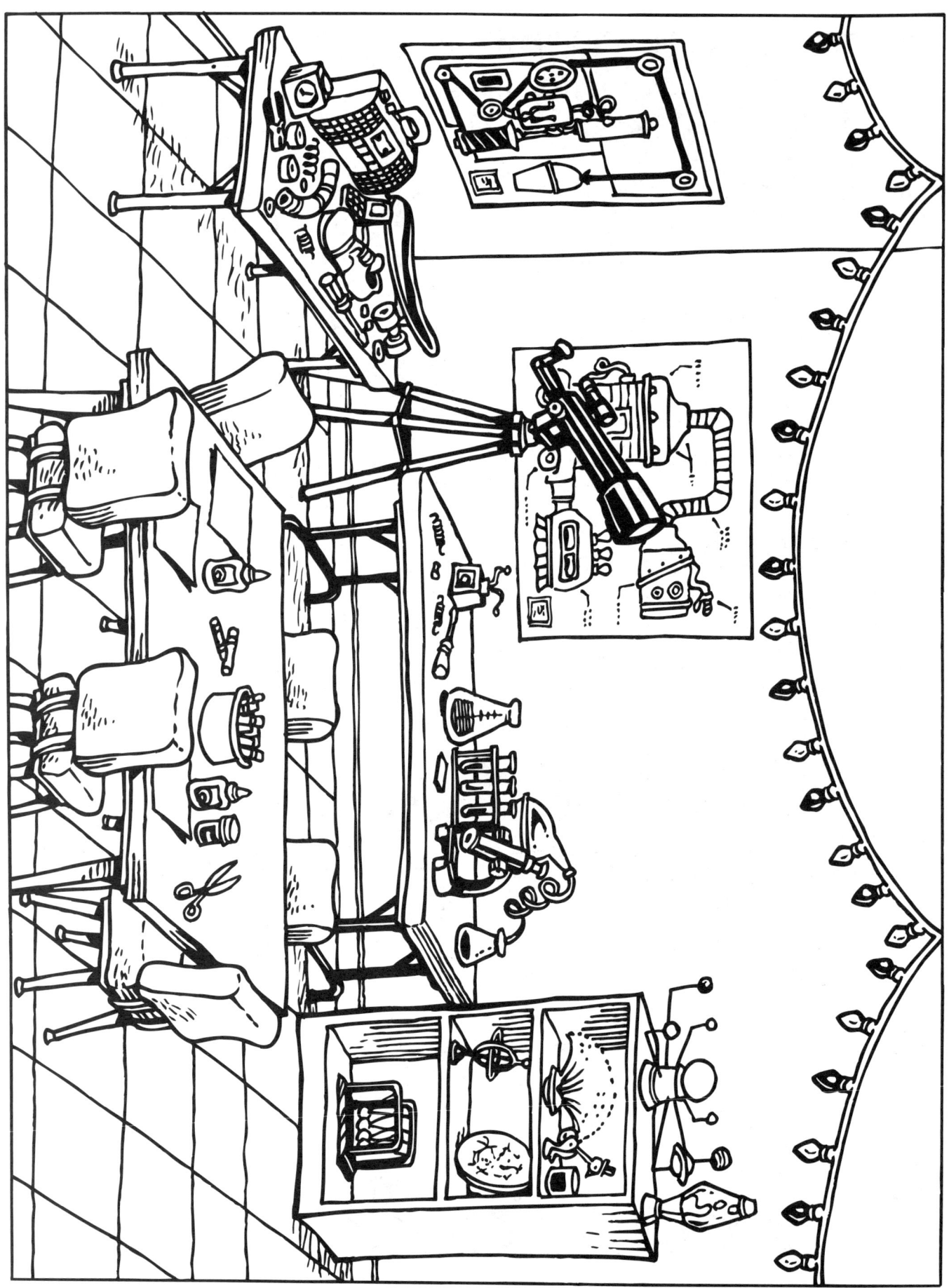

Theme Ideas

The Bonus Theme Ideas offered in every session will add an unforgettable dimension to *Agents in Action*. Here are additional ways to fill your church with the sights and sounds of a special-agent adventure.

Scenery

Use the decorating ideas on pages 29-32 to decorate the classrooms and activity centers.

Using a rubber stamp and a stamp pad with black-light ink, stamp students' hands every day as they arrive at *Agents in Action*. Place a black light at the entrance or in a central location, and ask students to place their hands under the light to show that they have the stamp proving they are allowed entrance.

Sounds

The *Agent* Music CD provides lively songs to help your students learn Bible truths. These memorable songs help students and adults alike discover what it means to live courageously for God in everyday life. Consider purchasing a special-agent instrumental music CD to add a fun atmosphere to your program. Play special-agent music throughout your hallways and outdoor areas.

At the beginning and end of each Worship Center segment, ask a volunteer to dress in theme-related clothing and blow an air horn. You may also use this sound to signal transition times in your schedule.

Groups of children will enjoy creating their own chants or cheers to say while moving between centers or while entering the assembly area.

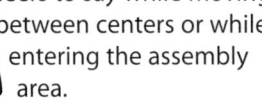

Special Days

Build interest and create enthusiasm for *Agents in Action* by asking students, teachers and helpers to bring in or wear items to enhance the fun. Consider doing one or more of the following:

>> **Hat Day** Children and leaders wear fun, funny and fantastic hats that they bring from home or that they make at *Agents in Action* using a variety of art supplies.

>> **Funny Hair Day** Encourage everyone involved in *Agents in Action* to come up with his or her most outrageous hairstyle.

>> **Special Agent Clothing** Ask children and leaders to wear sunglasses, dark jeans and brightly colored T-shirts one day.

>> **Color of the Day** Using the color of your choice, children and leaders wear the color of the day in their clothing or even their hair!

>> **Wacky Sunglasses Day** Encourage everyone involved in *Agents in Action* to wear sunglasses—the more colorful the better!

Staff Names and Group Names

Commander: Director

Senior Agents: Teachers and Helpers

Special Agents: Students

Technological Objects (Goofy Gadgets, Ready Robots, Cyber Cats, Terrific Techies, etc.): Group Names

Curriculum Resources

Familiarize yourself with the theme-related ideas provided throughout the curriculum. Each session includes a page of ideas for decorating, snacks, additional activities, etc.

Bible Story Center Tips

Most of us can still remember a childhood story told by a good storyteller. What makes a good storyteller so memorable? A good storyteller draws listeners in to the story, helping them imagine the story themselves and thus making it their own. You may not feel like one of the world's great storytellers, but fortunately, effective storytelling is a skill that you can develop by following the suggestions in this curriculum and by practicing a few simple principles. Here are some ideas and tips to help you become more confident and memorable!

A Good Beginning and Ending

A good beginning is essential, because it is much easier to capture an audience than it is to recapture them after their attention has wandered.

Bible Story Introduction

To help you make the most of the opening minutes of the Bible story, each story in *Agents in Action* begins with an introduction. In the introduction, you will find a question or comment that connects an element of the Bible story with a familiar childhood experience. In addition, to help you keep the interest of older children, a creative Bible storytelling technique is suggested for each lesson. As children are involved in interviews, role-playing, using storytelling props, etc., they will be motivated to follow along with the story action.

Special Agent Option Activity

To enhance the special-agent theme of this course, each Bible story also gives directions for an optional Special Agent Option activity that makes use of a box labeled Top Secret. In the Bible story for younger children, the object(s) in the box is (are) used as the basis for an interactive way of telling the Bible story.

The Special Agent activity for older children provides one or more creative clues that are removed from the box at the end of the story. As you guide children to solve the clues or reveal the hidden message, children will discover the lesson's daily mission for special agents.

Bible Story Conclusion

Each story also provides a conclusion—a brief summary of the basic focus of the story and how the Bible truth presented in the story connects with everyday life. This conclusion is called God's Word and Me. In the conclusion, one or more discussion questions are provided for you to use in helping children express their understanding of the lesson's focus and the Bible verse. A concluding prayer is suggested for elementary-age children. If the Bible story is told in a large group of 12 to 16 children, form small groups for the discussion time.

Suggested Materials for Younger Children's Special Agent Option

Lesson 1: Toy people, toy animals, green and blue paper, brown paper

Lesson 2: Toy shovels, sand shovels, large scoops or spoons

Lesson 3: Paper plates, marker, tongue depressors, tape

Lesson 4: Sheepskin fabric, kazoo, flashlight, earthenware jar

Lesson 5: Brown construction paper strips, basket

Lesson 6: Large hand mirror

Lesson 7: Small index cards, markers

Lesson 8: Seeds, dry dirt, small rocks, weeds, small plant, resealable plastic bags

Lesson 9: Wooden blocks

Lesson 10: Precut magazine pictures of food or toy food

Lesson 11: Pieces of flannel fabric, blue fabric and purple fabric

Lesson 12: Sheet of paper, marker

Lesson 13: Envelope with letter inside, toy horse, toy boat, red or orange construction paper, toy tree

Storytelling Tips

>> Practice telling the story aloud. Tell your story to yourself or someone in your family. Make notes or briefly outline the story.

>> Have your open Bible at hand while you are telling the story. Occasionally referring to the Bible reinforces the idea that the Bible stories are true and are found in the Bible. With preschoolers, frequently repeat that the stories are true and are written in the Bible for us to read.

>> While the Bible story is being told, other teachers and helpers sit separately among the children. Encourage them to fully participate with children, reacting appropriately and having fun! Their listening presence will encourage children to listen attentively as well, and they can help redirect children's attention back to the storyteller if needed.

>> Use dramatic facial expressions and vary your tone of voice according to the story action.

>> If students indicate a familiarity with the story, ask volunteers to tell some of the story action. Be sure to clarify and supplement information as needed.

>> Keep your story brief. A good rule of thumb for a beginning teacher is to limit your story to one minute for each year of the children's age. If you have more than one age level in your group, target for the middle of the group, but be ready to shorten the story if the younger ones are restless.

>> Work at maintaining eye contact with your children throughout the story. Know your story well enough that you can glance at your Bible and your notes and then look up.

Suggested Materials for Older Children's Special Agent Option

Lesson 1: Pencil, paper, crayons, red cellophane

Lesson 2: Toothpick or cotton swab, lemon juice, paper, cotton balls, iodine, water

Lesson 3: Blank crossword puzzle, pen

Lesson 4: Pen, paper

Lesson 5: Purple grape juice concentrate, paintbrushes, cup, water, baking soda, bowl, toothpick or cotton swab, paper

Lesson 6: Two sheets of paper, marker, flashlight

Lesson 7: Markers, two large sheets of paper

Lesson 8: Pen, several pads of paper, pencils

Lesson 9: Six mini-candy tubes or discarded film canisters, pen, small strips of paper

Lesson 10: Several pages of comic strips, straight pin, paper, markers

Lesson 11: Paper, ruler, markers, pencils

Lesson 12: White candle, scissors, newspaper, white paper, several resealable baggies filled with either dirt or dry coffee grounds

Lesson 13: Paper, pens

Art Center Tips

The Art Center is a place where children can become absorbed in a creative activity as a way of expressing their understanding of how the lesson's focus relates to their lives. Each art activity incorporates discussion of ways children can accomplish the lesson's daily mission in everyday life. In each art activity, the questions you ask and the comments you make will encourage students to apply Bible truth to everyday life. When students' hands are busy, they often talk freely!

Choose the Appropriate Activity

In each session, an art activity is provided for older children (elementary age) and for younger children (preschool age). Provide two centers, one for each age level. If you cannot provide two centers, choose the activity for which you have the most children. Each activity also includes a way to modify the activity (using the same or similar materials) for either younger or older children.

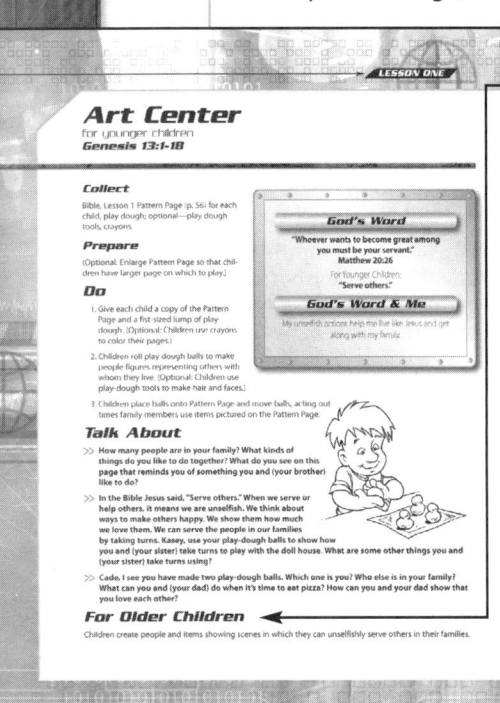

Before You Begin

Preparation is the key to making an art experience a joyful, creative one. No one enjoys a long stretch of waiting for a stapler or scissors. So make sure you have the following supplies on hand: newspaper (to protect surfaces), functional scissors, usable glue bottles and sticks, working markers, usable crayons and chalk, an adequate supply of tape, paint smocks (or men's old shirts) and butcher paper or newsprint end rolls (ask at your local newspaper office).

Before Every Activity

Before students arrive at your center, cover the work table(s) with newspaper or plastic table cover, securing it with masking tape, if needed. Set out materials in an orderly fashion, making sure you have enough materials for the number of children who will visit the Art Center.

If table space is limited, set out materials on a nearby shelf or supply table. Allow students to get and return materials to the appropriate places.

If most of your students are younger, use older students as helpers (for distributing supplies, stapling, etc.) during the Art Center time.

As Children Create

While children are working on their art creations, look for natural opportunities to ask the questions listed at the bottom of each Art Center page to help children relate the lesson focus to their daily lives. As children create, they are relaxed and eager to talk. Guided discussion will take the activity beyond art to discovery of Bible truth.

Comment on colors, lines and ideas you see represented. As you invite children to tell you about their work, many opportunities will arise for you to ask the discussion questions printed in bold type at the bottom of the page or to make comments that will help children understand the lesson focus.

Game Center Tips

The Game Center can be the perfect place for your students to let off steam, work out the wiggles and be open to guided discussion that relates the lesson focus to students' lives.

Choose the Appropriate Game

In each session, a game is provided for older children (elementary age) and for younger children (preschool age). Provide two centers, one for each age level. If you cannot provide two centers, choose the game for which you have the most children. Each game also includes a suggested modification (using the same or similar materials) for either younger or older children.

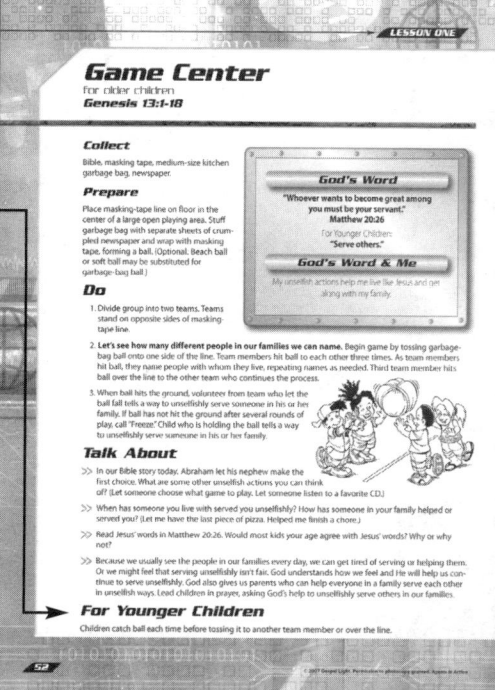

Creating a Play Area

Before leading a game, give yourself ample time to set up the play area. You may have little space in your classroom for a play area, so consider alternatives: outdoors, a gymnasium or a vacant area of the church from which sound will not carry to disturb other programs.

Once you have chosen the area, plan what you will need.

>> Will you need to move furniture?

>> Will you need to mark boundaries? Use chalk or rope outdoors; yarn or masking tape works indoors. (Remove masking tape from carpets after each session.)

>> How much space will you need? Carefully review the game procedures to plan what amount and shape of space will be needed.

>> From time to time, take stock of your classroom area. Is it time to remove that large table or unused bookshelf? Should the chairs be rearranged or the rug put in a different place? Small changes in arrangement can result in more usable space!

Forming Groups or Teams

To keep students' interest high and to keep cliques from forming, use a variety of ways to determine teams or groups.

>> Group teams by clothing color or other clothing features (wearing a sweater, wearing tennis shoes, etc.).

>> Place equal numbers of two colors of paper squares in a bag. Students shake the bag and draw out a square to determine teams.

>> Group teams by birthday month (for two teams, January through June and July through December); adjust as needed to make numbers even.

>> Group teams by the alphabetical order of their first or last names.

>> Group teams by telling them to stand on one foot: Those standing on a right foot form one team; those standing on a left foot form the other team.

Game Center Tips continued...

After playing a round or two of a game, announce that the person on each team who is wearing the most (red) should rotate to another team. Then play the game again. As you repeat this rotation process, vary the method of rotation so that students play with several different students each time.

Leading the Game

Explain rules clearly and simply. It's helpful to write out the rules to the game. Make sure you explain rules step-by-step.

Offer a practice round. When playing a game for the first time with your group, play it a few times just for practice. Students will learn the game's structure and rules best by actually playing the game.

Guiding Conversation

Using guided conversation turns a game activity into discovery learning! Make use of the discussion questions provided in the curriculum throughout the game time. You might ask a game's winners to answer questions or to consult with each other and answer as a group. You might discuss three questions between the rounds of a game or ask a question at the beginning of the round, inviting answers when the round is over.

Coloring/Puzzle Center Tips

The Bible story or verse coloring and puzzle pages provided for each lesson in *Agents in Action* provide an activity that you can use in several ways. These pages may be used as the basis of a separate activity center in which the youngest children (preschoolers and early elementary age) complete the coloring page and the older children (older elementary age) work on the puzzle. The coloring and puzzle pages often directly connect with a lesson's Bible story or verse, or sometimes provide additional Bible information. In order to complete the puzzle pages, students need Bibles for reference.

Alternatively, these pages can be used to supplement an existing center. For example, a Bible story coloring page can be provided for younger children to extend their interest in the Bible story. Or children who complete an art activity before others can be challenged to complete the coloring or puzzle page. Coloring and puzzle pages can also be kept for use when an activity runs short.

The coloring and puzzle pages may also be sent home with children on a weekly basis as a way of extending their Bible learning into the home. In addition, the coloring pages can be copied onto transparencies, projected and traced onto butcher paper and used for wall murals or bulletin boards.

Preparation

>> It's easiest to copy at one time all the pages needed rather than photocopying on a weekly basis. Store the pages in marked folders for easy use.

>> If you plan to use markers for the coloring pages, photocopy those pages onto heavier stock to avoid marker bleed-through.

>> Provide a variety of art materials for coloring; in addition to crayons and markers, colored pencils and watercolors add interest.

>> Have the puzzle answer sheets (pp. 242-245) available for children who are working on the Bible puzzle pages.

Discussion Opportunities

While students are coloring or working on the puzzles, ask the questions suggested on the coloring or puzzle pages. Using these questions will help you connect the coloring or puzzle activity to the lesson focus. Encourage student participation by introducing each question with a statement such as **I'm looking for four students wearing red to answer this question.** Another way to attract the interest of students is to say, **Someone whose name begins with the letter J can answer this question.**

Consider storing each child's coloring and/or puzzle pages in a folder. As time permits, refer to these pages as a way of reviewing past lessons. At the end of *Agents in Action*, give pages to children to take home.

Worship Center Tips

The Worship Center is a large-group gathering time for preschool- and elementary-age children that is best scheduled at the beginning or the end of each session. The goal is to help children participate in meaningful worship and build enthusiasm for discovering more about what it means to live courageously as God's disciples in real-life situations. Fun games, lesson-related music, saying or reading God's Word and prayer are all provided in the Worship Center.

Plan to have an enthusiastic youth-group-type leader guide the Worship Center activities. Ask him or her to dress in theme-related clothing—perhaps with a unique hat or vest, fake disguise items, etc. to help establish his or her character. Consider giving a name to the leader (Agent Pete, Director Debbie, etc.) to catch kids' attention.

Playing either "God's Kids" or "Mission of Love" as children gather for the Worship Center will help catch children's interest for *Agents in Action*.

Games

Each week a wacky game is suggested that will catch everyone's attention and involve children in team-building camaraderie. Sometimes the games connect to the Bible story and sometimes they do not. Often the game requires representatives from two or more teams. The number of children on a team may vary, depending on group size. Although not all children (especially preschoolers) will feel comfortable getting up in front to lead or participate in a game, they will enjoy being part of a team and cheering for their teammates.

Worship Times

Adults sometimes see children's worship time as occupying kids with frenzied repetitions of "Father Abraham" or as simply teaching children to worship in the same way as adults. But children need informal worship opportunities at their own level of understanding. Worship experiences designed to meet children's needs help them respond in love and praise to their heavenly Father.

Worship is indeed a time to show reverence and respect for God, but it doesn't mean always sitting still and being quiet. The activities offered in the Worship Center involve children and help them interact with each other and with teachers in singing praise to God and hearing His Word.

A Place of Worship

Worship is also enhanced by setting apart a place especially for praising Him. To create a space in your classroom for the Worship Center, prayerfully consider the ages and abilities of the children in your group, the kind of worship experience appropriate for them and the time and space available.

Consider ideas such as displaying a contemporary picture of Jesus, spreading a rug on the floor upon which children sit and playing a theme-related song as a signal to begin worship.

If taking an offering, singing a particular response or placing candles on an altarpiece are part of your church's adult worship, occasionally add those elements to the Worship Center as well. Give a simple explanation to help children understand why each of these acts is part of worship.

Keep in mind that the Worship Center is not just a place for entertainment or observation; your goal is to see every child participate in a positive way that is in keeping with his or her development.

Music Just for You!

Consider making copies of the *Agent* Music CD to help your students become familiar with the songs used during *Agents in Action*. A variety of musical styles are represented, making it easy for you to customize your worship time to include your students' favorites.

Leading Songs

Each of the upbeat songs on the *Agent* Music CD is designed to help children be aware of the opportunities they have every day to show that they are special agents for God—His disciples.

Children may participate by singing, clapping, playing rhythm instruments, holding up word charts, operating the overhead projector or adjusting the CD player. Help children understand that all these activities have one goal: to honor and praise God. Your example of sincere worship sets the tone—it is the strongest teaching about worship the children will receive.

Learning new songs can be difficult for some teachers. Listen to the song on the *Agent* Music CD. Then play the song again and sing along. Practice it several times (listen to it while driving in the car, while you cook, etc.). You may want to choose three or four favorite songs from the *Agent* Music CD and repeat them at each session, rather than teaching a variety of new songs. The younger the children are, the more repetition should be provided.

To teach a new song to children, print the words on a large chart or use the song charts in this book (pp. 246-254) to make a transparency to project on an overhead projector or to make PowerPoint slides. Project the words on a place where they may be seen easily by all the children.

As you play the song, sing along with the song, inviting children to join in with you. It is usually a good idea to sing only one stanza and/or chorus the first time through. If you are using an overhead, cover the entire transparency with a blank sheet of paper. As you sing, move the paper to reveal words one line at a time.

Choosing Additional Songs

If your church chooses to lead students in additional worship songs, select songs with the same prayer and sensitivity with which you'd plan adult worship. Utilizing simple worship choruses and hymns from among your own church's favorites will prepare children for the transition to adult-level worship in a gradual, age-appropriate manner. In this way, children will become familiar with a body of songs used in adult worship.

Whatever songs you use, be sure to explain any words or concepts that are unfamiliar to children. If unfamiliar words are used, take the time to give a brief definition of the word. Use a children's Bible dictionary if needed. For example, **The word "holy" means to be chosen or set apart. When we sing that God is holy, it means that He is perfect and without sin.** If you cannot put the words or concepts of a song in terms a child can truly understand, recognize that the song is probably appropriate only for adult worship.

Bible Verse

The simple verse activity provided encourages students to hear and/or say the Scripture in a creative way that invites their participation. While children may often memorize the verse as part of this activity, Bible memory is not the primary goal. Instead, the goal is simply the interactive reading or hearing of God's Word.

If the reading abilities of children and the number of teachers permit, children may find and read the verse in Bibles as part of this activity.

Consider printing out each week's verse on a computer banner for easy reading.

Prayer Time

Prayer is an integral part of worship. Don't deny children this privilege because they seem unable to hold still with folded hands and bowed heads for long periods of time. Instead, involve children in prayer in ways that will help them understand that prayer is something they can do. Don't insist that students pray in a particular posture; keep prayer times short and make them times of high involvement. Remember that your prayers give the students in your class a model for prayer that they will follow. Keep your prayers brief and use simple words. Long sentences and long prayers make prayer seem boring and not something for a child.

Each Worship Center provides prayer activity ideas for a large-group prayer at the end of the worship time. In addition to these ideas, you may also invite students to say sentence prayers, record requests and answers in a prayer journal, list prayer requests on a large sheet of paper, and allow children to pray with eyes open so that they are able to read and recall requests.

Agents in Action Lessons

In this section are each lesson's instructions. Before each session, photocopy and distribute the lesson to each teacher and leader.

LESSON ONE

Families

Bible Story:
Abraham's Unselfish Action
Genesis 13:1-18

Teacher's Devotional

The family is the world's most intimate place. It is the place where our behaviors are built. For some, family is a place we leave, never wanting to return; for others, it's a place we never want to leave! But however our own families affected us, our goal in this lesson is to help kids consider, "How can I honor God with attitudes and actions that will help me get along in my family—particularly with my brothers and sisters?" Abraham and Lot give us an instructive illustration.

Abraham was Lot's uncle and they lived in a close family relationship for years. They traveled together through unfamiliar territory and relied on each other in danger. When faced with the crisis of overcrowding, Abraham offered Lot first choice of whatever land he wished to take. Lot didn't seem to have hesitated to take the land that looked superior; he immediately chose the grassy plain near Sodom.

The point of including this event in Scripture may look like it's only about kind actions; however, it seems that the deeper lesson is the reason why Abraham was able to share unselfishly. Abraham knew he could give Lot first choice and allow him to take what looked better because he was certain that he could count on God. And as Lot's animals pounded down the dusty hills toward the green plains below, God repeated His promises to Abraham. His blessing wasn't limited to what looked good.

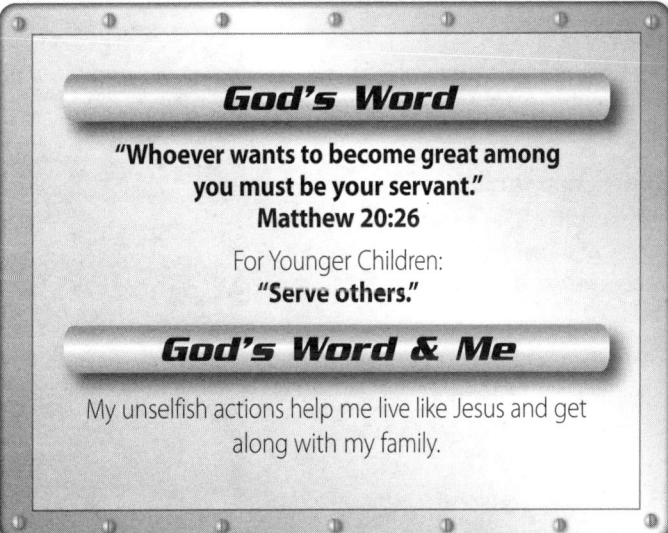

God's Word

"Whoever wants to become great among you must be your servant."
Matthew 20:26

For Younger Children:
"Serve others."

God's Word & Me

My unselfish actions help me live like Jesus and get along with my family.

Selfishness cripples adults and children alike. It comes from a fear that we will not have enough of what we need. This fear comes from the lie that God is not really good enough to meet our needs and therefore He cannot be trusted. Ultimately, we become unable to truly trust others because of our own worries and fears.

The youngest of the children we teach are just beginning to build an understanding of what it means to serve and value others and, even more importantly, how to demonstrate service in everyday family life. Jesus' words in Matthew 20:26 give us the challenge of being a servant, and God Himself gives us the strength to meet this challenge.

© 2007 Gospel Light. Permission to photocopy granted. *Agents in Action*

LESSON ONE

Planning Page

Choose which centers you will provide and the order in which children will participate in them (see pp. 14-18 for schedule tips and pp. 24-25 for guidelines in combining older and younger children). Also plan who will lead each center (for staffing tips see pp. 19-21). Use the reproducible planning sheet (p. 238) to record your plans.

Bible Story Center

Bible Story
Abraham's Unselfish Action • Genesis 13:1-18

Younger Child Option
Move toy people and animals to show story action

Older Child Option
Use red acetate to discover the daily mission "unselfish service"

Game Center

Younger Child Option
Participate in a relay to discover pictures of family members and talk about ways to obey Jesus' words and show love to them

Materials
Bible, four to six magazine pictures of different family members, large paper plates

Older Child Option
Play a game like volleyball to name family members who they can unselfishly serve as a way to follow Jesus' words

Materials
Bible, masking tape, medium-size kitchen garbage bag, newspaper

Art Center

Younger Child Option
Make play dough balls representing family members and move them on Pattern Page to discuss ways of obeying Jesus' command to serve others

Materials
Bible, Lesson 1 Pattern Page (p. 56), play dough

Older Child Option
Make magnetic photo frames to display pictures of family members and talk about ways of serving them unselfishly to obey Jesus' command

Materials
Bible, scissors, magnetic tape, empty CD cases, decorating materials

Worship Center

For the Younger and Older Child
Participate in large-group activities to review Bible verse and to worship God together

Materials
Bibles, *Agent* Music CD and player, at least two dozen balloons of varying sizes, masking tape, construction-paper squares in at least four colors (one for each child), song charts (pp. 246, 254)

Coloring/Puzzle Center

Younger Child Option
Review the Bible story while completing coloring page

Materials
Lesson 1 Coloring Page (p. 57) for each student, crayons

Older Child Option
Review ways of serving others while completing puzzle page

Materials
Lesson 1 Puzzle Page (p. 58) for each student, pencils

LESSON ONE

Bonus Theme Ideas

Bonus Theme Ideas can be used at any time during this session: as an additional activity center, to extend the session for a longer time or for added theme excitement.

Top Secret Verse Puzzles

Purchase one or more 24-piece puzzles. Before class, put the puzzle(s) together. Turn the puzzle over and use permanent marker to write the words of Matthew 20:26 on the back of the puzzle(s). Take the puzzle(s) apart. During the session, let children put the puzzle(s) together to discover the Bible verse. (Optional: Purchase two identical puzzles. Mail individual puzzle pieces of one set to children along with an invitation to come to Agents in Action and bring their puzzle pieces. Use puzzle pieces from second set to supplement pieces brought by children.)

Special Agent Information

Daily Mission Display

In a central area, set up a display on which you will reveal each lesson's daily mission based on the lesson's Bible verse. Cover a bulletin board with black paper. Print "Daily Missions" on a strip of white paper and attach to bulletin board. Also attach to the bulletin board 13 manila envelopes on which you have printed "Top Secret" in varying colors. Each week remove one of the envelopes. Replace the envelope with a paper on which you have written in large letters the daily mission. (See the Special Agent Option in the Bible Story for Older Children in each lesson.)

Special Agent Information

Sundae Fun

Set out strawberry jam, strawberry yogurt, Cheerios and washed and sliced strawberries in separate containers with plastic spoons. Give each child a plastic spoon and a transparent plastic cup or small bowl. Children build sundaes by layering items in their cups or bowls. (Optional: Top with whole strawberry.)

Special Agent Information

Post a note alerting parents to the use of food. Also, check registration forms for possible food allergies.

© 2007 Gospel Light. Permission to photocopy granted. *Agents in Action*

LESSON ONE

Bible Story Center
for younger children
Genesis 13:1-18

Collect

Bible.

Introduction

Put hands together in tent shape. Make a tent shape with your hands if you have ever slept in a tent. Volunteers respond. **Listen to hear about some families who lived in tents all the time!**

Tell the Story

Abraham and Lot lived with their families in tents. Abraham and Lot had many helpers who lived near them in more tents. And Abraham and Lot also had many, many cows and donkeys and sheep and goats. Everywhere you looked there were people and animals!

Special Agent Option

In a box labeled "Top Secret," place a variety of items that can be used to act out the Bible story—toy people to represent Abraham, Lot and their helpers; toy animals such as sheep, goats and cows; green and blue paper or card stock to represent grass and water; brown paper or card stock folded in half to represent tents. At the appropriate times in the story, remove items from box. Set up items and move them to show story action.

Every day Abraham's helpers and Lot's helpers took the animals to eat green grass and to drink cool water.

Then one day, there was not enough grass to eat or enough water to drink for all their animals. The helpers began to argue over whose animals would eat the grass and drink the water.

"We must stop this arguing. We need to move apart from each other to find enough grass and water for all our animals," Abraham said. So Lot and Abraham climbed to the top of a hill. They could see far, far away.

Abraham said, "You may choose first, Lot. You may choose the land you want."

Lot pointed to good land, where there was plenty of water and grass. "I'll move to that land," Lot said.

Lot took his family and his helpers and his animals to live in the good land.

Abraham took his family and his helpers and his animals and walked to another place to live. His animals would have enough water and grass, too. God knew that Abraham was kind to Lot. God promised to take care of Abraham. Abraham was glad he had been kind and let Lot choose first.

God's Word & Me

Abraham and Lot lived in the same family. When Abraham and Lot could have argued about who was going to get the best land, Abraham was unselfish. He didn't try to keep the best for himself. He let Lot choose first.

With our brothers and sisters and moms and dads, there are always times when we can be unselfish and let others choose first. In the Bible, Jesus said, "Serve others." When we serve others, it means that we are unselfish. We show how much we love and care for them. We think about what would make others happy. Pray, **Dear God, please help us show our love to the people we live with. In Jesus' name, amen.**

LESSON ONE

Bible Story Center
for older children
Genesis 13:1-18

Collect

Bible, name tags or simple Bible-times costumes.

Introduction

What would be good about moving to a new city? What might be bad about moving to a new city? Volunteers answer. **Today we're going to hear about something good and something bad that happened to a family who moved to a new place.** Before telling the Bible story, ask for volunteers to pantomime the actions of these animals (sheep and goats) and these story characters (Abraham, Sarah, Lot, Abraham's servants, Lot's servants). Give each volunteer a name tag or simple Bible-times costume to wear. Volunteers stand in front of group. As you tell the Bible story, children pantomime the actions of their assigned characters (hold hand behind ear to listen to God's words, pretend to put items in sacks, walk in place, hold hand over eyes to "see" the new land, chew grass, etc.). Encourage children to exaggerate the motions for more interest.

Special Agent Option

Before class, use a blue crayon to write the daily mission "unselfish service" on several sheets of paper. Then write any other words (school, book, pencil, etc.) over the phrase on each paper with red crayon. Place papers and several sheets of red acetate (use notebook covers available in office supply stores) in a box labeled "Top Secret." At the end of the story, volunteers remove items and lay acetate on top of the colored area to read the daily mission.

Tell the Story

Abraham was a man who lived in the city of Ur. Ur was a big city, full of fountains and trees and houses made of brick and plaster. Abraham and his wife, Sarah, had lived in Ur all their lives.

Abraham loved God. He often talked with God. And one day, God told Abraham something VERY SURPRISING. He told Abraham, "I want you to go to a new land. I will show you where to go."

Abraham believed God and began to get ready to move. Because this move would be like a long camping trip, the people in Abraham's household packed up everything they would need for traveling—pots and pans, clothes and tents, rugs and blankets, water and food. They tied the bundles onto camels and donkeys and herded the sheep and goats. Abraham's father and his nephew Lot also went with them on this journey. Soon the whole family was off—walking to a place they knew nothing about!

Abraham's family walked for weeks and months and then years! Sometimes Abraham's family must have wondered if they would ever get to the land God had promised! But Abraham trusted God. He was sure God would take care of him. He knew that, sooner or later, they were going to reach the new land where God had promised to bring them.

After many years of traveling and many adventures, they came to a place of hills and valleys covered with good grass that would feed many sheep and goats and cows. "This is the land I promised to you," God told Abraham. It was beautiful! The land was called Canaan.

© 2007 Gospel Light. Permission to photocopy granted. *Agents in Action*

Now, during all this time Abraham and his family had traveled, their flocks of sheep and herds of goats had grown and grown. There were so MANY animals, that there wasn't enough water or grass for all of them. Both Abraham and his nephew Lot had HUGE flocks of animals. And in the crowded valley, the servants who took care of these animals began to fight over whose flocks should get the water and the grass.

When Abraham heard about the fighting, he said to Lot, "Let's not have any quarreling between you and me, or between your servants and mine. Look around! The whole land is here for us. You may choose where you would like to go. Take your animals in that direction and I'll go the other way. Then there will be plenty for all of us."

Lot looked and saw that the whole plain, or flat area, that went down to the sea was beautiful. He could see bright streams of flowing water and fields of green grass. So Lot chose this plain for himself and his family. He said good-bye to Abraham's family and moved down to the plain.

Because Abraham unselfishly gave Lot first choice, the fighting stopped! There was peace. After Lot had moved away, God said to Abraham, "Look around. All the land that you can see I will give to you and your family forever. Your family will grow and I will give you many grandchildren! Go, walk all through the land. I am giving it to you."

God's Word & Me

Abraham and Lot could have spent time arguing about who was the greatest and who should get the best land. But instead, Abraham was willing to serve Lot by letting Lot choose first. Abraham's unselfish attitude and actions stopped an argument.

One time Jesus' disciples argued about who was the greatest. Listen to what Jesus said to them. Read Matthew 20:26. **In our families, there are always going to be times when we have to choose if we are going to obey Jesus' words or not. Obeying Jesus and unselfishly serving others in our families—especially our brothers and sisters—will help our homes be better places to live.**

>> **What are examples of situations in which kids your age have to choose to be unselfish in the way they treat the people they live with?** (When families are choosing what movie to watch. When a family member won't share a video game. When someone needs help to finish a chore. When dividing the last piece of dessert.)

>> **Why is it hard to be unselfish and serve the people in our families?**

>> **What can you do when it's hard to unselfishly serve others?** (Remember when the person has helped me. Ask a parent to help me plan a fair solution. Pray to God for help.) Pray with children, asking His help in unselfishly serving the people in our families.

LESSON ONE

Game Center
for younger children
Genesis 13:1-18

Collect

Bible, four to six magazine pictures of different family members (baby, young child, teenager, parent, grandparent, etc.), large paper plates.

Prepare

Place pictures on the floor at one end of large open playing area. Cover each picture with a paper plate. Set up one game for each group of four to six children.

Do

1. Children line up at end of playing area opposite from plates and pictures. Children take turns running across the playing area and removing a plate and identifying the person pictured. Child tells a way to help the person pictured.

2. Repeat activity as time permits, mixing up order of pictures for each round. (Optional: Vary the method children use to move across the playing area for each round. Children may hop, jump, crawl, walk backwards or tiptoe.)

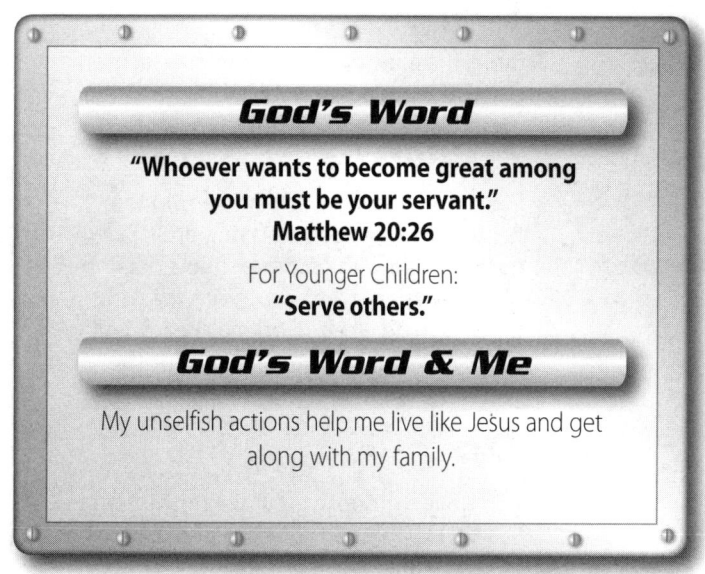

God's Word

"Whoever wants to become great among you must be your servant."
Matthew 20:26

For Younger Children:
"Serve others."

God's Word & Me

My unselfish actions help me live like Jesus and get along with my family.

Talk About

>> **In the Bible Jesus says, "Serve others." When we serve others, we help them. We show how much we love them. In our Bible story today, Abraham showed love to his nephew Lot. Abraham let Lot choose first.**

>> **Karis, thank you for letting Lily take the first turn. Letting others take the first turn is a way to serve them.**

>> **Justin, when you play with your (sister), when can you let her have the first turn?**

>> **When we remember to show love to the people we live with, it helps us be happy together.** Pray briefly, **Dear God, thank You for the people in our families. Please help us to show how much we love each other. In Jesus' name, amen.**

For Older Children

Staple two paper plates together with tops facing each other. Set out pictures in an open area of the room. Children take turns tossing plates like Frisbees to see which picture they land on or near. Child tells a way to show unselfish service to the person pictured and/or a way the person pictured has shown unselfish service to him or her.

LESSON ONE

Game Center
for older children
Genesis 13:1-18

Collect

Bible, masking tape, medium-size kitchen garbage bag, newspaper.

Prepare

Place masking-tape line on floor in the center of a large open playing area. Stuff garbage bag with separate sheets of crumpled newspaper and wrap with masking tape, forming a ball. (Optional: Beach ball or soft ball may be substituted for the garbage-bag ball.)

Do

God's Word
"Whoever wants to become great among you must be your servant."
Matthew 20:26

For Younger Children:
"Serve others."

God's Word & Me
My unselfish actions help me live like Jesus and get along with my family.

1. Divide group into two teams. Teams stand on opposite sides of masking-tape line.

2. **Let's see how many different people in our families we can name.** Begin game by tossing garbage-bag ball onto one side of the line. Team members hit ball to each other three times. As team members hit ball, they name people with whom they live, repeating names as needed. Third team member hits ball over the line to the other team who continues the process.

3. When ball hits the ground, volunteer from team who let the ball fall tells a way to unselfishly serve someone in his or her family. If ball has not hit the ground after several rounds of play, call "Freeze." Child who is holding the ball tells a way to unselfishly serve someone in his or her family.

Talk About

>> **In our Bible story today, Abraham let his nephew make the first choice. What are some other unselfish actions you can think of?** (Let someone choose what game to play. Let someone listen to a favorite CD.)

>> **When has someone you live with served you unselfishly? How has someone in your family helped or served you?** (Let me have the last piece of pizza. Helped me finish a chore.)

>> Read Jesus' words in Matthew 20:26. **Would most kids your age agree with Jesus' words? Why or why not?**

>> **Because we usually see the people in our families every day, we can get tired of serving or helping them. Or we might feel that serving unselfishly isn't fair. God understands how we feel and He will help us continue to serve unselfishly. God also gives us parents who can help everyone in a family serve each other in unselfish ways.** Lead children in prayer, asking God's help to unselfishly serve others in our families.

For Younger Children

Children catch ball each time before tossing it to another team member or over the line.

LESSON ONE

Art Center
for younger children
Genesis 13:1-18

Collect

Bible, Lesson 1 Pattern Page (p. 56) for each child, play dough; optional—play dough tools, crayons.

Prepare

(Optional: Enlarge Pattern Page so that children have larger page on which to play.)

Do

1. Give each child a copy of the Pattern Page and a fist-size lump of play dough. (Optional: Children use crayons to color their pages.)

2. Children roll play dough balls to make people figures representing others with whom they live. (Optional: Children use play dough tools to make hair and faces.)

3. Children place balls onto Pattern Page and move balls, acting out times family members use items pictured on the Pattern Page.

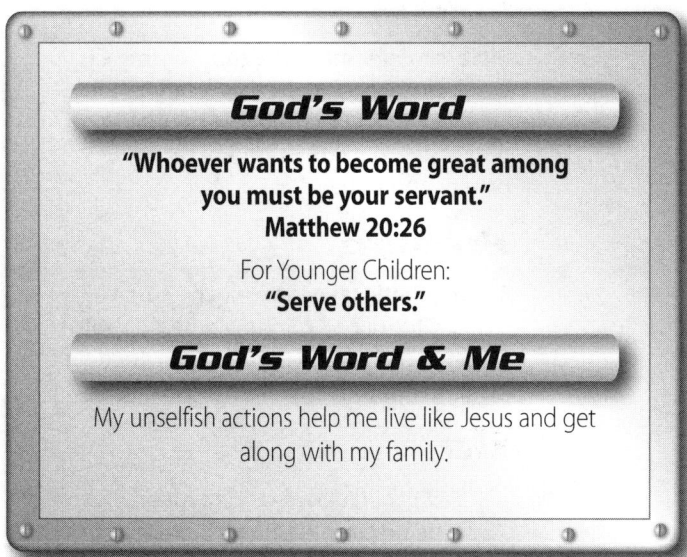

God's Word

"Whoever wants to become great among you must be your servant."
Matthew 20:26

For Younger Children:
"Serve others."

God's Word & Me

My unselfish actions help me live like Jesus and get along with my family.

Talk About

>> How many people are in your family? What kinds of things do you like to do together? What do you see on this page that reminds you of something you and (your brother) like to do?

>> In the Bible Jesus said, "Serve others." When we serve or help others, it means we are unselfish. We think about ways to make others happy. We show them how much we love them. We can serve the people in our families by taking turns. Kasey, use your play-dough balls to show how you and (your sister) take turns to play with the doll house. What are some other things you and (your sister) take turns using?

>> Cade, I see you have made two play-dough balls. Which one is you? Who else is in your family? What can you and (your dad) do when it's time to eat pizza? How can you and your dad show that you love each other?

For Older Children

Children create people and items showing scenes in which they can unselfishly serve others in their families.

LESSON ONE

Art Center
for older children
Genesis 13:1-18

Collect

Bible, scissors, magnetic tape, empty CD cases, decorating materials (puffy paint, glitter glue, foam cutouts); optional—paper and markers, or digital camera, printer and paper.

Prepare

Cut magnetic tape into 3-inch (7.5-cm) strips. (Optional: Arrange a time to photograph and print a picture of each child and his or her family.)

Do

1. Each child places strip of magnetic tape on the back of each empty CD case.
2. Children decorate 1-inch (2.5-cm) border around edge of CD case with decorating materials.
3. Child takes home decorated CD case, trims family photo as needed before inserting and taping photo inside the case to create a picture frame that can be displayed on refrigerator. (Optional: Child draws picture of family to insert into case.)

God's Word

"Whoever wants to become great among you must be your servant."
Matthew 20:26

For Younger Children:
"Serve others."

God's Word & Me

My unselfish actions help me live like Jesus and get along with my family.

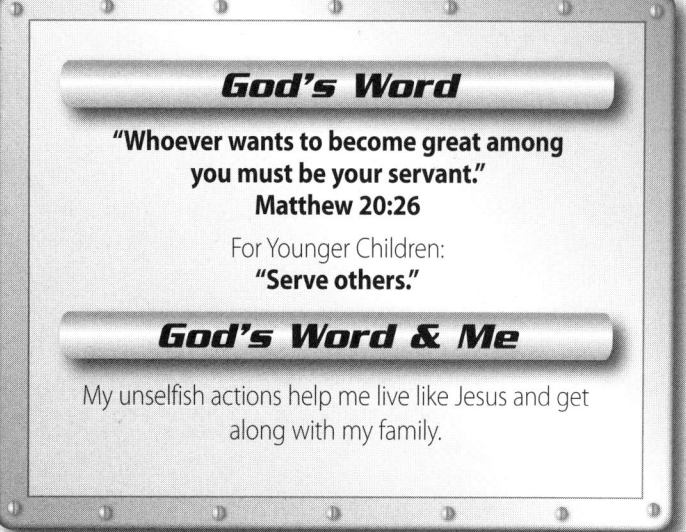

Talk About

>> Read Matthew 20:26 aloud. **How might your family be different if everyone remembered these words of Jesus? What are some examples of ways to unselfishly serve others in your family?**

>> **When do you think kids your age have a hard time unselfishly serving others?** Pray, asking God's help to serve and help others at home.

>> **In today's Bible story, Abraham unselfishly served Lot by letting him make the first choice. When are some times brothers and sisters might argue about who should get the first choice? How might you follow Abraham's example and stop the argument?** (Talk with brother or sister about a fair plan. Agree on a plan to take turns choosing first.)

For Younger Children

Children use stickers to decorate CD cases.

LESSON ONE

Worship Center
for younger and older children
Genesis 13:1-18

Collect

Bibles, *Agent* Music CD and player, at least two dozen balloons of varying sizes, masking tape, construction-paper squares in at least four colors (one for each child), song charts (pp. 246, 254).

Preparation

Inflate and tie balloons. In an open area of the room, use masking tape to designate start and finish lines approximately 10 feet (3 m) apart.

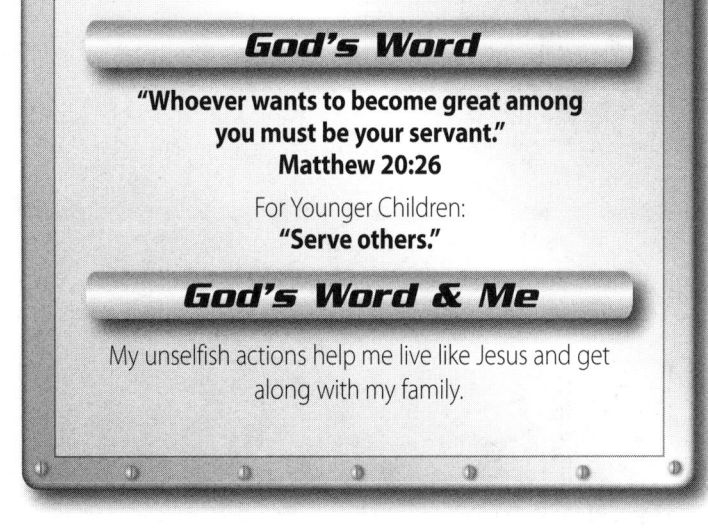

God's Word

"Whoever wants to become great among you must be your servant."
Matthew 20:26

For Younger Children:
"Serve others."

God's Word & Me

My unselfish actions help me live like Jesus and get along with my family.

Team Game

Divide group into two or more teams of special agents. (Optional: Volunteers from each team choose names for their teams.) Invite two children from each team to stand at the start line. **Today we're going to see how our teams of special agents can help each other.** Give a balloon to each pair of children. At your signal, pairs carry balloon to finish line and back without using their hands (between shoulders, between elbows, etc.). (If balloon drops, pairs pick up balloon and continue.) Pairs repeat action, each time with an additional balloon, trying to see which pair can carry the most balloons. Team members cheer for their team's agents.

Bible Verse Game

Repeat Matthew 20:26 aloud with children. Mix up colors of paper squares and distribute randomly to children. Then as you call out each color, children holding those colors stand up and say words of verse together. (Variation: Children run to front of room before reciting the verse.)

Song

Lead children in singing "God's Kids." Add motions and/or clapping if desired.

Prayer

Every day we have opportunities to unselfishly serve the people we live with. Hold up one hand. For each finger, see if you can think of one way to help or serve the people in your family. Invite volunteers to tell ways. **Let's ask God's help in showing His love to our moms, dads, brothers and sisters.** Lead children in prayer.

Song

Lead children in singing "Train Me Up." Add motions and/or clapping if desired.

LESSON ONE · Pattern Page

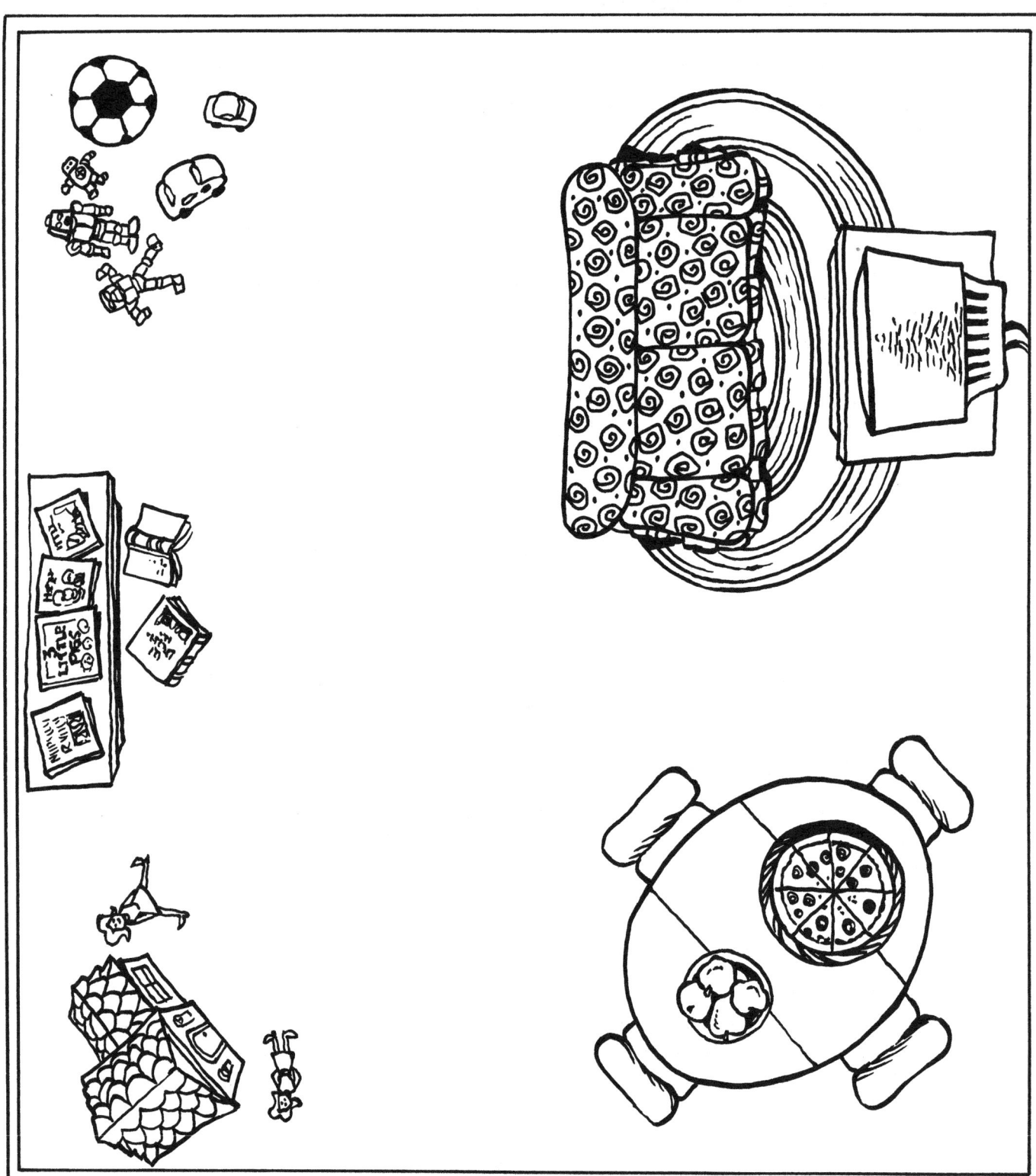

LESSON TWO

Fighting

Bible Story:
Isaac Makes Peace
Genesis 26:12-33

Teacher's Devotional

Peace is very important—everyone wants peace! But peace that is the result of military action or political forces is often what people think of when they talk about peace. However, these kinds of enforced peace are only fragile cessations of war or danger. Such peace does not go deeply enough to change warlike attitudes! The kind of peace that comes from God is another kind of peace entirely!

Isaac returned to Gerar, his birthplace, because he needed to find water for his flocks and family. Retracing his father's steps, he re-dug his father's wells. God's blessing on Isaac (and the water) was so abundant that the people of Gerar grew jealous. They filled in Abraham's wells and ordered Isaac to leave—which he did, quietly and without argument. After Isaac moved twice—and dug more wells—angry locals took those wells, too! Isaac could have argued, demanded his rights based on his father's work or could even have taken revenge—but he didn't. Later, the king who had banished him came to make peace with him, saying, "We saw clearly that the Lord was with you." Had Isaac stuck up for his rights or struck back in retaliation, God's favor would not have been so obvious.

Isaac was willing to give up even something as precious as water to make peace. The basis of Isaac's peaceful attitude was his trust in God. He knew that even in crisis over the most needed resource, God was ultimately his source of supply. His peacemaking flowed from his certainty that he could trust God's blessing. He then did what was right and trusted God for the outcome. Genuine peace followed!

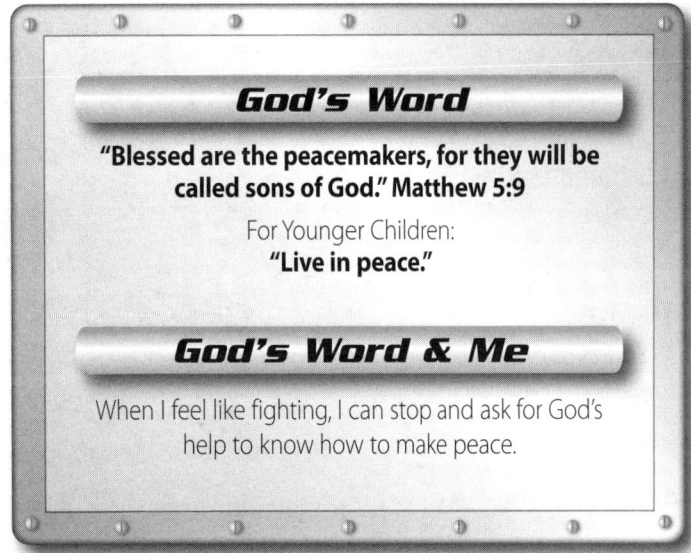

God's Word

"Blessed are the peacemakers, for they will be called sons of God." Matthew 5:9

For Younger Children:
"Live in peace."

God's Word & Me

When I feel like fighting, I can stop and ask for God's help to know how to make peace.

As we try to help kids understand what to do when they feel like fighting, encourage them to remember that even in crisis, we can stop to pray. We can trust God to give us wisdom to know the best possible response—sometimes walking away, sometimes getting protection from an adult and sometimes using words to communicate legitimate concerns. The situations in which your students live and the threat of physical violence may vary widely. Listen carefully to the comments your students make and ask God to help you be sensitive to their circumstances. Help children realize that trusted adults can help them work out plans to live in peace.

LESSON TWO

Planning Page

Choose which centers you will provide and the order in which children will participate in them (see pp. 14-18 for schedule tips and pp. 24-25 for guidelines in combining older and younger children). Also plan who will lead each center (for staffing tips see pp. 19-21). Use the reproducible planning sheet (p. 238) to record your plans.

Bible Story Center

Bible Story
Isaac Makes Peace • Genesis 26:12-33

Younger Child Option
Use toy shovels, sand shovels and large scoops or spoons to pretend to dig wells

Older Child Option
Use grape-juice concentrate to discover the daily mission "make peace"

Game Center

Younger Child Option
Drink water in a relay race and talk about ways God helps them to live in peace

Materials
Bible, a paper cup for each child, water, trash can

Older Child Option
Play a game of Peacemaker Tag and talk about God's help to know what to do when tempted to fight

Materials
Bible

Art Center

Younger Child Option
Make puppets to show Isaac's kind actions and talk about ways God helps them live in peace with kind actions and words

Materials
Bible, Lesson 2 Pattern Page (p. 70), sturdy construction paper or cardstock, scissors, crayons or markers

Older Child Option
Decorate peace cups to share with others, and talk about what peacemakers who obey God are like

Materials
Bible, scissors, at least two different colors of gift-wrap cellophane, clear plastic cups (two for each student), glue sticks

Worship Center

For the Younger and Older Child
Participate in large-group activities to review Bible verse and to worship God together

Materials
Bibles, *Agent* Music CD and player, song charts (pp. 246, 250), two buckets and a large plastic cup for each team, uncooked beans or pasta

Coloring/Puzzle Center

Younger Child Option
Review the Bible story while completing coloring page

Materials
Lesson 2 Coloring Page (p. 71) for each student, crayons

Older Child Option
Review results of actions while completing puzzle page

Materials
Lesson 2 Puzzle Page (p. 72) for each student, pencils

© 2007 Gospel Light. Permission to photocopy granted. *Agents in Action*

LESSON TWO

Bonus Theme Ideas

Bonus Theme Ideas can be used at any time during this session: as an additional activity center, to extend the session for a longer time or for added theme excitement.

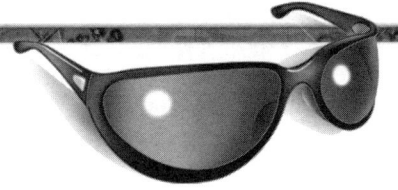

Who's Who?

On a length of butcher paper, print the name of each child who attends *Agents in Action*. Leave an open area around each name. (Optional: Take a picture of each child and display it near the child's name.) Title the paper "Agent Roster." Display the paper at an entrance or in a large room where children meet. Near the paper set out one or more inkpads in a variety of colors and several boxes of disposable wipes. Each week, child records attendance by making a fingerprint below his or her name. Children may also create and write their special-agent names on the paper. Variation: Make agent badges for children to wear as name tags. Include child's name, photo and fingerprint. Laminate and attach lanyard for child to wear.

Special Agent Information

Special Agent ID

Record several "special agents" (children, leaders and/or church staff) saying the words of the Bible verse. Play recordings as children arrive, during an activity center or as part of a large-group time to see who will be the first to ID the voice. Repeat this activity each lesson using different special agents. Variation: Video tape special agents who are wearing disguises (hats, sunglasses, jackets, etc.). You may also take photos of children, leaders or church staff, cut out facial features (eyes, noses, mouths) to display for children to guess.

Special Agent Information

Banana Sticks

Place granola or crushed flake cereal on a paper plate and set out a bowl of any flavor of yogurt. (If you have a large group, make duplicate plates and bowls.) Cut bananas into thirds. Slowly insert craft stick into one end of banana. Children roll bananas in yogurt and then in the granola or crushed cereal before eating.

Special Agent Information

Post a note alerting parents to the use of food. Also, check registration forms for possible food allergies.

© 2007 Gospel Light. Permission to photocopy granted. *Agents in Action*

LESSON TWO

Bible Story Center
for younger children
Genesis 26:12-33

Collect

Bible.

Introduction

Use your arms to make a big circle if you have or someone you know has ever dug a hole in the ground. What kinds of tools were used? Volunteers respond. **Listen to hear about a time Isaac's helpers had to dig in the ground again and again.**

Special Agent Option

In a box labeled "Top Secret," place a variety of toy shovels, sand shovels, large scoops or spoons—one for each child. During the story, let each child use shovels, scoops or spoons to pretend to dig wells.

Tell the Story

In Bible times, people did not have sinks and faucets in their homes. People got their water outdoors. They would dip buckets or jars into deep holes in the ground called wells. Isaac needed to dig a well, so his family and his helpers and his animals could have good water to drink. Dig, dig, dig—Isaac's helpers worked hard. The hole got deeper and deeper. Then water began to fill up the hole!

Everyone was happy—EXCEPT Isaac's neighbors. They shouted, "That well is OURS!" They started a big argument. Isaac did not want to argue with his neighbors. He wanted to make peace with them. So Isaac let them have the well. Isaac moved to another place. He told his helpers to dig another well. Dig, dig, dig—the helpers worked hard. Soon water began to fill up the hole. They had found water again!

But then Isaac's neighbors came again. "That well is OURS!" they shouted. They were so angry. They may have even pushed and shoved Isaac's helpers.

Isaac STILL wanted to make peace with his neighbors. And Isaac knew that God would help him have the water he needed. So again Isaac moved to another place. And he told his helpers to dig ANOTHER well. Dig, dig, dig—the helpers worked hard. Soon water began to fill up the hole.

One night soon after, God said to Isaac, "Do not be afraid, Isaac. I will always be with you." Isaac thanked God for being with him.

Isaac's neighbors came again. But this time they did not shout. They did not push. They said, "We know God is with you. We will not argue with you anymore."

Isaac was very happy! He invited the neighbors to stay for dinner. Isaac was glad God helped him make peace with his neighbors.

God's Word & Me

Isaac worked hard to make peace with his neighbors. Isaac was a peacemaker. Isaac wanted to live in peace with others instead of arguing or fighting with them.

We can make peace with our neighbors, too. Who are our neighbors? (Everyone!) **In the Bible, Jesus said, "Live in peace." When we live in peace, it means that we can ask God's help in knowing what to do when we feel like fighting.** Pray, **Dear God, please help us to make peace. In Jesus' name, amen.**

LESSON TWO

Bible Story Center
for older children
Genesis 26:12-33

Collect

Bible, five large blue construction paper circles to represent wells, newspaper sheets.

Introduction

When have you been hot and thirsty? Where were you? What did you want to drink? Volunteers respond. **In our Bible story today, a whole bunch of people wanted water to drink. Some of these people wanted water so much they were willing to fight for it. Let's find out what happened.** As you tell the Bible story, set out a paper circle to represent each location where Isaac and his servants dug wells. Invite volunteers to crumple newspaper sheets and toss onto circles to represent filling wells with dirt.

Special Agent Option

Before class, place purple grape juice concentrate and several paintbrushes into a cup. Mix equal parts water and baking soda in a bowl. Dip cotton swab into mixture and print the daily mission "make peace" on several sheets of paper. Allow to dry. Place sheets in a box labeled "Top Secret." At the end of the story, cover table or floor with plastic tablecloth. Volunteers remove the papers and paint over them with juice concentrate to read the daily mission.

Tell the Story

One hot and dusty day in Old Testament times, Isaac, Rebekah, their family and herdsmen trudged along beside their sheep and cattle. There was a famine where they had been living. A famine is a time when there isn't enough rain for crops to grow and drinking water becomes scarce. Isaac and his family were going to the city of Gerar (JIHR-ahr). Isaac's father, Abraham, had lived there long before. They hoped that there was still water in the wells Abraham had dug years before.

But Gerar wasn't empty. People called Philistines lived there. Not long after Isaac and his family arrived, the king of the Philistines, Abimelech, told his people to leave Isaac's family alone—and they did, at first. Isaac's family found water in the wells, settled down and planted crops. God blessed their work: They harvested 100 times what they had planted! The number of sheep and cattle they owned grew and grew!

When the Philistines saw Isaac's BIG harvest and BIG flocks, they got jealous! Soon they wanted revenge! So they filled with dirt all the wells Isaac's father had dug! And King Abimelech told Isaac to move AWAY.

Even though Isaac, his family and all his servants had settled in and made themselves feel at home, Isaac did what the king asked. He didn't argue; he didn't try to change Abimelech's mind. He simply moved away from Gerar and settled in a valley away from the town.

After they looked for a place to set up camp in the valley, they searched for the most important thing—WATER! Isaac's men found more old wells that Isaac's father, Abraham, had dug. After long days of cleaning out the wells, they had water to drink! They also dug a new well that gave cool, fresh water. BUT it wasn't long until they had unhappy visitors.

"Didn't we tell you to LEAVE?" the herdsmen from Gerar asked Isaac's men. "THIS is OUR well because this is OUR land," they growled.

© 2007 Gospel Light. Permission to photocopy granted. *Agents in Action*

The Bible says that Isaac and his people kept the peace, moved on and dug another well in a new place. GUESS who came to take THIS well away? That's right, the herdsmen of Gerar came after them AGAIN and told them to leave!

No doubt some of Isaac's herdsmen grumbled as they packed up to move AGAIN. It wasn't FAIR! They hadn't hurt anybody. But Isaac was determined to keep the peace between himself and the Philistines.

Once again, Isaac and his family, his herdsmen and their families settled at a new place Isaac found. And they began to do the FIRST thing they had to do—dig another WELL. They must have been pretty good at it by now!

But this time, they had moved far enough away. No one came to fight with them over the water! And although Isaac was glad to have some peace, he moved on after a while to a place called Beersheba. God talked to Isaac at Beersheba and reminded him of His promises to Isaac's father, Abraham. Isaac settled in at Beersheba and guess what they did next? That's right! They dug a WELL!

Meanwhile, King Abimelech and one of his advisors came to Beersheba. Isaac met them and said, "Why have you come here? You sent me away from your land!"

King Abimelech answered, "We saw clearly that God has helped you. We decided that we should make an agreement with you. Promise us that you will do us no harm because we have never harmed you but only sent you away in peace."

WELL! That wasn't exactly how Isaac remembered it! But he was glad that the king wanted peace. So he made the agreement and made a feast for the visitors. That day, Isaac's servants found water in the newest well they were digging. Now they had water —and peace!

God's Word & Me

The Bible doesn't tell us if Isaac found it easy or hard to make peace with his neighbors. But the Bible does tell us the results of Isaac's actions. He was able to live in peace and not suffer the trouble that often comes with fighting.

Listen to these words Jesus said as a way of teaching His followers the benefit that comes when we make peace with others. Read Matthew 5:9. **There may be times when you feel like fighting. You might even feel like you have a good reason for fighting. But paying attention to Jesus' words about being peacemakers will help us remember to stop and ask God's help in knowing what to do to make peace. When Jesus lived on Earth, His life, death and resurrection made it possible for us to become peacemakers.** (Talk with interested students about salvation. See "Leading a Child to Christ" on p. 12.)

>> **What often results from fighting?** (Kids get in trouble or get hurt. Kids aren't friends anymore.)

>> **When are some times that kids your age might feel like fighting?** (Someone has been mean. Someone has hurt them or taken what belongs to them.)

>> **What might kids choose to do instead of fighting?** (Walk away. Try to talk to the person. Get protection from an adult.) **What action might you choose? Which action do you think would have the best result?**

>> **Think about a time when you might feel like fighting with someone.** Pray with children, asking God's help in knowing what to do to make peace.

Game Center
for younger children
Genesis 26:12-33

Collect
Bible, a paper cup for each child, water, trash can.

Prepare
Fill one cup for each child with a small amount of water. Place cups on table to represent a "well."

Do
Line children up in at least two teams for a relay race. At your signal, first child in line for each team runs to the "well," drinks one cup of water and throws cup into trash can before returning to his or her team. Continue until each child has run to the well. Fill new cups and play again as time allows. (Optional: Children clap and call out "live in peace" while waiting their turn. Children skip, hop or crawl to the well for variety.)

Talk About

>> **In today's Bible story, Isaac's neighbors wanted to take his wells. Isaac didn't argue or fight. Instead, Isaac lived in peace with his neighbors.**

>> **Dakota, when is a time someone your age might feel like arguing or fighting?** (Someone is mean. Someone doesn't want to take turns or share.) **God can help us know what to do so that we can live in peace with our friends.**

>> **Jaden, when someone wants to take something you are playing with, what can you do to live in peace?** (Tell the person I will share in a few minutes. Ask an adult for help. Find another toy for the person. Find a new toy for me.)

>> **Jesus said, "Live in peace." We need God's help to live in peace with others.** Pray briefly, **Dear God, please help us know how to live in peace with others. In Jesus' name, amen.**

For Older Children
Set up a series of wells. To complete relay, children run from one well to the next, drinking small amount of water at each well.

God's Word
"Blessed are the peacemakers, for they will be called sons of God." Matthew 5:9

For Younger Children:
"Live in peace."

God's Word & Me
When I feel like fighting, I can stop and ask for God's help to know how to make peace.

LESSON TWO

Game Center
for older children
Genesis 26:12-33

Collect
Bible.

Do

1. Play Peacemaker Tag. Designate several children to be Peacemakers and several children to be It. (For example, if there are 20 children, designate 3 to be Peacemakers and 3 to be It.) Explain that the Peacemakers cannot be tagged, but will free children who are tagged.

2. Start playing the game. When a child is tagged, he or she freezes with hands in a fighting pose. Child remains frozen until freed by a Peacemaker. Once a child is freed, he or she becomes a Peacemaker and helps to free others. (If playing area is small, children take baby steps to move around during the game.) Play until most children have been tagged and then freed to become Peacemakers. Repeat game as time permits, with different children taking the roles of Peacemakers and It.

God's Word

"Whoever wants to become great among you must be your servant."
Matthew 20:26

For Younger Children:
"Serve others."

God's Word & Me

My unselfish actions help me live like Jesus and get along with my family.

Talk About

>> Read Matthew 5:9. **What might someone do who is a peacemaker?** (End an argument. Look for ways to live in peace with others. Help two friends get along.)

>> **When are some times kids your age can be peacemakers?** (When a brother or sister refuses to help you. When someone at school starts an argument.)

>> **What can kids your age do to be peacemakers?** (Talk to someone instead of fighting. Be patient. Walk away until the person isn't so angry.)

>> **What can we do to obey Jesus' words in Matthew 5:9 when we're tempted to fight?** (Pray and ask God for help. Ask an adult for advice.)

>> **Sometimes it's hard to think of what to do to live in peace with others. God promises to help us know the right things to do.** Lead children in prayer, asking God to help us resist the urge to fight and become kids who live in peace.

For Younger Children

Have children stand on one side of the room. Stand on the other side of the room and announce that you are a Peacemaker. Run or walk across to grab one child's hand and bring the child back to your starting position. Then that child runs or walks across the room to bring someone else back to the Peacemaker side, and so on, until all have become Peacemakers.

© 2007 Gospel Light. Permission to photocopy granted. *Agents in Action*

LESSON TWO

Art Center
for younger children
Genesis 26:12-33

Collect

Bible, Lesson 2 Pattern Page (p. 70), sturdy construction paper or card stock, scissors, crayons or markers.

Prepare

Make one copy of Pattern Page for each child onto paper or card stock. Cut slit in each page (see sketch). Make a sample of the puppets.

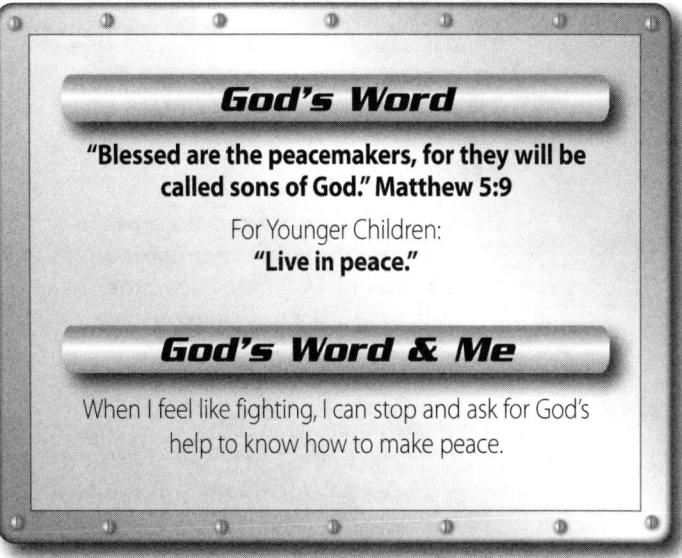

God's Word

"Blessed are the peacemakers, for they will be called sons of God." Matthew 5:9

For Younger Children:
"Live in peace."

God's Word & Me

When I feel like fighting, I can stop and ask for God's help to know how to make peace.

Do

1. Insert puppets into your sample page to briefly show Bible story action. **Today in our Bible story a man named Isaac dug a well to get water. His neighbors were mad and told him to leave! Isaac was kind and moved to a new place. But when he dug a new well, the same thing happened. Finally, Isaac's neighbors became his friends.** Reinsert neighbors puppet to show happy faces. **Isaac was glad God helped him make peace.**

2. Give each child a Pattern Page. Child cuts off puppets and colors page.

3. Child inserts puppets into page to show Bible story action.

Talk About

>> Jesus said, "Live in peace." Our Bible story tells that Isaac wanted to live in peace, instead of fighting or arguing with others.

>> One way to live in peace is to talk kindly to others. Sam, what are some kind words you can say to people in your family to make your home more peaceful? (Please. Thanks. You're welcome. I love you.)

>> Another way to live in peace is to act in kind ways, even when someone is unkind. Kaylee, if someone throws a ball at you, how can you live in peace and be kind? (Find someone else to play with. Tell the person that throwing the ball hurts.) Pray briefly, **Dear God, please help us remember to live in peace. In Jesus' name, amen.**

For Older Children

Using the Pattern Page as a guide, children make and illustrate their own pages and puppets, showing situations in which kids their age need to live in peace.

Art Center
for older children
Genesis 26:12-33

Collect

Bible, scissors, at least two different colors of gift-wrap cellophane, clear plastic cups (two for each student), glue sticks.

Do

1. **Today you may each make a peace cup, one for you and one for a friend.** Children help each other by cutting cellophane into a variety of 1-inch (2.5-cm) shapes.

2. Give each child two cups. Children use glue sticks to glue outsides of cups. Then children select different colored pieces of cellophane and press them onto glued area on their cups, forming designs of their own choosing. (Note: For younger children, suggest they glue one area of a cup at a time.)

3. Children take home peace cups and give to others with whom they want to live in peace.

God's Word

"Blessed are the peacemakers, for they will be called sons of God." Matthew 5:9

For Younger Children:
"Live in peace."

God's Word & Me

When I feel like fighting, I can stop and ask for God's help to know how to make peace.

Talk About

>> Read Matthew 5:9. **How might someone act who is a peacemaker? Why do you think Jesus said peacemakers are called "sons of God?"** (They show others that God loves everyone and wants people to live in peace.)

>> **Why does God want us to get along with others and be peacemakers?** (When we get along, we show God's love to each other. God knows that living in peace is the best way to live.)

>> **When might kids your age have a hard time acting as peacemakers?** Pray together, asking God's help in being peacemakers.

For Younger Children

Children attach stickers to cups instead of using cellophane.

LESSON TWO

Worship Center
for younger and older children
Genesis 26:12-33

Collect

Bibles, *Agent* Music CD and player, song charts (pp. 246, 250), two buckets and a large plastic cup for each team, uncooked beans or pasta.

Preparation

For each team, fill one bucket with beans or pasta. Place filled bucket in an open area of the room. Place empty bucket at the other end of the open area.

Team Game

Divide group into two or more teams of special agents. Invite an equal number of volunteers from each team to line up at the start line. **Let's see how long it takes our teams of special agents to fill up their wells.** Give first player on each team a plastic cup. At your signal, players dip cup into bucket of beans or pasta, run to the empty bucket and pour beans or pasta into the bucket. Players run back to team and give cup to next players in line. Relay continues until one team's bucket is full. Team members cheer for their team's agents.

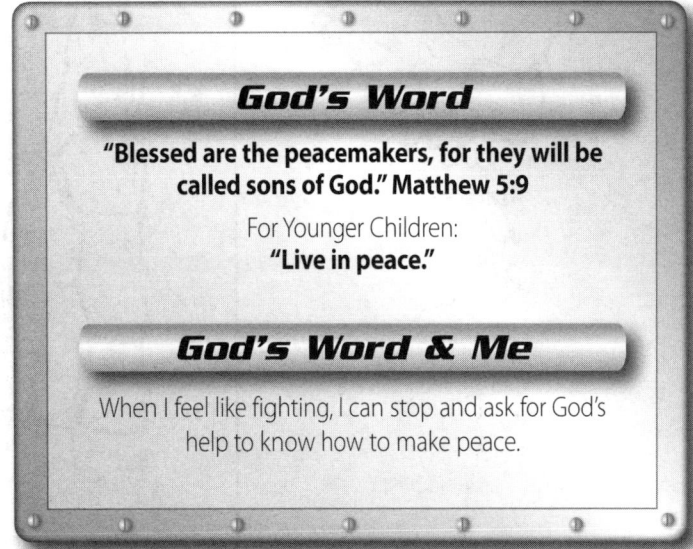

God's Word

"Blessed are the peacemakers, for they will be called sons of God." Matthew 5:9

For Younger Children:
"Live in peace."

God's Word & Me

When I feel like fighting, I can stop and ask for God's help to know how to make peace.

Bible Verse Game

Repeat Matthew 5:9 aloud with children. **Shaking hands is something people do to show that they have made an agreement. While the music plays, move around the room to see how many people you can shake hands with. When you shake hands, say the first part of the verse: "Blessed are the peacemakers." When the music stops, freeze in place.** Play "Psalm 34:12-14" for approximately 10 seconds. Repeat process again, encouraging children to shake hands with different people and repeating the second part of the verse. (Optional: Invite children to create their own special-agent handshake to use when shaking hands with others.)

Song

Lead children in singing "Mission of Love." Add motions and/or clapping if desired.

Prayer

We know that kids, grown-ups and even the leaders of countries sometimes feel like fighting. For all of us, in whatever situations we're in, we can stop and ask God's help in knowing how to be peacemakers. Let's see how many different peaceful actions and words we can think of (share, help, care, take turns, shake hands, high five, hug, say "I'm sorry" or "I forgive you," etc.). Lead children in prayer.

Song

Lead children in singing "God's Kids." Add motions and/or clapping if desired.

LESSON TWO · Pattern Page

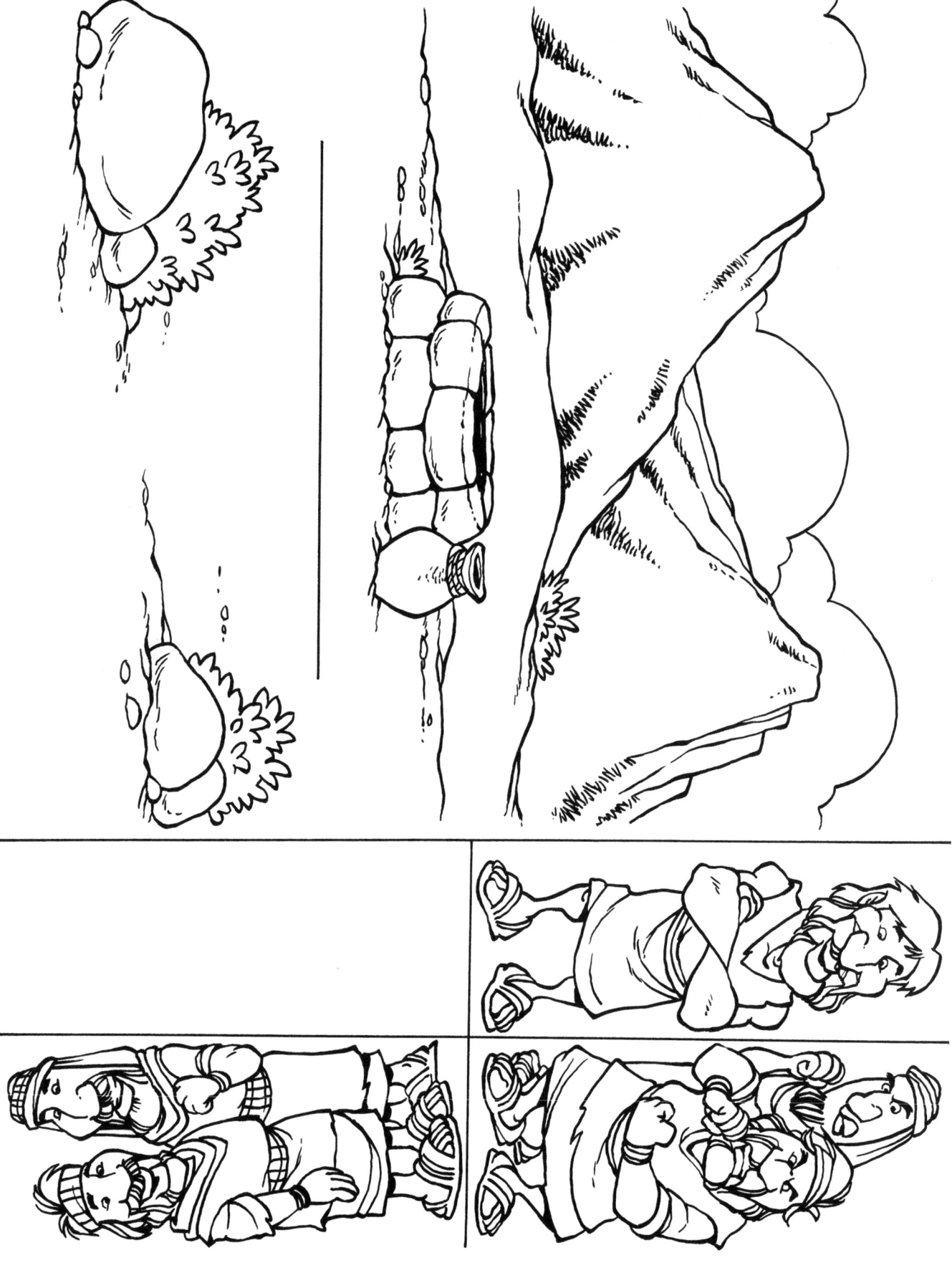

70
© 2007 Gospel Light. Permission to photocopy granted. *Agents in Action*

Isaac chooses not to fight.
Genesis 26:12-33

LESSON TWO · Coloring Page

What can you do when someone is mad and wants to fight?

© 2007 Gospel Light. Permission to photocopy granted. *Agents in Action*

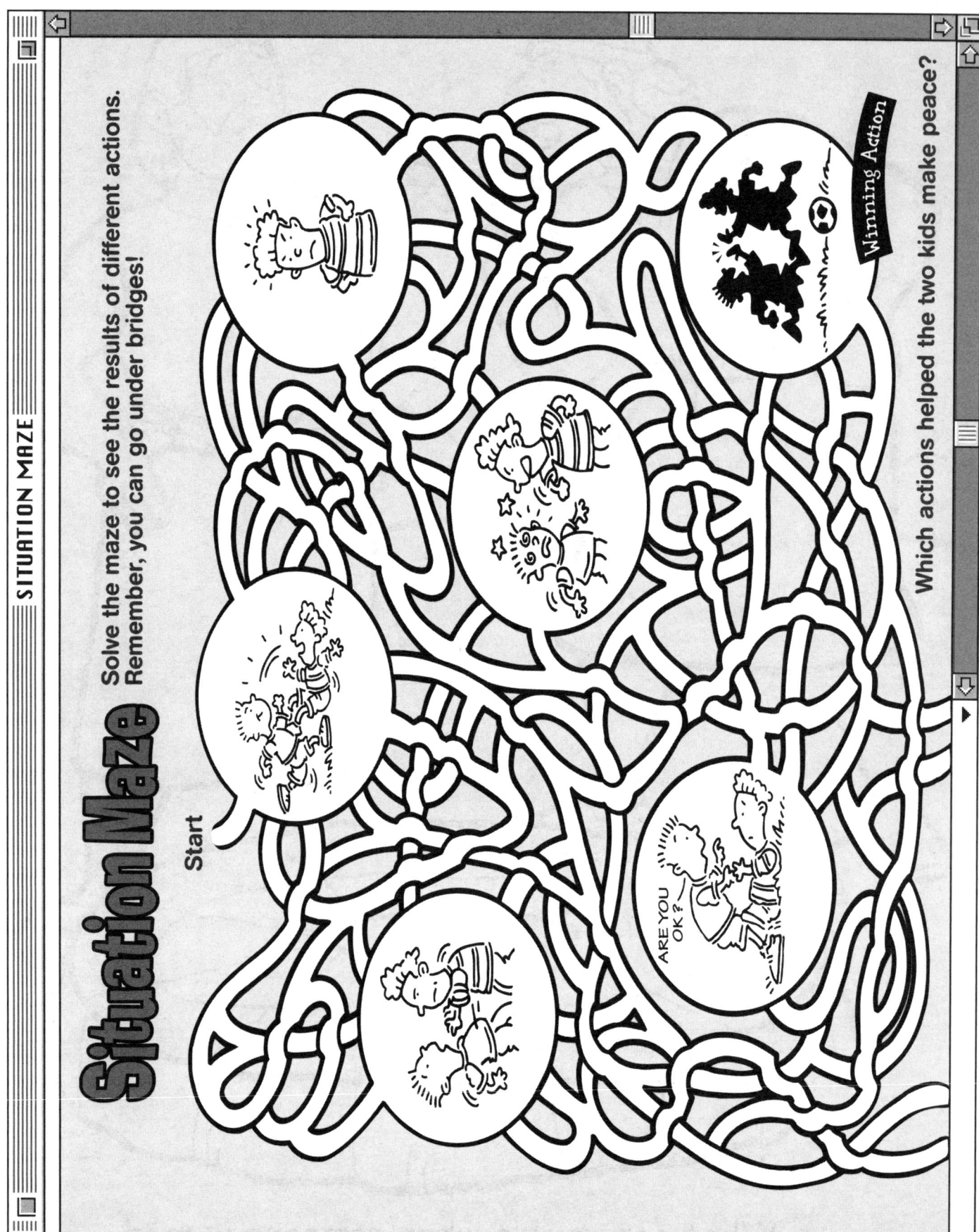

LESSON THREE

Honesty

Bible Story:
Jacob's Lies Lead to Trouble
Genesis 27:1-46

Teacher's Devotional

It's increasingly tough to see the value of honesty and telling the truth. In our world, creating one's own version of the facts is far more popular. Even news agencies now report findings of opinion surveys as if the opinions were as true as the facts themselves! Restructuring events, speaking in hyperbole—accepted ways of lying flourish.

This isn't new. Although there is no written record of Rebekah's words, Jacob's actions indicate that his mother must have often told him he should have been the favored one and deserved the blessing and birthright. Once Jacob believed this, he was blinded to the possibility that God could intervene. Instead, he and his mother concocted their own solutions to this perceived unfairness. First, Jacob deceived Esau with the stew. Once he had taken his brother's birthright, he and his mother saw more deception as the only solution. In fact, Rebekah had already made a plan for deceiving her husband so that Jacob would get what she believed he deserved. Deception then blinded them both to the consequences of their actions—until it was too late.

An old maxim says: "Oh, what a tangled web we weave, when first we practice to deceive!" It is basic to human nature to believe that once we've fallen off the "honesty wagon," we can't be forgiven. Instead, we scramble to keep up appearances and despair inwardly that we can't come clean on this one. But that lie traps us into deceiving again, finding ourselves in a far bigger mess than we ever anticipated!

God's Word

"Do not steal, do not give false testimony."
Matthew 19:18

For Younger Children:
"Be honest."

God's Word & Me

Obeying God's command to be honest helps others trust me.

Kids may choose dishonesty for a variety of reasons: fear of getting in trouble, desire for something unobtainable or perhaps thinking that small lies don't matter. In your discussion with your children, help them understand the value of an honest reputation in both big and little things. Also be sure to communicate that God is always ready to forgive, no matter how great our sin. As we choose to place our trust in Him instead of in our deceit, we can take our problems to Him and ask God to surprise us with His creative answers!

LESSON THREE

Planning Page

Choose which centers you will provide and the order in which children will participate in them (see pp. 14-18 for schedule tips and pp. 24-25 for guidelines in combining older and younger children). Also plan who will lead each center (for staffing tips see pp. 19-21). Use the reproducible planning sheet (p. 238) to record your plans.

Bible Story Center

Bible Story
Jacob's Lies Lead to Trouble • Genesis 27:1-46

Younger Child Option
Move paper-plate puppets to show story action

Older Child Option
Solve a crossword puzzle to discover the daily mission "be honest"

Game Center

Younger Child Option
Give honest answers during games, and talk about times to obey God's command to be honest

Materials
Bible, four paper plates, masking tape, buttons or coins

Older Child Option
Play a game to toss rings around cones, and talk about the results of honesty or dishonesty

Materials
Bible, 3 to 5 sturdy paper plates, scissors, 3 to 5 sports cones, small snacks or other small prizes

Art Center

Younger Child Option
Make paper-bag puppets and use them to practice obeying God by telling the truth

Materials
Bible, Lesson 3 Pattern page (p. 84), markers, scissors glue, lunch-size paper bags

Older Child Option
Decorate and stack papers to make an Honesty Pyramid, and give examples of ways to obey God and be honest

Materials
Bible, different colors of large construction paper, markers, stickers and other decorating materials, glue, tape

Worship Center

For the Younger and Older Child
Participate in large-group activities to review Bible verse and to worship God together

Materials
Bibles, *Agent* Music CD and player, song charts (pp. 249, 251), nine inflated balloons (plus several extras), permanent marker

Coloring/Puzzle Center

Younger Child Option
Review the Bible story while completing coloring page

Materials
Lesson 3 Coloring Page (p. 85) for each student, crayons

Older Child Option
Review the Bible verse while completing puzzle page

Materials
Lesson 3 Puzzle Page (p. 86) for each student, pencils

LESSON THREE

Bonus Theme Ideas

Bonus Theme Ideas can be used at any time during this session: as an additional activity center, to extend the session for a longer time or for added theme excitement.

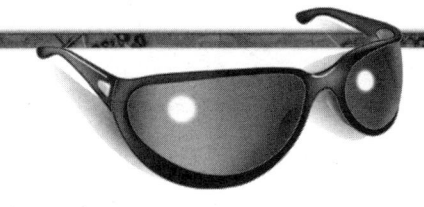

Special Agent Practice

Before class, draw an X on a large sheet of butcher paper or cardboard. In class, divide group into teams of special agents. Assign each team a color and give each child a balloon of the same color. Use permanent marker to write child's initials on his or her balloon. Teams form a circle around the paper or cardboard you prepared. At your signal, children blow up their balloons, but don't tie them. (Note: Some children may need help blowing up balloons. Provide beanbags or crumpled paper balls for preschoolers to toss onto the paper.) At your signal, children let go of their balloons, aiming them toward the X. See which team's balloons get the closest to the X. Children collect their balloons and play again as time and interest allow.

Special Agent Information

Special Agent ID

To remind children that God's special agents live all over the world, create a 3-D display showing where missionaries from your church or denomination live. Cover a large box with black or dark-blue paper. In addition to displaying one or more pictures of the earth as viewed from space (available on the Internet) and other colorful maps, attach the missionaries' photos and names on the sides of the box creating a collage. Throughout *Agents in Action*, use a digital camera to take pictures of your community. Print out the pictures and add them to the display. (Optional: Invite children to bring pictures or postcards from places they visit on vacation to add to the display.)

Special Agent Information

Star Snacks

Provide a variety of star-shaped cookie cutters for children to cut bread into star shapes. Set out plastic knives and bowls with three kinds of jam (strawberry, grape and peach or apricot). Explain to children that the color of a star varies according to how hot it is (red for a cool star, orange for a medium star, purple for the hottest). Children spread jam on their stars, choosing how hot they want their stars to be.

Special Agent Information

Post a note alerting parents to the use of food. Also, check registration forms for possible food allergies.

© 2007 Gospel Light. Permission to photocopy granted. *Agents in Action*

LESSON THREE

Bible Story Center
for younger children
Genesis 27:1-46

Collect

Bible.

Introduction

Everyone put your hands on your head. Now, if you have a brother or sister, put your hands on your shoulders. Volunteers respond. **Listen to find out what happened when two brothers grew up.**

Tell the Story

Jacob and Esau were twin boys who lived long ago in Bible times. Esau had been born first. In Bible times, that meant that Esau would be given special things.

Jacob and Esau were all grown up now. Their father, Isaac, told Esau, "I am getting old. I want to give you my blessing before I die." The blessing meant that Isaac wanted to promise Esau that Esau would be the new leader of the family. But first, Isaac asked Esau to go hunting and cook Isaac's favorite food. Esau went out hunting right away!

But Jacob and Esau's mother, Rebekah, wanted Jacob, instead of Esau, to be the new leader. She told Jacob, "We will get the blessing for YOU while Esau is gone. Do what I say, Jacob."

Isaac was so old that he could not see anything. Rebekah told Jacob to put on Esau's clothes. She put hairy goatskins on Jacob's hands and neck because Esau had a lot of hair. Now that Jacob felt and smelled like Esau, Isaac would think Jacob was Esau! Rebekah made Isaac's favorite meal. She told Jacob to take the food to Isaac.

Jacob took the food to his father. He then said something that was not true. "It's me, Esau," Jacob said. "I've made your food." Isaac asked how he found the food so quickly. "Oh, God helped me!" Jacob said. Jacob lied again!

Isaac smelled Esau's clothes that Jacob was wearing. He felt the goatskins on Jacob's hands. The tricks worked. Isaac said, "It sounds like Jacob's voice, but these hands feel like Esau's hands. It must be Esau who is here with me." Isaac ate, and then he said the words of blessing. Isaac thought he had blessed Esau, but he was really blessing Jacob!

When Esau found out Jacob had tricked their father, he burst out crying. Isaac was sad, too; but it was too late. Esau was so angry, he wanted to hurt Jacob! Jacob had to go away and stay with his uncle. He had to stay away for many, many years.

> **Special Agent Option**
>
> In a box labeled "Top Secret," place four paper plates on which you have drawn faces (see sketch below). Tape a tongue depressor to each puppet so that you can use the plates as puppets. At the beginning of the story, remove puppets from box and use them to act out the story.

God's Word & Me

What happened because Jacob did not tell the truth? (Isaac was tricked. Esau was angry. Jacob had to go away.) **Jacob's lies made lots of trouble for EVERYONE in his family! Telling the truth is much better than making trouble!**

In the Bible, Jesus said, "Be honest." When someone asks us a question, it's important to say what is true. Telling the truth to others is a way to obey God. Pray, **Dear God, please help us to be honest and tell the truth. In Jesus' name, amen.**

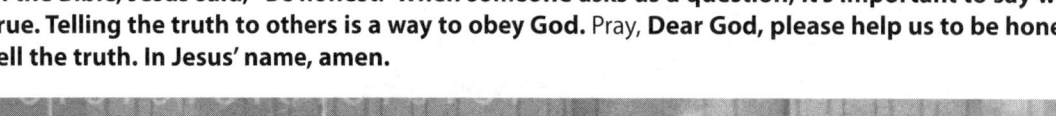

LESSON THREE

Bible Story Center
for older children
Genesis 27:1-46

Collect

Bible, highlighters in four colors.

Prepare

Make five copies of Genesis 27:1-36. Use a highlighter to mark the spoken words of Isaac, Esau, Rebekah and Jacob.

Introduction

What is something that would be fun about having a twin brother or sister? What might be hard? Volunteers respond. **In our Bible story today, we're going to hear about the problems of two brothers who were twins.** Give prepared copies of Genesis 27:1-36 to four volunteers. At the appropriate time in the story, ask volunteers to read spoken words of Isaac, Esau, Rebekah and Jacob. Read the narration yourself.

Special Agent Option

Before class, enlarge a blank crossword puzzle from a newspaper or crossword puzzle book. Print the daily mission "BE HONEST" in several places in the puzzle. Fill in extra boxes with random letters. (To simplify this puzzle, fill in extra boxes with only two or three other letters.) Make several copies of the prepared puzzle. Place puzzles in a box labeled "Top Secret." At the end of the story, volunteers remove puzzles and discover the daily mission.

Tell the Story

Jacob and Esau were the twin sons of Isaac. These boys were very different from each other but they were twins. It was now many years since Jacob had bought Esau's birthright for a bowl of stew. (The birthright was the special gifts he would receive as the oldest son.) Now Jacob and Esau were grown men. Their parents, Isaac and Rebekah, were much older, too. Isaac was so old that he couldn't see any longer. He was blind.

Isaac called Esau into his tent. "I'm getting old. I may not live much longer," Isaac said. "I want to give you my blessing." (The blessing was a prayer that God would show favor on Esau. It was also a promise that Isaac would give the majority of his wealth to Esau and that Esau would have authority as the leader of the family after Isaac died.)

Then Isaac said, "But first, go hunting and bring back some meat. Cook it the way I like it. After we eat, I will give you my blessing."

Rebekah heard Isaac and Esau talking. She didn't want Esau to be the leader. She wanted HER favorite son, Jacob, to be the leader of the family! So Rebekah made a plan—a very sneaky plan.

"Jacob! Jacob! Come here!" she called.

"Here I am, Mother," said Jacob. "What is it?"

"Your father is about to give Esau the blessing. Now, I have a plan so that you can get your father's blessing instead of Esau. But you'll have to hurry! Get two young goats."

Jacob did as his mother asked. Rebekah made a delicious goat stew cooked the way Isaac liked it. Rebekah brought out some of Esau's clothes and helped Jacob put them on. Then she tied some goatskins on the smooth skin of Jacob's hands and arms. She told Jacob to take the food to Isaac and pretend to be Esau.

© 2007 Gospel Light. Permission to photocopy granted. *Agents in Action*

Jacob took the food to his father. "Who's there?" asked Isaac.

"It's me, Esau," Jacob lied. "I've made your food just the way you like it. Sit up and eat and then you can give me your blessing."

But Isaac suspected something was wrong. He asked, "How did you get back so quickly?"

"God helped me," Jacob lied again.

"Come closer," Isaac ordered. When Jacob came closer, Isaac touched the goat skin on Jacob's hand. It felt like Esau's hand. Isaac could smell Esau's clothes. They smelled like the outdoors, like Esau. So Isaac believed Jacob's lie. Isaac ate the food Jacob brought and then he gave Jacob the blessing that should have been Esau's. As soon as Isaac blessed him, Jacob left the tent.

Right after Jacob left Isaac's tent, Esau came back from hunting. He cooked Isaac's favorite meal and then hurried to take it to Isaac. But when he got to the tent, he found that Isaac had already eaten.

"Who are you?" Isaac demanded.

"I am your son, Esau! I brought the food you asked me for. I'm here for the special blessing you promised to give me."

Isaac began to shake all over. "Who was it that fixed the meal I just ate? I gave him my special blessing, and I can't take back the blessing!"

Because Esau was SO very angry at Jacob's lies, Rebekah told Jacob to leave home. Jacob's lie caused so much trouble that he had to run away from home. He had to stay away from his family for many years.

God's Word & Me

Jacob's dishonest actions caused a lot of problems for him and his family. Being honest and telling the truth helps prevent a lot of problems from happening.

Read Matthew 19:18. **Jesus said these words and we can also read them in the Old Testament part of the Bible** (see Exodus 20:15-16). **God wants us to tell the truth to each other and be honest in the way we treat others. If you are honest, everyone around you—your friends, your family, your teachers—know that they can count on you. You will be a person who can be trusted to be honest. We can ask God to help us when it is hard to be honest.**

>> **When might someone your age need to choose between honesty and dishonesty?** (When your parent asks if you watched a TV show you're not allowed to watch. When a friend wants to copy your homework.)

>> **What are some of the reasons it's good for people to know that you are honest?**

>> **What difference would it make in your school if everyone was honest?**

>> **When is it hard for kids your age to be honest and tell the truth?** Pray with children, asking God's help in obeying His command to be honest.

LESSON THREE

Game Center
for younger children
Genesis 27:1-46

Collect

Bible, four paper plates, masking tape, buttons or coins.

Prepare

Lay four paper plates in a row on the floor a few feet apart. Place masking-tape lines one, two, three and four feet from row.

Do

Let's play some games where we have to be honest and tell the right answers. (1) Demonstrate hiding a button (or coin) inside one of your fists while holding both fists behind your back. Ask a volunteer to guess which hand is holding the button and which hand is empty. Tell the correct answer and then open fists and show the button. Help children form pairs. Give each pair a button (or coin). Partners take turns hiding and guessing. (2) Children line up behind the one-foot masking-tape line. Children take turns tossing a button (or coin) onto one of the plates and depending on the result of the toss, they say "I did it" or "I missed it." Move to more challenging tosses. Continue play as time permits.

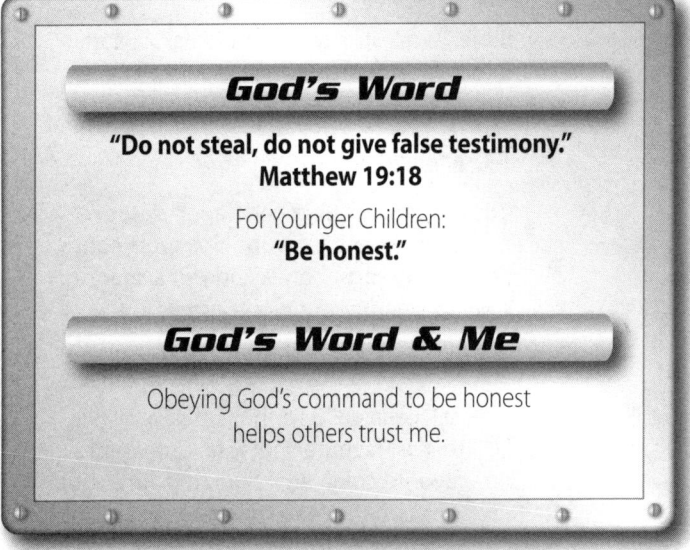

God's Word

"Do not steal, do not give false testimony."
Matthew 19:18

For Younger Children:
"Be honest."

God's Word & Me

Obeying God's command to be honest helps others trust me.

Talk About

>> **It's fun to play games! What did you have to do or say to be honest in the games we played today?** (Stand behind the line. Tell the truth about which hand was holding the button.) **When people are honest, it's more fun to play games together.**

>> **Jesse, when is a time your mom or dad asks you a question? You can tell the truth and be honest when your dad asks you if you put away your toys.**

>> **Jesus said, "Be honest." When we obey these words of Jesus, other people know they can trust us. They know we will say what is right.** Pray briefly, **Dear God, please help us remember to always tell the truth. In Jesus' name, amen.**

For Older Children

Double or triple the distance between the plates and masking-tape lines, depending on children's ages. Children say words of Bible verse before each button (or coin) toss.

LESSON THREE

Game Center
for older children
Genesis 27:1-46

Collect

Bible, 3 to 5 sturdy paper plates, scissors, 3 to 5 sports cones, small snacks or other small prizes.

Prepare

Cut the center out of the paper plates to make rings that fit around the sport cones. Set out the sport cones and put a snack or small prize under one of them.

Do

1. Ask each child to think of several things (favorite snack, favorite game, favorite color, etc.) that are true about him or her. **We're going to play a game in which we tell what is true about ourselves.**

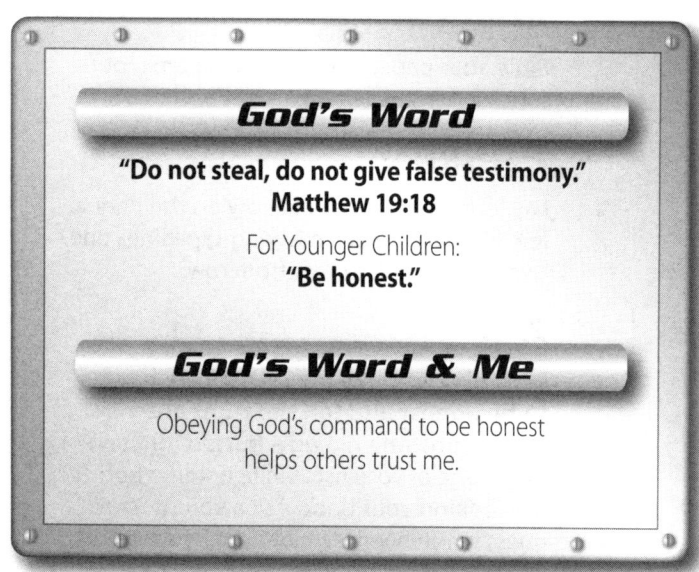

God's Word

"Do not steal, do not give false testimony."
Matthew 19:18

For Younger Children:
"Be honest."

God's Word & Me

Obeying God's command to be honest helps others trust me.

2. Ask for three to five volunteers and give each one a ring. Have each volunteer take a turn to tell something true about him- or herself, and then toss ring to hook it on a cone. (Adjust distance children stand from rings according to age and ability.) After three tries, child may simply place the ring on the cone. When everyone has hooked a ring on a cone, children lift up their cones to see who gets the prize. Repeat game with new volunteers until everyone has had a chance to play. Pass out the rest of the snacks or prizes for everyone who didn't get one during the game.

Talk About

>> **When are some times that kids might choose not to tell the truth?** (Parent or teacher wants to know if they've done something. When playing a game. When something gets broken.)

>> **Who is someone you know who always tells the truth to you? How do you feel about that person?** (I can trust the person. I like to be with him or her.) **If you know that someone lies to you, how does that make you feel? What are the results in a family when kids are not honest?**

>> Read Matthew 19:18. **When we obey God's command to tell the truth, how can it help our friendships?** (It makes them stronger. Our friends will feel they can trust us to be honest.)

>> **When we are tempted to lie, what can we do?** (We can remember Jesus' command to tell the truth. We can pray to God for help to be honest.) Lead children in prayer, asking God to help us always be honest.

For Younger Children

Make an obstacle course with the cones. Have children finish sentences about their favorite items ("My favorite food is [pizza]") and then run around the cones. Give each child a snack or prize when he or she finishes the obstacle course.

© 2007 Gospel Light. Permission to photocopy granted. *Agents in Action*

LESSON THREE

Art Center
for younger children
Genesis 27:1-46

Collect
Bible, Lesson 3 Pattern page (p. 84), markers, scissors glue, lunch-size paper bags.

Prepare
Make one copy of Pattern Page for each child. (Optional: Precut facial features for children.)

Do
1. Each child chooses facial features from Pattern Page to color, cut and glue onto the bottom of a paper bag to create a puppet face. Children color clothing and hair on paper bags.
2. Show children how to put paper bags over their hands, using fingers to wiggle the "head" of their puppets. Children use puppets to say words that are true (God loves me. My name is [Penni]. I like to eat apples.)

Talk About
>> **Noah, what true things can you say with your puppet?** Every day when you talk to your mom or dad or your friends, you can say what is true. When you are honest, people know they can trust you. They know you will say what is right.

>> **Morgan, who is someone you can tell the truth to?** Your (grandma) is glad when you tell her the truth. It's good to be honest.

>> **Jesus said, "Be honest."** Pray briefly, **Dear God, help us tell the truth and be honest. In Jesus' name, amen.**

For Older Children
Provide a variety of decorative materials (chenille wire, fabric scraps, trim, etc.) for children to use in making puppets. After making puppets, children use them to say two true things about themselves and one untrue thing. Other children try to guess what is true and untrue. (Optional: Children write items on paper. Read items aloud. Group tries to guess which child wrote the items as well as which are true and untrue.)

God's Word
"Do not steal, do not give false testimony."
Matthew 19:18

For Younger Children:
"Be honest."

God's Word & Me
Obeying God's command to be honest helps others trust me.

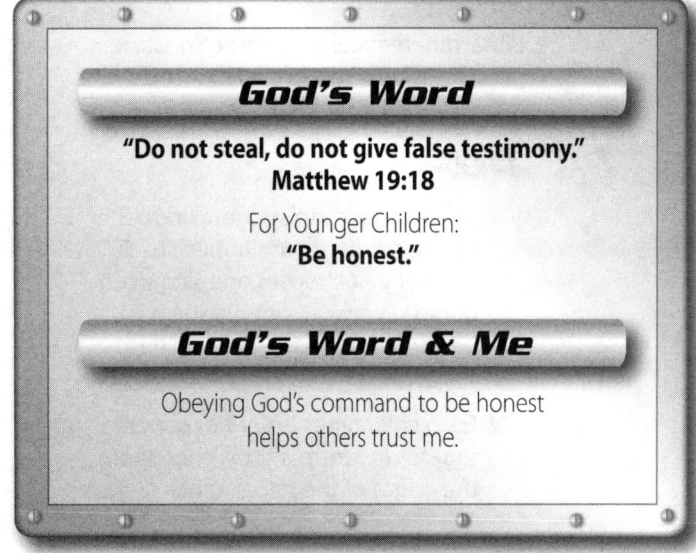

© 2007 Gospel Light. Permission to photocopy granted. *Agents in Action*

LESSON THREE

Art Center
for older children
Genesis 27:1-46

Collect

Bible, different colors of large construction paper, markers, stickers and other decorating materials, glue, tape.

Do

1. Invite children to suggest slogans or phrases about being honest. Each child or pair chooses one slogan or phrase and writes it on a sheet of construction paper. Children decorate papers.

2. Each child tapes his or her paper together to form a tube, overlapping the edges of the paper 1 inch (2.5 cm).

3. When everyone is finished, have children stack their tubes in a pyramid. Children read slogans aloud.

God's Word

"Do not steal, do not give false testimony."
Matthew 19:18

For Younger Children:
"Be honest."

God's Word & Me

Obeying God's command to be honest helps others trust me.

Talk About

>> **Why do you think kids sometimes choose to be dishonest?** (They are afraid of getting into trouble. They want to do something they are not allowed to do.)

>> **What might happen if a kid is often dishonest? What might result if a kid tries to always tell the truth and be honest?** (If we lie, others might not trust us. If we tell the truth, we could help our friendships and we show our love for God.)

>> Read Matthew 19:18. **This verse gives two examples of ways to be honest: don't steal and don't tell lies about others in a court. What are some examples of ways kids today can be honest?** (Play fair in a game. Do your own work on a test.) **God wants us to obey His command and always tell the truth because it helps others trust us. Honesty helps others, but telling lies hurts others.** Pray, asking God to give us the strength to always tell the truth.

For Younger Children

Print "Be Honest" on each sheet of construction paper. Children decorate the papers. (Optional: Tape papers together and let children stack them in a pyramid.)

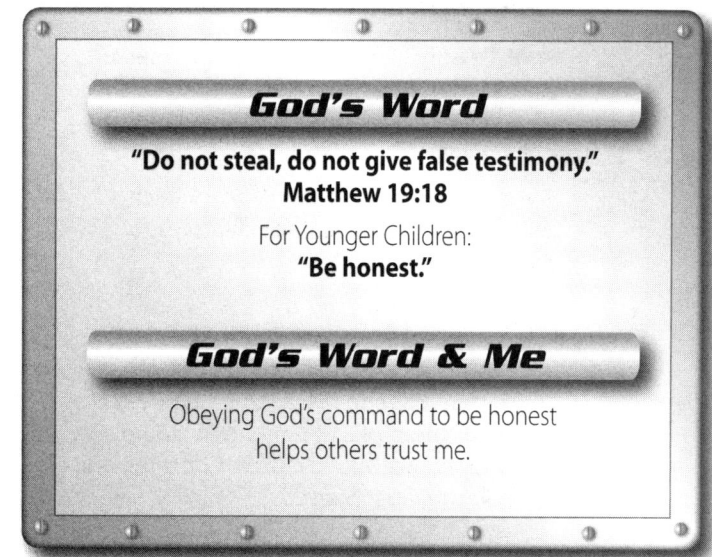

LESSON THREE

Worship Center
for younger and older children
Genesis 27:1-46

Collect

Bibles, *Agent* Music CD and player, song charts (pp. 249, 251), nine inflated balloons (plus several extras), permanent marker.

Preparation

Use permanent marker to write each word of Matthew 19:18 and the reference on a separate balloon.

Team Game

Ask all children and leaders to stand up and play "Sit Down If." Tell the children that you are going to read a list beginning with the phrase "Sit down if . . . ." If the phrase honestly describes them, they sit down. The last three or four children left standing are the winners. Play the game using phrases such as, "you have a pet bird", "you sleep in a bunk bed", "you like to eat spinach", "you ate pancakes for breakfast", "your birthday is in (July)", "you are wearing shorts", "you have a younger brother or sister", etc. Toward the end of the game, you might have to think of phrases that fit the children in your group in order to determine the winners.

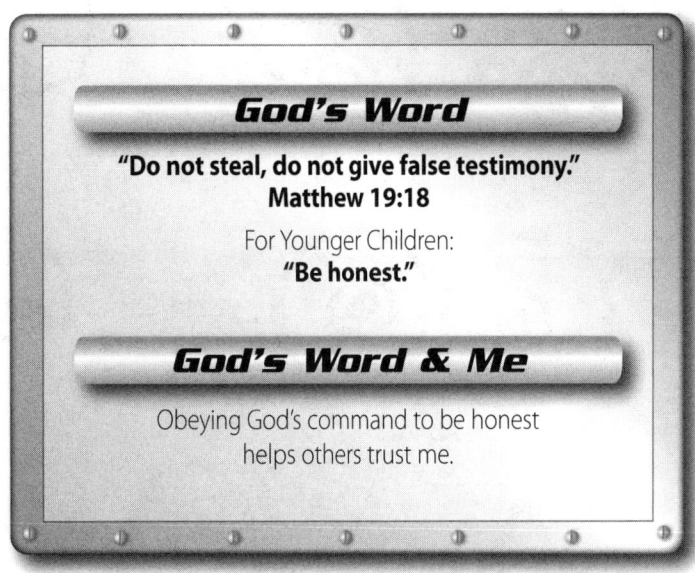

God's Word

"Do not steal, do not give false testimony."
Matthew 19:18

For Younger Children:
"Be honest."

God's Word & Me

Obeying God's command to be honest helps others trust me.

Bible Verse Game

Tap prepared balloons to children around the room. Invite children to continue tapping balloons around the room. After 10 or 15 seconds, say, "Catch." Children try to grab the nearest balloon. Children holding balloons run to the front of the room and quickly arrange themselves in verse order. (Give help to non-readers as needed.) Read Matthew 19:18 together. Repeat as time permits.

Song

Lead children in singing "Gotta Give It Up!" Add motions and/or clapping if desired.

Prayer

Think of what you'll be doing after you leave church today. Think of the people you will be with. What can you do and say to be honest? Clap your hands when you've thought of a way to be honest. As time permits, invite children to tell responses. **Let's ask God to help us be honest in all the things we do and say.** Lead children in prayer.

Song

Lead children in singing "Psalm 34:12-14." Add motions and/or clapping if desired.

PINBALL PARLOR!

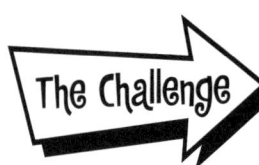

Matthew 19:18

The Challenge

"Do not steal, do not give false testimony."

Follow the arrows to find the path that goes through all the words of the verse.

How many situations can you think of in which kids your age need to be honest?

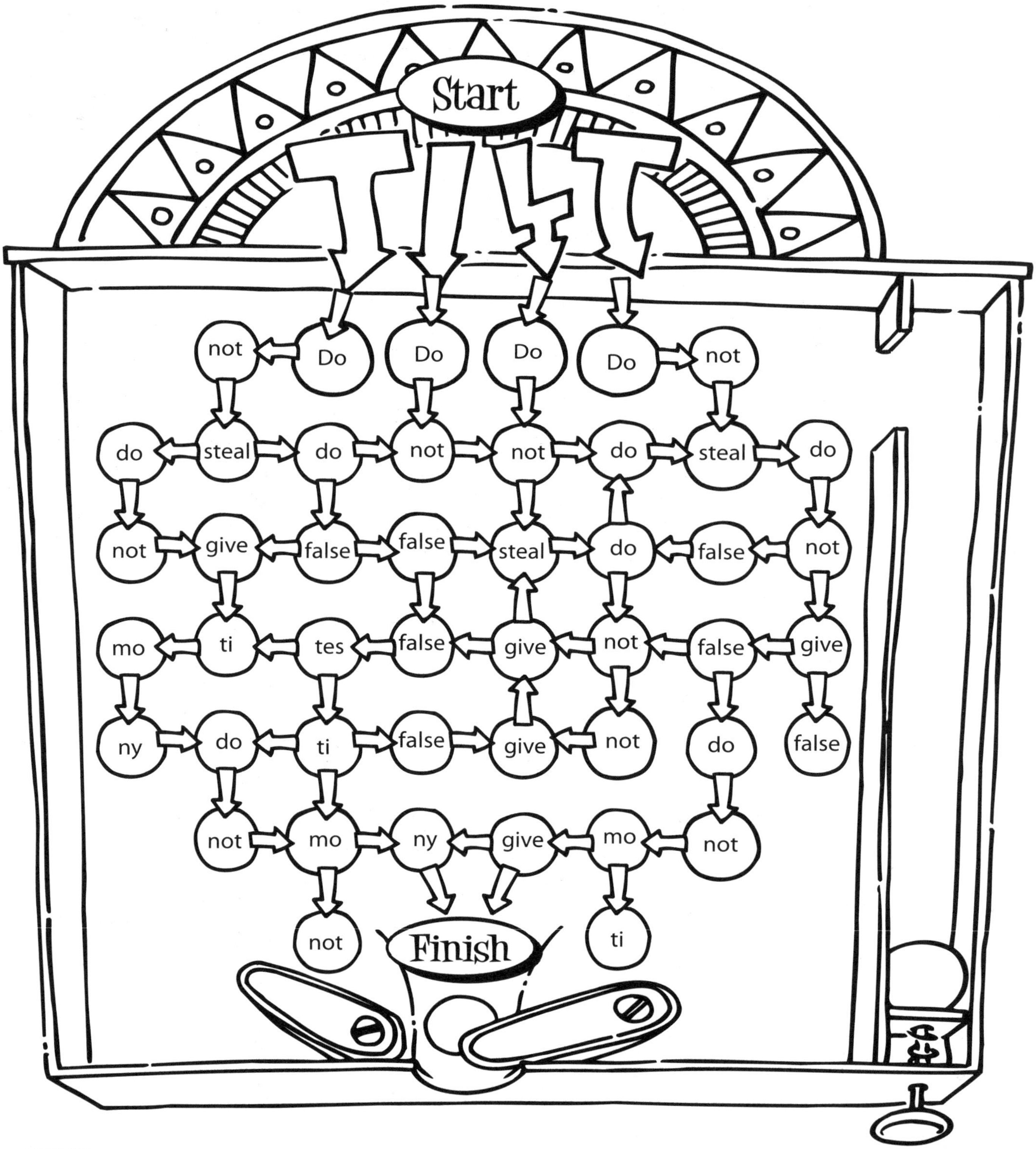

LESSON FOUR

Fear

Bible Story:
Gideon Needs Proof
Judges 6—7

Teacher's Devotional

We'd all like for our children to live free of fears, emotional scars and painful events. But pain and loss come: death of a loved one, divorce, loss of a friend, separation from family members—the list of possible losses is long. Fearful losses and tough times give rise to questions that are not easy to answer. *Why did Grandma die? Is it my fault you got divorced? Why did God let that person hurt my friend? Why didn't God stop this bad thing from happening—doesn't He love us?*

Let kids know it is OK to cry and to express anger, fear, abandonment or sadness. It is even OK to express those feelings to God. (Look at the psalms David wrote. He was honest with God about his emotions!) There are no easy answers to life's fearful times. And our quick adult answers may belittle a child's feelings and well shut down the chance to talk honestly with a child. Curb the urge to speak for God to tell a child why something happened. Answers may come over time, or they may never come.

Because we know God loves us, we can wholeheartedly trust Him. We can be sure that He is with us, cares about us and grieves with us. We can be thankful that no matter how bad the situation, He knows all about it. He is working it together for His glory and for our good—no matter how things look (see Romans 8:28).

When fearful times come, don't try to tough it out! Just as God patiently proved His love to Gideon over and over, God waits for us to trust Him enough to come to Him with our fears, our questions and our frustrations. He waits with open arms to hear us, hold us and help us walk together through the tough times.

God's Word

"Do not let your hearts be troubled. Trust in God; trust also in me." John 14:1

For Younger Children:
"Trust in God's care."

God's Word & Me

When I'm afraid or worried, I can trust in God to help me.

LESSON FOUR

Planning Page

Choose which centers you will provide and the order in which children will participate in them (see pp. 14-18 for schedule tips and pp. 24-25 for guidelines in combining older and younger children). Also plan who will lead each center (for staffing tips see pp. 19-21). Use the reproducible planning sheet (p. 238) to record your plans.

Bible Story Center

Bible Story
Gideon Needs Proof • Judges 6—7

Younger Child Option
Show and use story props to help tell the story

Older Child Option
Fly and catch special-agent shuttles (paper airplanes) to discover the daily mission "trust in God"

Game Center

Younger Child Option
Move through an obstacle course and talk about ways God helps when feeling afraid

Materials
Bible; *Agent* Music CD and player; furniture, boxes or blocks to create an obstacle course

Older Child Option
Identify common fears and talk about what it means to trust in God's care when feeling afraid or worried

Materials
Bible, large sheet of butcher paper, marker, masking tape, scissors, slips of paper, pencils

Art Center

Younger Child Option
Make dot-art posters of their names and talk about God's care for each child

Materials
Bible, paper, marker, several colors of tempera paints, shallow baking pans, cotton swabs, newspaper

Older Child Option
Sculpt open hands to represent God's help and discuss ways of showing trust in God

Materials
Bible, modeling clay or air-drying play dough, paper plate for each child, markers

Worship Center

For the Younger and Older Child
Participate in large-group activities to review Bible verse and to worship God together

Materials
Bibles, *Agent* Music CD and player, song charts (pp. 247-248), balloons, permanent marker, masking tape

Coloring/Puzzle Center

Younger Child Option
Review the Bible story while completing coloring page

Materials
Lesson 4 Coloring Page (p. 99) for each student, crayons

Older Child Option
While completing puzzle page, review ways of acting when feeling afraid

Materials
Lesson 4 Puzzle Page (p. 100) for each student, pencils

LESSON FOUR

Bonus Theme Ideas

Bonus Theme Ideas can be used at any time during this session: as an additional activity center, to extend the session for a longer time or for added theme excitement.

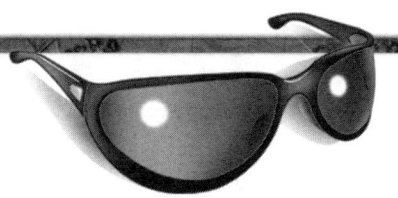

Secret Pal Agents

Invite children to be secret pal agents. Secretly give each child the name of another child who is attending *Agents in Action*, along with a letter to be taken home with instructions for how to be a secret pal. You may designate two or more sessions to which secret pals bring small items (stickers, candy, party favors, etc.) labeled with their secret pal's name. Establish a central location at which secret pal gifts can be left. (Have ready a few extra items in case some children forget to bring their secret pal gifts.) Plan a special way to identify the secret pal agents—children bring signed cards to give to their secret pals, or tell each child to whisper "S.P.A." (Secret Pal Agent) to his or her secret pal sometime during the session.

Special Agent Information

Agent Rescue

Play a game of tag with a twist. When an "agent" is tagged, he or she must freeze and place hand on body where tagged. After another agent rescues the player by tagging him or her, player rejoins game. (Variations: Designate several children as rescuers, changing rescuers every so often. If playing tag with younger children, leaders and helpers take turns being "It" and trying to tag children.)

Special Agent Information

Dip It!

On separate plates, place toothpicks, cheese cubes, diced fruit and minimarshmallows. Make dip by using a whisk to mix ¾ cup plain yogurt with two tablespoons maple syrup. Place dip into one or more bowls. Children use toothpicks to pick up the food items, dip and enjoy!

Special Agent Information

Post a note alerting parents to the use of food. Also, check registration forms for possible food allergies.

© 2007 Gospel Light. Permission to photocopy granted. *Agents in Action*

LESSON FOUR

Bible Story Center
for younger children
Judges 6—7

Collect
Bible.

Introduction
Make a scared face if you've ever felt afraid. What might kids do when they are afraid? Volunteers respond. **Listen to hear what God's people did when they were afraid.**

Tell the Story
God's people, the Israelites, had disobeyed God. Now they were in trouble! The Midianites were their enemies. They stole all the Israelites' food! The Israelites were afraid! But finally, they asked God for help.

Special Agent Option
In a box labeled "Top Secret," place one or more of these story props: a piece of sheepskin fabric, a kazoo, a flashlight, an earthenware jar. (Optional: Provide a kazoo for each child.) At appropriate times in the story, remove items from box and use them (play kazoo, turn on flashlight) or show them to children.

One day an Israelite named Gideon was hiding from the Midianites. He was hiding so that the Midianites would not find him and steal the small amount of wheat he was getting ready to eat! God sent an angel to talk to Gideon. The angel said, "God is with you, mighty warrior!" What a funny way to describe someone who is hiding!

God told Gideon to save Israel from the Midianites. Gideon didn't think he could save Israel. But God said, "I will be with you and help you!"

Gideon was afraid! He asked the angel to prove he was speaking from God. The angel did!

Soon, many people came to help Gideon fight the Midianites. But Gideon still was afraid. He asked God to show him he was doing right.

"I will put a sheepskin out on the ground tonight," Gideon said. "Please make it wet. Leave everything around it dry. Then I will know I am doing what You said." And God did what Gideon asked! Then Gideon asked God to make the sheepskin dry and the ground wet! God did that, too! Finally, Gideon was not afraid. He knew God would help him.

God told Gideon to give each man in his army a trumpet and a big water jar. In each jar, the men hid a torch. In the middle of the night, the men quietly circled the Midianite camp. Then, they ALL blew their trumpets. They ALL smashed their jars. They ALL waved their lighted torches. They ALL shouted, "FOR THE LORD AND FOR GIDEON!"

When the Midianites saw the light and heard the noise, they ran away! All Gideon's army had to do was chase them OUT of Israel! God helped Gideon when he was afraid.

God's Word & Me
Gideon must have been glad that God helped him when he was afraid. There might be times that we feel afraid, too. When we're afraid, we can remember that God will help us.

In the Bible, Jesus said, "Trust in God's care." When we trust in God, it means that we remember that God cares for us and that He will help us. One way God helps us is by giving us people who love us. Pray, **Thank You, God, for caring for us. Thank You for helping us when we are afraid. In Jesus' name, amen.**

LESSON FOUR

Bible Story Center
for older children
Judges 6—7

Collect

Bible, instant camera.

Introduction

What are some things people do to protect themselves when they are afraid? (Wear seatbelt. Lock doors. Buy burglar alarm.) **Today we're going to hear about what a man in Bible times used to protect himself and his army.** After you tell each section of the story, assign characters (Gideon, stranger, messengers, soldiers, Midianites) to different volunteers. Volunteers pose, illustrating the action of that section of the story. Use an instant camera to photograph children posing. Display photographs in story order. (Optional: Provide Bible-times costumes for children to wear, or provide props such as trumpet, jar, sheepskin, etc. for children to use while posing.)

Special Agent Option

Before class, write the daily mission "trust in God" on several sheets of paper. Fold papers to make paper airplanes representing special-agent shuttles. Place papers in a box labeled "Top Secret." At the end of the story, volunteers remove special-agent shuttles and fly them to children. Children unfold papers and read daily mission aloud. (Optional: Refold papers and fly again as time permits.)

Tell the Story

One of God's followers, Gideon, was threshing grain—tossing it into the air to separate the hulls from the grain. Usually people do this in the open air, so the breeze carries off the hulls. But Gideon was doing it while he HID! He was down in a large pit under an oak tree! You see, the Midianites, Israel's enemy, were everywhere. And they were taking everything—flocks, herds and food! Gideon was scared and was hiding and hoping the Midianites wouldn't find him and take his grain! But someone DID find him.

A stranger came right up to Gideon and said, "The Lord is with you, mighty warrior!" Gideon must have been surprised when he heard these words. The stranger said that Gideon was going to defeat the Midianites! Gideon didn't see how THAT could happen! He wasn't brave or strong—he was scared! But the stranger said, "I will be with you." The stranger was God. GOD would help Gideon!

The Bible tells us that God's Spirit was with Gideon and then Gideon blew a ram's horn and sent messengers to call warriors from all over the country of Israel. Thousands of Israelites came to help defeat the Midianites!

But Gideon was still afraid. He asked God to do something to prove he would really defeat the Midianites. Gideon laid a sheepskin out at night and asked God to make the ground around it dry but the sheepskin wet. Well, God did just that! And then God did it again in a different way—He made the sheepskin dry and the ground wet. God wanted Gideon to be convinced of God's help!

Next, God told Gideon, "There are too many soldiers. With so many, Israel might think they beat the Midianites by their own strength. Send anyone home who is afraid!" Gideon obeyed, and all but 10,000 men went home. And Gideon obeyed again when God told him to send even MORE people home! Now there were only 300 soldiers. There were THOUSANDS of Midianites! But God had told Gideon that He would defeat the enemy.

© 2007 Gospel Light. Permission to photocopy granted. *Agents in Action*

Gideon and his men got ready. Instead of weapons, they carried horns and torches inside clay jars. Gideon told them, "God has said we will defeat the Midianites. Now watch me and do what I do!" In the middle of the night, they made a big circle around the valley where the Midianites were sleeping. They blew their horns, broke their jars, lifted their torches and SHOUTED!

The shouting and bright lights woke the Midianites. Scared and confused, they began to fight EACH OTHER! They began to RUN! All Gideon and his men had to do was to CHASE them! God had defeated the Midianites!

God's Word & Me

At the beginning of this story, Gideon was afraid. He had a hard time trusting in God's care without proof. As we grow up and face new situations, there may be times when we are afraid. Briefly tell about a time you were afraid and how God helped you. **We might find it hard to trust in God's care. But listen to what Jesus said.** Read John 14:1.

Jesus said these words to help us know that even when we are afraid, we can remember that God's care and help are bigger than all our fears. We can tell Him when we are afraid, like Gideon did. He knows we need His help. God doesn't promise us that we will never feel afraid, but even when we are afraid, we can trust in Him to care for us.

>> **Why might someone who's afraid not trust in God's help and care?** (Get scared. Forget about God's promises.)

>> **What has God given to help us when we're afraid?** (Promises of His help found in the Bible. Parents. Friends.)

>> **What does it mean to trust in God's help?** (Believe that He is able to care for you and help you know what to do. Depend on His power.)

>> **When are some times kids your age might be afraid?** (Going to a new school. Have a hard test to take. Walking or riding the bus to school.) Pray with children, asking God's help when kids are afraid.

LESSON FOUR

Game Center
for younger children
Judges 6—7

Collect

Bible; *Agent* Music CD and player; furniture, boxes or blocks to create an obstacle course.

Prepare

Clear an open space in your classroom and set up an obstacle course, making at least one or two challenging obstacles for the age of your children.

God's Word

"Do not let your hearts be troubled. Trust in God; trust also in me." John 14:1

For Younger Children:
"Trust in God's care."

God's Word & Me

When I'm afraid or worried,
I can trust in God to help me.

Do

1. **When we feel afraid or worried, it can seem like we are having a hard day. We can trust God to help us, even when things seem hard. Let's see if you can go through this hard obstacle course.** Demonstrate how to correctly move through obstacle course.

2. Children take turns moving through the obstacle course. Invite all children to give thumbs-up signal and say "God helps me" as each child begins the course. Play "Be Strong and Courageous" as children move through obstacle course. As time permits, rearrange course and let children move through it again.

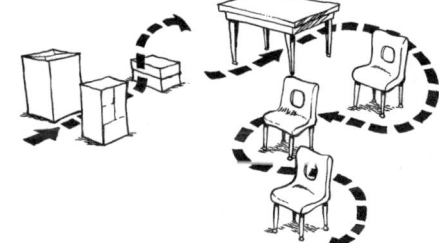

Talk About

>> Our Bible story today tells us about Gideon. Gideon was afraid when God asked him to lead an army in battle. But God helped Gideon. Sometimes we might feel afraid, too. God promises to help us. Jesus said, "Trust in God's care." When we trust God, it means that we remember God's love and help.

>> **If you were afraid, who could you ask for help?** (Mom. Grandpa. Teacher.) **God cares for us by giving us people to help us.**

>> **Some children might be afraid at bedtime. Why might some children be afraid at night? What can those children remember to do?** (Ask God to help them. Remember that God cares for them.) **We all feel afraid sometimes. We can remember that God cares for each one of us and will help us. We can trust God.**

>> **When can we trust God? Give me a thumbs-up and say, "All the time!"** Pray briefly, **Dear God, thank You for taking care of us when we are afraid or worried. In Jesus' name, amen.**

For Older Children

Photocopy Lesson 4 Pattern Page (p. 98) for each child. Use paper cutter to cut apart verse cards. Collect obstacle course items and let children arrange the course. Shuffle all verse cards and place a stack at each obstacle. Divide group into two teams. As players take turns moving through the course, they collect verse cards. After completing obstacle course, teams try to assemble verse cards in order. Players repeat obstacle course as needed to collect the correct cards.

LESSON FOUR

Game Center
for older children
Judges 6—7

Collect
Bible, large sheet of butcher paper, marker, masking tape, scissors, slips of paper, pencils.

Prepare
Print John 14:1 on butcher paper and post it on the wall. Cut 12-inch (30.5-cm) strips of masking tape and place on table or shelf edges. Cut 2-inch (5-cm) strips and attach randomly to prepared butcher paper.

Do
1. Give each child several slips of paper and pencils. Ask children to think of typical fears of kids their age and write each fear on a separate slip of paper. Talk with children as needed to help them think of fears. Collect completed slips of paper and place them around the room.
2. Each child wraps masking tape strip around one hand—sticky side out. (Note: Let children help each other wrap hands.) At your signal, children run around the room and collect papers by pressing taped hands to the papers. Children remove papers from taped hands and tape the papers to the verse poster. Continue until all papers have been collected.
3. Read fears aloud. End by saying the words of the verse.

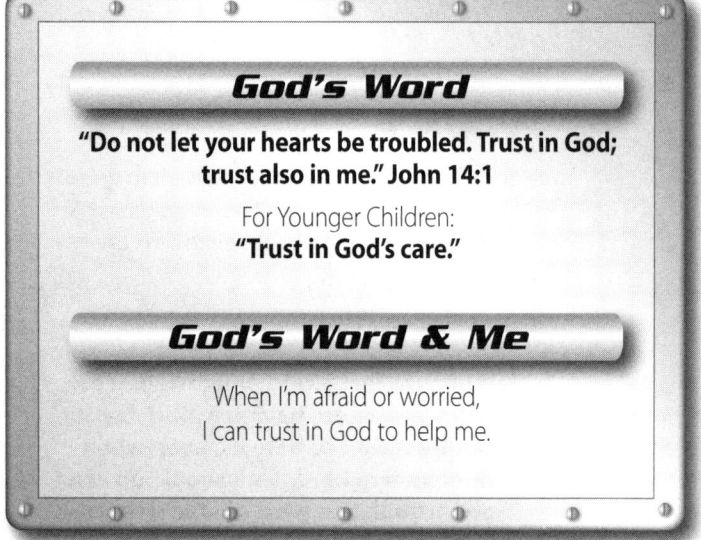

God's Word

"Do not let your hearts be troubled. Trust in God; trust also in me." John 14:1

For Younger Children:
"Trust in God's care."

God's Word & Me

When I'm afraid or worried, I can trust in God to help me.

Talk About

>> **Which of these fears do you think would be the scariest for a kid your age? Why?**

>> **In our Bible story today, a man named Gideon was so afraid** that he asked God to let him know that God would help him. When we're afraid, we can ask God for His help, too. **How would it make a difference to know that God will help you when you feel afraid?** (Give me courage. Remind me that God will help me know what to do.)

>> Read John 14:1. **What does it mean to trust God for help when we're afraid?** (Pray for His help. Believe that He is with us and that He will help us know what to do.)

>> **It can be hard to admit that we have fears or worries, but everyone is afraid or worried sometimes. God understands how we feel. Let's ask His help.** Lead children in prayer, thanking God for His care and asking for His help.

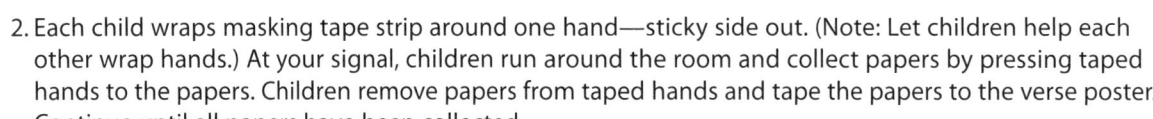

For Younger Children

Print the letters of the word "trust" on separate slips of paper and number each paper in order. Make several sets, each set on a different color paper or using a different colored marker. Hide the papers around the room. At your signal, children collect them and sort by color. Help children put papers in order to spell "trust."

LESSON FOUR

Art Center
for younger children
Judges 6—7

Collect

Bible, paper, marker, several colors of tempera paints, shallow baking pans, cotton swabs, newspaper; optional—markers, or small squares of colored construction paper and glue sticks.

Prepare

Draw big bubble letters for each child's first name on paper. Pour ½-inch (1.3 cm) of paint into baking pans. Lay cotton swabs next to each pan on a table covered with newspaper.

Do

1. Set out prepared papers and let each child find his or her name. Give help as needed.

2. Children fill in bubble letters, using cotton swabs to dip into one color of paint and dot spots inside the bubble letters. (Optional: Instead of using paint, children color letters or glue paper squares onto letters.) Remind children to use different swabs for each color of paint and to use one end of each swab for painting and one end to hold.

God's Word

"Do not let your hearts be troubled. Trust in God; trust also in me." John 14:1

For Younger Children:
"Trust in God's care."

God's Word & Me

When I'm afraid or worried, I can trust in God to help me.

Talk About

>> I'm glad to know that God cares for each person. Morgan, who is sitting at our table with us today? God cares for (Jayce). God cares for (Lily). God cares for (James).

>> In our Bible story today, a man named Gideon learned that God cared for him. God helped Gideon when Gideon was afraid. God will care for us and help us, too—even when we feel afraid.

>> Jesus said, "Trust in God's care." We can trust that God will care for us. He will always help us. One way God helps us is by listening to us when we pray. Pray briefly, **Dear God, thank You for caring for us. Help us remember to trust You when we feel afraid. In Jesus' name, amen.**

For Older Children

Older children draw bubble letters to fill in with dots. Encourage children to use dots in creative patterns. If time permits, allow dot-art to dry. When dry, children cut around the dot-art paintings and glue onto sheets of colored construction paper.

© 2007 Gospel Light. Permission to photocopy granted. *Agents in Action*

LESSON FOUR

Art Center
for older children
Judges 6—7

Collect

Bible, modeling clay or air-drying play dough, paper plate for each child, markers.

Do

1. Pass out a paper plate and fist-sized lump of clay or dough to each child.

2. **We often use our hands to help other people. Today you may make hand sculptures as reminders of God's help.** Children create clay or dough hand sculptures representing God's help. Children write names on paper plates.

Talk About

>> **In our Bible story today, Gideon was so afraid that he asked God for proof that God would help him. Gideon discovered that he could trust in God. That's what God wants us to know, too. Listen to what Jesus said:** Read John 14:1.

>> **What do you think a kid your age can do to show that he or she trusts in God?** (Pray to God when feeling afraid. Remember God's promises of care and help.)

>> **How might it make a difference in a kid's life to trust in God?** (Give him or her courage. Feel less afraid.) **One of the ways God helps us when we're afraid or worried is to give us people who care about us.** Lead children in prayer, thanking God for His help.

For Younger Children

Instead of making sculptures, give children play dough. Children form flat circles with their play dough and then make handprints in the dough.

God's Word

"Do not let your hearts be troubled. Trust in God; trust also in me." John 14:1

For Younger Children:
"Trust in God's care."

God's Word & Me

When I'm afraid or worried, I can trust in God to help me.

LESSON FOUR

Worship Center
for younger and older children
Judges 6—7

Collect

Bibles, *Agent* Music CD and player, song charts (pp. 247-248), balloons, permanent marker, masking tape.

Preparation

Inflate balloons. Using permanent marker, print the word "FEAR" on balloons—one letter on each balloon. Make a set of balloons for each team. In an open area of the classroom, use masking tape to designate start and finish lines approximately 10 feet (3 m) apart. Place inflated balloons by finish line.

God's Word

"Do not let your hearts be troubled. Trust in God; trust also in me." John 14:1

For Younger Children:
"Trust in God's care."

God's Word & Me

When I'm afraid or worried, I can trust in God to help me.

Team Game

Divide group into two or more teams of special agents. (Optional: Volunteers from each team choose names for their teams.) Invite four children from each team to stand at the start line. **Let's see how fast your team of agents can pop their "fears."** At your signal, first player on each team runs to balloons and pops the balloon with the letter "F" on it. Player runs back to team. Continue until each team has popped all their balloons. (Optional: Instead of popping balloons, children move balloons from one side of the room to the other.) Teams cheer for their agents.

Bible Verse Game

Repeat John 14:1 aloud with children. With a volunteer, say the words of the verse and demonstrate the clapping pattern shown in sketch, repeating the pattern for each word of the verse. Then invite children to find partners and say verse while doing actions. Repeat as time permits, finding new partners or forming larger groups (trios, quadruplets, etc.) each time. Challenge: Older children may create more complicated clapping patterns.

Song

Lead children in singing "Be Strong and Courageous."

Prayer

It's easy to say we believe in God's help, but sometimes in situations that make us worried or afraid, it's hard to remember His promises of love and care. Listen to what David, a famous king in the Old Testament, said about his trust in God. Read or ask a volunteer to read Psalm 28:7 aloud. **Let's ask God to help us always trust in Him.** Lead children in prayer.

Song

Lead children in singing "All of the Time." Add motions and/or clapping if desired.

LESSON FOUR · Pattern Page

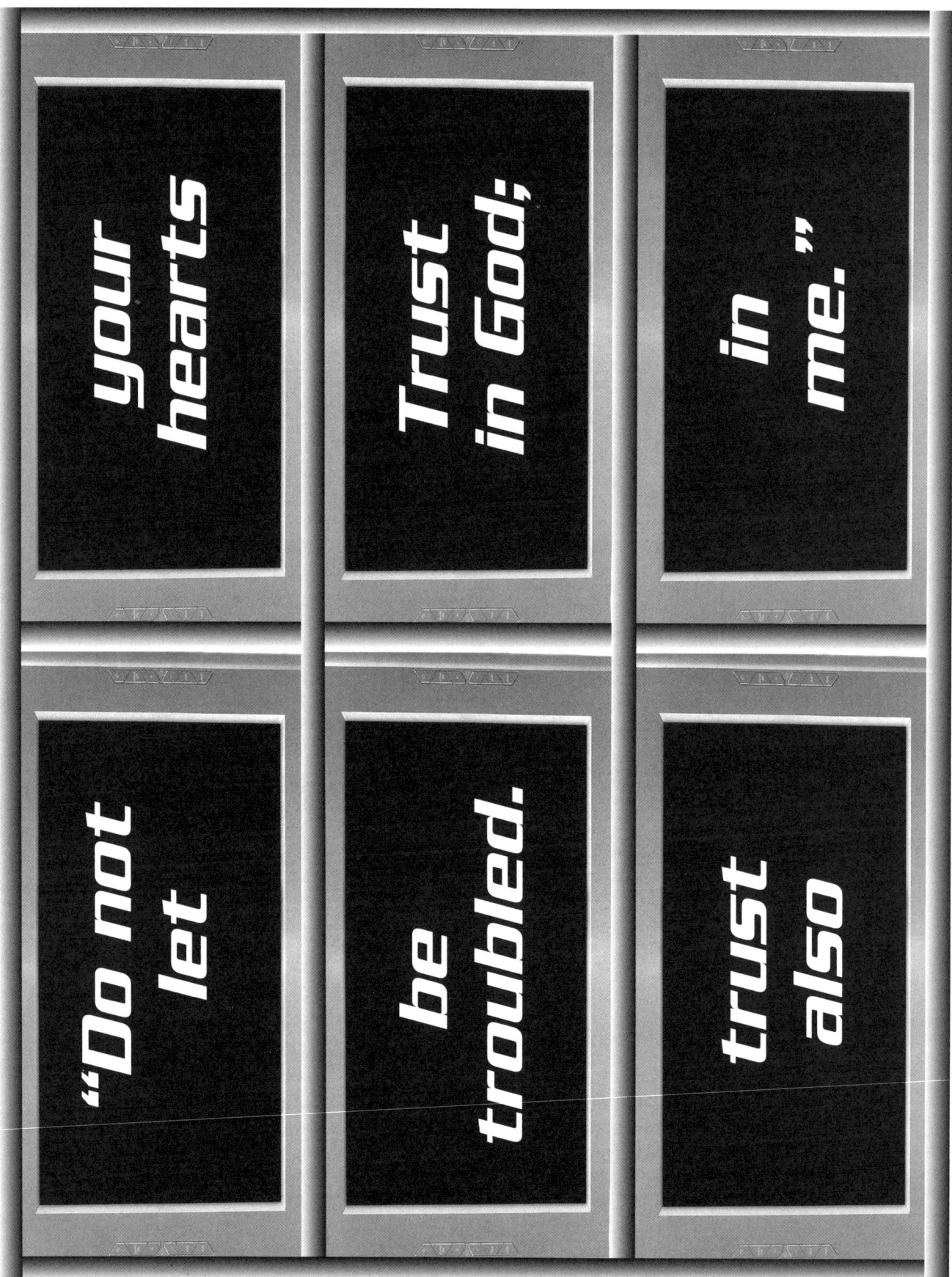

98

LESSON FOUR • Puzzle Page

WORD PUZZLE

What are some things people use for protection from scary things? Complete the word puzzle to find one answer to this question. Copy the lines in each puzzle square on the matching square in the grid. (A1 is done for you.)

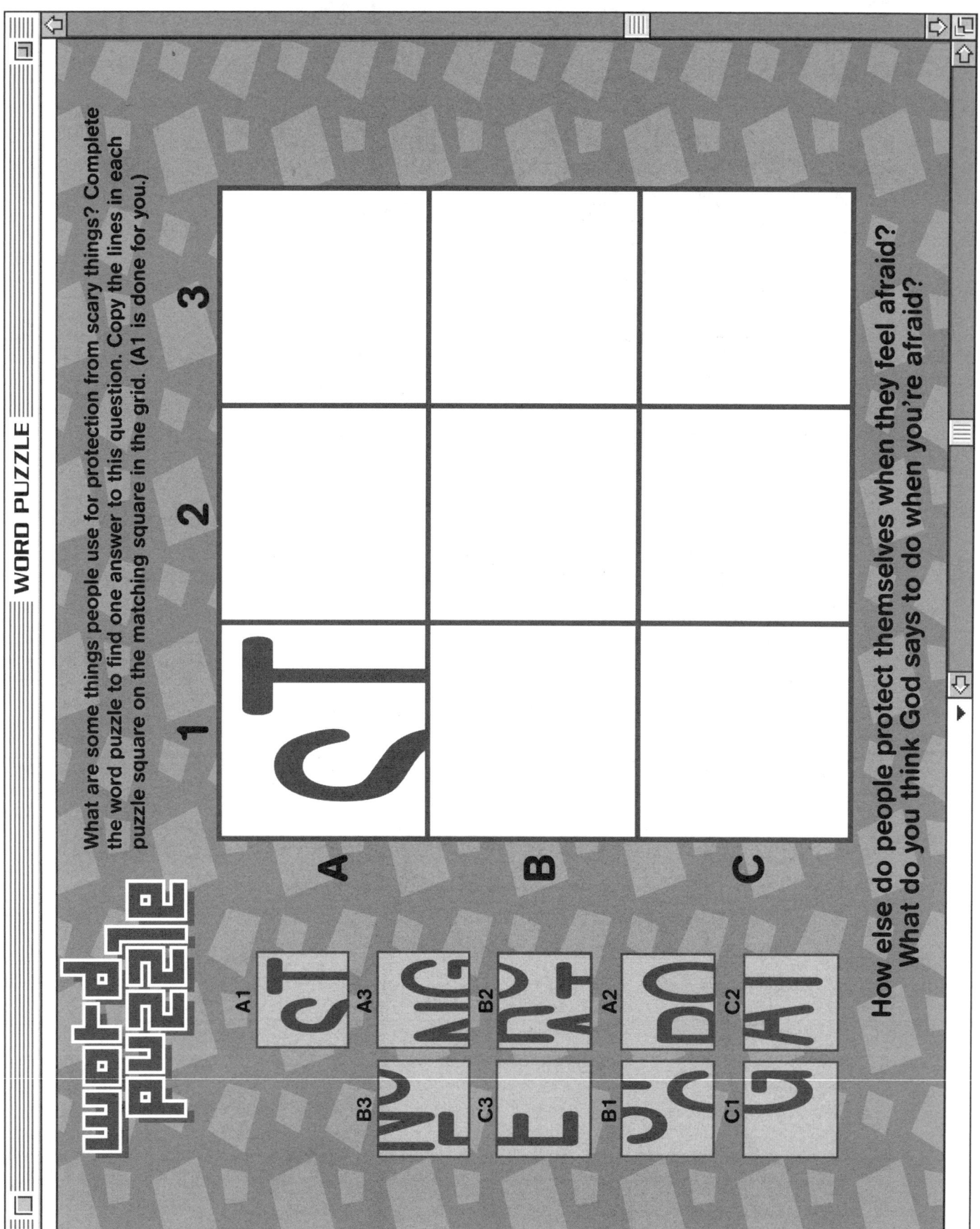

How else do people protect themselves when they feel afraid? What do you think God says to do when you're afraid?

LESSON FIVE

Future

Bible Story:
Ruth's Adventure
Ruth

Teacher's Devotional

We frail humans don't deal well with too much change, too quickly; dramatic or constant change weighs on us and causes fear and worry. We lose sleep, lose hair, lose weight or even think we'll lose our minds! Ruth knew such stress; her story gives us hope and shows us how to live positively through stressful times.

Ruth was a Moabite and lived in Moab. She had married a foreigner from Israel. But later, her husband died. No doubt she was already stunned by the fearful changes of widowhood. But Ruth then had to choose between an unknown foreign destination or her own family and home. Ruth chose even greater change in order to remain with her mother-in-law, Naomi.

Ruth chose a new life in a foreign land and committed to trusting in the God of Israel (see Ruth 1:16-18). As she committed her future to God's care, she simply did what work He had put nearest at hand. She worked diligently to feed her aging mother-in-law and herself—and of course, God was also at work! Boaz, a wealthy landowner and (surprise!) distant relative of Naomi, noticed Ruth in his fields. Ruth watched God's plan unfold as God restored Naomi's land, renewed her own hope and revealed great purpose for her family—ancestors of David and of Jesus, a surprising ending to a seemingly hopeless story!

Children today, even preschoolers, may be faced with change, fear and stress. Even children whose lives are seemingly problem-free today may experience worry about what might happen in the future. Help children develop an understanding that God is always present, always loving, always aware and always busy on their behalf. God's promise of His presence can remind children and adults alike to focus on the God of Israel instead of on our uncertain futures.

God's Word

"I am with you always, to the very end of the age." Matthew 28:20

For Younger Children:
"God is always with you."

God's Word & Me

God promises to be with me, no matter what happens now or in the future.

© 2007 Gospel Light. Permission to photocopy granted. *Agents in Action*

Planning Page

LESSON FIVE

Choose which centers you will provide and the order in which children will participate in them (see pp. 14-18 for schedule tips and pp. 24-25 for guidelines in combining older and younger children). Also plan who will lead each center (for staffing tips see pp. 19-21). Use the reproducible planning sheet (p. 238) to record your plans.

Bible Story Center

Bible Story Ruth's Adventure • Ruth

Younger Child Option
Gather narrow brown construction paper strips to help tell the story

Older Child Option
Complete pencil rubbings to discover the daily mission "God is with me"

Game Center

Younger Child Option
Pretend to pack and move to a new house and talk about God's promise to be with us wherever we go

Materials
Bible, *Agent* Music CD and player, grocery bag for each child

Older Child Option
Take turns being blindfolded and led around the room, and talk about God's promise to be with us

Materials
Bible, blindfolds

Art Center

Younger Child Option
Decorate covers and draw pictures for books that tell about God's promise to be with us no matter how old or young we are

Materials
Bible, Lesson 5 Pattern Page (p. 112), card stock, plain paper, stapler, crayons or markers; optional—instant camera.

Older Child Option
Create pasta mazes and discuss what it means to say that God is with us

Materials
Bible, a shoebox lid for each child, markers, uncooked pasta noodles (such as mini penne), glue, small beads or marbles

Worship Center

For the Younger and Older Child
Participate in large-group activities to review Bible verse and to worship God together

Materials
Bibles, *Agent* Music CD and player, song charts (pp. 246-247), large sheet of butcher paper, marker, tape, variety of small prizes or individually wrapped candy

Coloring/Puzzle Center

Younger Child Option
Review the Bible story while completing coloring page

Materials
Lesson 5 Coloring Page (p. 113) for each student, crayons

Older Child Option
Review God's promise to be with us while completing puzzle page

Materials
Lesson 5 Puzzle Page (p. 114) for each student, pencils

LESSON FIVE

Bonus Theme Ideas

Bonus Theme Ideas can be used at any time during this session: as an additional activity center, to extend the session for a longer time or for added theme excitement.

No. 1149 — Family Fun Event

Invite children and families to attend a special event that will create enthusiasm for *Agents in Action* and build relationships among families. Send home invitations (see p. 233) several weeks ahead of time. Plan this special event immediately following a session of *Agents in Action*, or on another day of the week. Depending on how much time is available, plan a meal (pizza or BBQ) or a snack (use one of the snacks suggested in the Bonus Theme Ideas for each lesson). For activity, play one or more of the Team Games or Bible Verse Games suggested in each lesson's Worship Center. Make sure to give each family member a name tag to wear and encourage your leaders to introduce family members to each other. Begin or end the event by singing "God's Kids" and "Mission of Love."

Special Agent Information

Agent Atmosphere

Catch children's attention by adding one or more of these eye-catching decorations to the rooms in which children meet. (1) Attach long metallic streamers at the top of each doorway through which children enter. (2) Cut out black or neon construction-paper footprints and tape to floor in a path from the entrance of your church building to room where children gather. (3) Build a dramatic entrance by cutting doors out of a refrigerator box. Paint box inside and out with black paint or cover with black construction paper. Place glow-in-the-dark stickers on inside of box. Attach rope lights or Christmas lights around outside of box or inside.

Special Agent Information

No. 1149 — Cupcake Creations

Give each child a cupcake and a plastic knife. Provide several colors of frosting and decorating items (candy confetti, theme fruit snacks, chow mein noodles, stick pretzels, sprinkles, etc.) in separate bowls. Children spread frosting onto cupcakes and create their own decorations.

Special Agent Information

> **Post a note alerting parents to the use of food. Also, check registration forms for possible food allergies.**

© 2007 Gospel Light. Permission to photocopy granted. *Agents in Action*

LESSON FIVE

Bible Story Center
for younger children
Ruth

Collect
Bible.

Introduction
Rub your hands in a circle over your stomach if you've ever been really hungry. Volunteers respond. **What do you do when you feel hungry? I'm glad that we can go to the refrigerator or cupboard or even to a grocery store to buy food when we're hungry. Listen to our Bible story to find out what a hungry woman did.**

Special Agent Option
In a box labeled "Top Secret" place narrow brown construction-paper strips representing "grain" (several for each child) and a basket. (If possible, use real stalks of grain.) At the appropriate time during the story, remove strips and place them in an open area around the room. Invite children to demonstrate Ruth's actions by collecting grain and putting them into basket. (Optional: Serve bite-size pieces of whole-grain bread to children. Check registration forms for possible food allergies and post a note alerting parents to the use of food.)

Tell the Story

The Bible tells about two women who loved and obeyed God. Their names were Ruth and Naomi. Ruth and Naomi had just moved to a new land. They must have wondered how they would get food to eat. They must have wondered if people would be kind to them in this new land.

Ruth and Naomi did not have money to buy food. They were hungry, so Ruth went to find some food. Ruth went to a field where workers were cutting grain called barley. The grain was used to make bread. The workers tied the grain into bundles. Some of the grain fell on the ground. The workers left the grain on the ground. Then people who did not have enough food to eat could pick up the grain. Ruth asked a man if she could pick up some of the grain.

The man said, "Yes." So Ruth picked up grain and put it into her basket. She worked very hard.

Boaz was the man who owned the field. He saw Ruth working hard. Boaz told Ruth, "From now on you may pick up all the leftover grain in my field. And when you are thirsty, please drink from our water jars." Boaz was kind to Ruth.

Later that day, Boaz brought some extra food to Ruth. She was hungry, but she didn't eat it all. She saved some to take home to Naomi. Then Ruth went back to work! She picked up all the grain she could carry in her basket. When it began to get dark, she went home.

Naomi had a happy surprise! Ruth brought home a lot of grain! There was enough to make many loaves of bread. Ruth gave Naomi the food she had saved for her. Now Naomi would not worry. She was glad that Ruth was kind to her. Ruth and Naomi were glad that God cared for them and helped them.

God's Word & Me

Ruth and Naomi knew that God was with them. Even when Ruth didn't know where her new home was going to be or how she was going to get food, God was with Ruth. God is with us, too. Sometimes things happen that might make us feel sad. We worry about what will happen. God promises to be with us.

In the Bible, Jesus said, "God is always with you." We can't see God, but we know that He is with us, caring for us and helping us. Pray, **Dear God, thank You for always being with us. Thank You for Your love. In Jesus' name, amen.**

LESSON FIVE

Bible Story Center
for older children
Ruth

Collect

Bible, Bible-times costume.

Introduction

What are some things you do every day? Is it easy or hard to do them? Volunteers respond. **Today we'll find out what happened when a woman had to do a hard job every day.** Dress up in a Bible-times costume and tell the story as Ruth. (Optional: Videotape someone ahead of time telling this story as Ruth. Play video during class.)

Tell the Story

Long ago, even before there were kings in Israel, there was a famine in the country. A famine is a time when there isn't enough rain for crops to grow and drinking water becomes scarce. Because there was not enough food or water, a woman named Naomi and her family left their home in Bethlehem.

With her husband and two sons, Naomi went to Moab to find food. While Naomi's family lived in Moab, her husband died. When her boys grew up, they both married Moabite girls; one son married Orpah and the other married Ruth. Then, to make matters worse, Naomi's sons died! Now Naomi and her daughters-in-law were very sad. Without husbands, it would be VERY hard to get enough food. *What would they DO?* they wondered.

Naomi had heard that there was food in Bethlehem again. She decided to go back home, where the rest of her family lived. *Maybe I'll find food there*, Naomi thought. Naomi also thought it would be better for Orpah and Ruth if they stayed in Moab. Orpah agreed with Naomi and decided to live with her relatives in Moab. But Ruth said, "Don't tell me to go back, Naomi. I won't leave you! Your people will be my people, and your God will be my God." Ruth stayed with Naomi.

Ruth and Naomi traveled together back to Israel. They arrived in Bethlehem during the spring barley harvest. Ruth went to the field of a man named Boaz. She gleaned there. That means she took leftover barley off the ground and put the grain in her basket. It was hard work out in the hot sun. But Ruth was determined to help Naomi no matter what.

Boaz was kind to Ruth. "Come to my field anytime," Boaz told Ruth. He told his workers to leave extra grain on the ground for Ruth to pick up. He had heard about Ruth, you see. Boaz was impressed with Ruth's kindness to Naomi.

When Naomi found out that Ruth was working in Boaz's field, she got very excited. Boaz was actually a relative of her husband! That meant that Naomi and Ruth might be able to convince Boaz to provide a home for Ruth.

Special Agent Option

Before class, use a pen to write the daily mission "God is with me" on the top sheet of several pads of paper. Press down hard. Throw away the top sheet of paper on all the pads. Place pads of paper and pencils into a box labeled "Top Secret." At the end of the story, volunteers remove items. Children gently rub pencils over the sheet of paper left on the pads to read the daily mission.

Naomi had a plan. She told Ruth to go to Boaz at night when he would be sleeping outdoors to guard his grain. She told Ruth just how to ask Boaz to be her protector. And according to the law, if Boaz would agree, it also meant he would MARRY Ruth!

Ruth did just what Naomi told her to do. She talked with Boaz, and Boaz was glad to help her and Naomi. He was glad to marry Ruth, too! So Ruth became Boaz's bride. Later, she and Boaz had a baby! They named the baby Obed. Now Naomi had a grandson who would keep her land in the family. Because of Ruth's kindness, Naomi was cared for and had a family again!

Best of all, many years later Obed would grow up and become a grandpa himself. He was the grandfather of King David—one of the ancestors of Jesus!

God's Word & Me

There were many times in Ruth's life when she didn't know what was going to happen in the future. Her husband died, she moved to a new land, she needed to get food—all of these situations were times when Ruth might have felt afraid or worried.

Listen to what Jesus said that is an awesome promise to remember when we're afraid or worried. Read Matthew 28:20. **Jesus said these words to His disciples when they were feeling worried about what was going to happen to them in the future. In our lives, there are going to be times when things happen to make us sad, or when we worry about what might happen to us in the future. God promises to be with us—now and in the future. We can trust in His love and care. We can trust that He will help us know what to do.**

- **When are some times kids your age especially need to remember God's promise to be with them?** (They have to move to a new place. Their dad or mom lose their jobs.)
- **When might kids worry about what will happen in the future?** (They hear stories about kids who get sick or hurt.)
- **Why can we trust in God's love and care?** (He has helped us in the past. He always keeps His promises.)
- **How can we show that we believe God's promise to be with us?** (Remember to pray to God and ask for His help when we are afraid or worried about the future.)
- **What could you do to encourage a friend to trust God?** (Tell God's promise.) Pray with children, thanking God for His promise to be with us, and asking His help in remembering to trust Him now and in the future.

LESSON FIVE

Game Center
for younger children
Ruth

Collect

Bible; *Agent* Music CD and player; grocery bag for each child; optional—backpacks, duffle bags or empty rolling suitcases.

Do

1. **Let's pretend we're moving to a new house today, just like a woman named Ruth did in today's Bible story.** Pass out grocery bags. (Optional: Distribute backpacks, duffle bags or empty rolling suitcases.) Children pretend to pack their "suitcases," naming items they pack.

2. Lead children around room, walking slowly as Ruth might have done. Play "All of the Time" on CD. Periodically stop music to act out eating and resting. Children take turns being leaders. Celebrate when you finally arrive to the "new house."

God's Word

"I am with you always, to the very end of the age." Matthew 28:20

For Younger Children:
"God is always with you."

God's Word & Me

God promises to be with me, no matter what happens now or in the future.

Talk About

>> **In our Bible story today, a woman named Ruth moved to a new home. God was with Ruth. God promises to be with us, too.**

>> **Angelica, where are some places you go?** God is with you everywhere you go.

>> **The Bible says, "God is always with you." Lanai, who do you see in this room? God is with (Maycee).** Have each child repeat the words "God is with me" while giving themselves a hug.

>> **God promises to be with us, no matter now we feel. God is with us when we're sad. God is with us when we're happy. God is with us when we're worried.** Pray briefly, **Dear God, thank You for promising to always be with us. In Jesus' name, amen.**

For Older Children

Place grocery bags at one end of open area in your room. (Optional: Use rolling suitcases, duffle bags or backpacks.) Children form two teams and line up on other side of the room. At your signal, first player on each team runs across the room, collects a bag, runs back to his or her team and gives the bag to the next player. This player holds the bag, runs across the room, collects a second bag, runs back to his or her team and gives both bags to the next player. Continue process, until each child has had a turn or there are no bags left.

LESSON FIVE

Game Center
for older children
Ruth

Collect

Bible, blindfolds.

Do

1. Help each child find a partner. Partners stand by doorway of room. Blindfold one child in each pair and have partners link arms. Partners without blindfolds lead their blindfolded partners to an area of the room or another room, if possible. Blindfolded partners try to guess where they are, and then remove their blindfolds to see if they're right.

2. Return to doorway and repeat with different children wearing blindfolds. (Note: If a child does not wish to wear a blindfold, he or she may continue acting as the leader for different partners.)

God's Word

"I am with you always, to the very end of the age." Matthew 28:20

For Younger Children:
"God is always with you."

God's Word & Me

God promises to be with me, no matter what happens now or in the future.

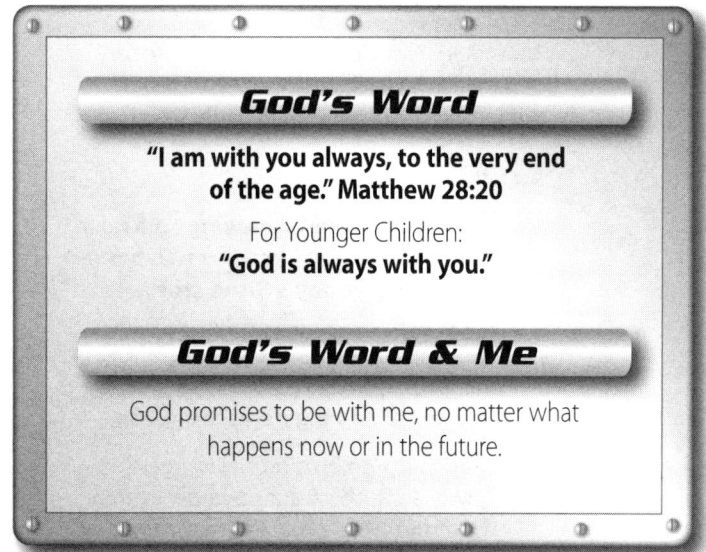

Talk About

>> **What was it like when you were blindfolded? What was hard? Who did you have to depend on?**

>> Read Matthew 28:20. **This verse is a promise we can depend on when we don't know what might happen. How can it help us to know that God is always with us?** (It's not as scary when we remember that God is with us. We can trust God to lead us in the right direction.)

>> **When are some times that kids at school need to remember that God promises to be with them?** (When they worry about getting good grades or taking hard tests. When they don't have very many friends.)

>> **What do you think is the best part about remembering God's promise to be with you?** (Even when I'm worried, I can know that God will be with me. God gives people to help me.) Lead children in prayer, thanking God for His promise to be with us.

For Younger Children

Help children form pairs and stand in a circle together. One child in each pair takes a turn to close his or her eyes while partners hold their hands and walk in a circle with them. (Optional: Some children may wish to be blindfolded.)

LESSON FIVE

Art Center
for younger children
Ruth

Collect

Bible, Lesson 5 Pattern Page (p. 112), card stock, plain paper, stapler, crayons or markers; optional—instant camera.

Prepare

Copy Pattern Page onto card stock, making one copy for each child. Staple Pattern Page book cover on top of three blank pages of plain white paper to make a blank book for each child.

Do

1. Give each child a book and read the words on the cover. **God promises to always be with you**. Children write their names on the cover and color it.

2. Children draw themselves as babies on page one. On page two, children draw pictures of themselves as they look now. (Optional: Take photo of each child and attach to page two.) On page three children draw themselves as grown-ups.

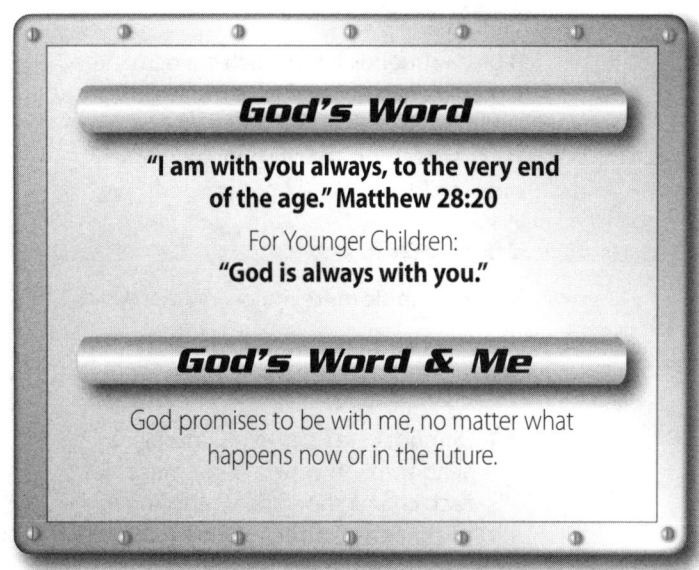

God's Word

"I am with you always, to the very end of the age." Matthew 28:20

For Younger Children:
"God is always with you."

God's Word & Me

God promises to be with me, no matter what happens now or in the future.

Talk About

>> Austin, what do you want to be when you grow up? No matter what you do or where you go when you grow up, God will always be with you.

>> Ben, what do you think you looked like when you were a baby? God was with you when you were a little baby. God is with you now, and God promises to be with you when you grow up.

>> Raise your hand to show that God is with you. Now put both arms up and shake your hands while we say, "Thank You, God, for promising to be with me always!" Lead children in repeating words. Pray briefly, **Thank You, God, for being with me now and when I grow up. In Jesus' name, amen.**

For Older Children

Children make their own covers by writing Matthew 28:20 and decorating the covers. Add two pages to the book so that children can draw pictures of themselves as teenagers and grandparents. Children may also write sentences on each page, describing things they did when they were younger or things they hope to do when older.

LESSON FIVE

Art Center
for older children
Ruth

Collect

Bible, a shoebox lid for each child, markers, uncooked pasta noodles (such as ziti), glue, small beads or marbles; optional—use cardstock sheets instead of shoebox lids for older children.

Prepare

Make a sample maze, following directions below.

Do

1. Demonstrate how to roll marble or bead through your sample maze. Give each child a shoebox lid. (Optional: Use sheets of card stock for older children.) Child draws a maze on the lid (or card stock), writing his or her name at start of maze and "God is with me" at the end of the maze.

2. Children glue uncooked pasta on maze lines. Give each child a marble or small bead. Child tilts lid (or card stock) to roll marble or bead through the maze.

God's Word

"I am with you always, to the very end of the age." Matthew 28:20

For Younger Children:
"God is always with you."

God's Word & Me

God promises to be with me, no matter what happens now or in the future.

Talk About

>> **Some mazes are easy to figure out, but some mazes can be really hard. How do you think our lives might be like mazes?** (We have to make choices about what to do. Sometimes it's confusing or hard to know what to do.)

>> **When we think about the future—what we're going to do next week or next year—we don't know what will happen. Sometimes not knowing what's going to happen in the future can make us worried or afraid. What might kids your age worry will happen to them in the future?**

>> Read Matthew 28:20. **What does this verse say God promises to do now and in the future?** (He promises to be with us.) **What does it mean to say that God is with us always?** (He helps us know what to do. He hears our prayers. He stays with us no matter where we are.) Pray, thanking God that He is with us now and in the future.

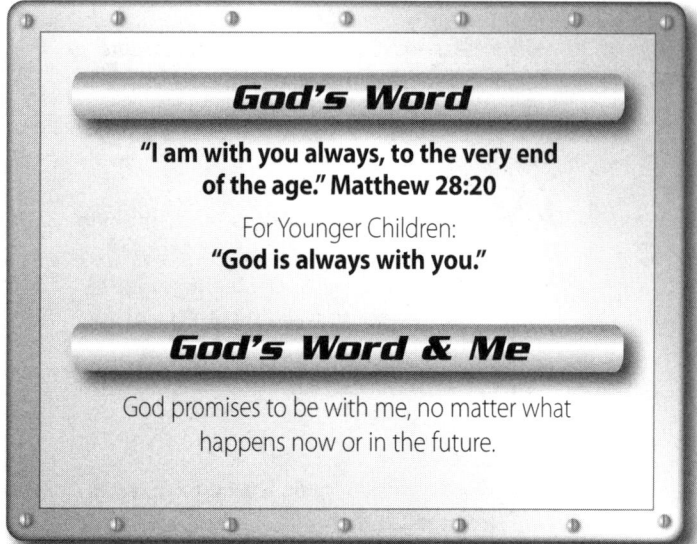

For Younger Children

Ahead of time, draw a simple maze on a sheet of paper that will fit inside shoebox lids and make photocopies. Children glue paper inside lids and then glue pasta onto the lines.

LESSON FIVE

Worship Center
for younger and older children
Ruth

Collect

Bibles, *Agent* Music CD and player, song charts (pp. 246-247), large sheet of butcher paper, marker, tape, variety of small prizes.

Preparation

Draw a large 12-square grid on butcher paper and add numbers and letters as shown (see sketch). Make sure each square is large enough for a child to stand in it. On a separate paper, draw a small version of the grid and tape it to wall.

Team Game

Place grid on floor. Invite volunteers to be special agents who stand in squares of grid and face the group. (Not all squares need to be used.) Ask special agents to hold hands behind their backs. Secretly give several special agents a small prize to hold behind their backs. **Today we're going to see which special agents are holding prizes.** Volunteer names coordinates (as in the game of Battleship) to choose a square on the grid. If the special agent standing in that square is holding a prize, he or she gives it to the child who guessed and moves off grid. Mark guess on small version of the grid. Continue until all prizes have been located. (At end of game, make sure each child has a prize.)

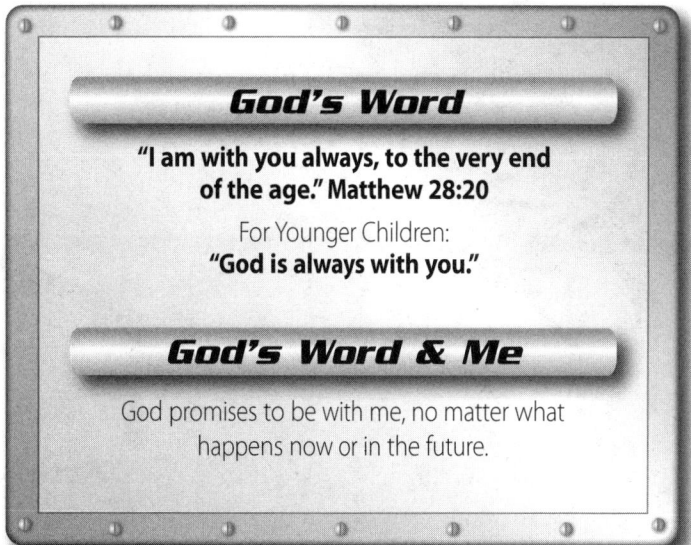

God's Word

"I am with you always, to the very end of the age." Matthew 28:20

For Younger Children:
"God is always with you."

God's Word & Me

God promises to be with me, no matter what happens now or in the future.

Bible Verse Game

Divide class into four groups and number each group. **Special agents sometimes send messages in code. Today we're going to say our Bible verse in a special kind of code.** Instruct Group 1 to say "I am with you" when you point to your eye. Instruct Group 2 to say "always" when you spread out your hands. Instruct Group 3 to say "to the very end" when you place your palms together. Finally, instruct Group 4 to say "of the age" when you hold up your arms in a V shape. Each time you make one of the motions, the appropriate group says their phrase of the verse. Practice several times so that each group remembers when it's their turn. Quicken the pace after several rounds.

Song

Lead children in singing "All of the Time." Add motions and/or clapping if desired.

Prayer

Let's thank God for His promise to be with us. Lead children in prayer, inviting them to say the words "Thank You, God, for always being with us" in unison.

Song

Lead children in singing "God's Kids." Add motions and/or clapping if desired.

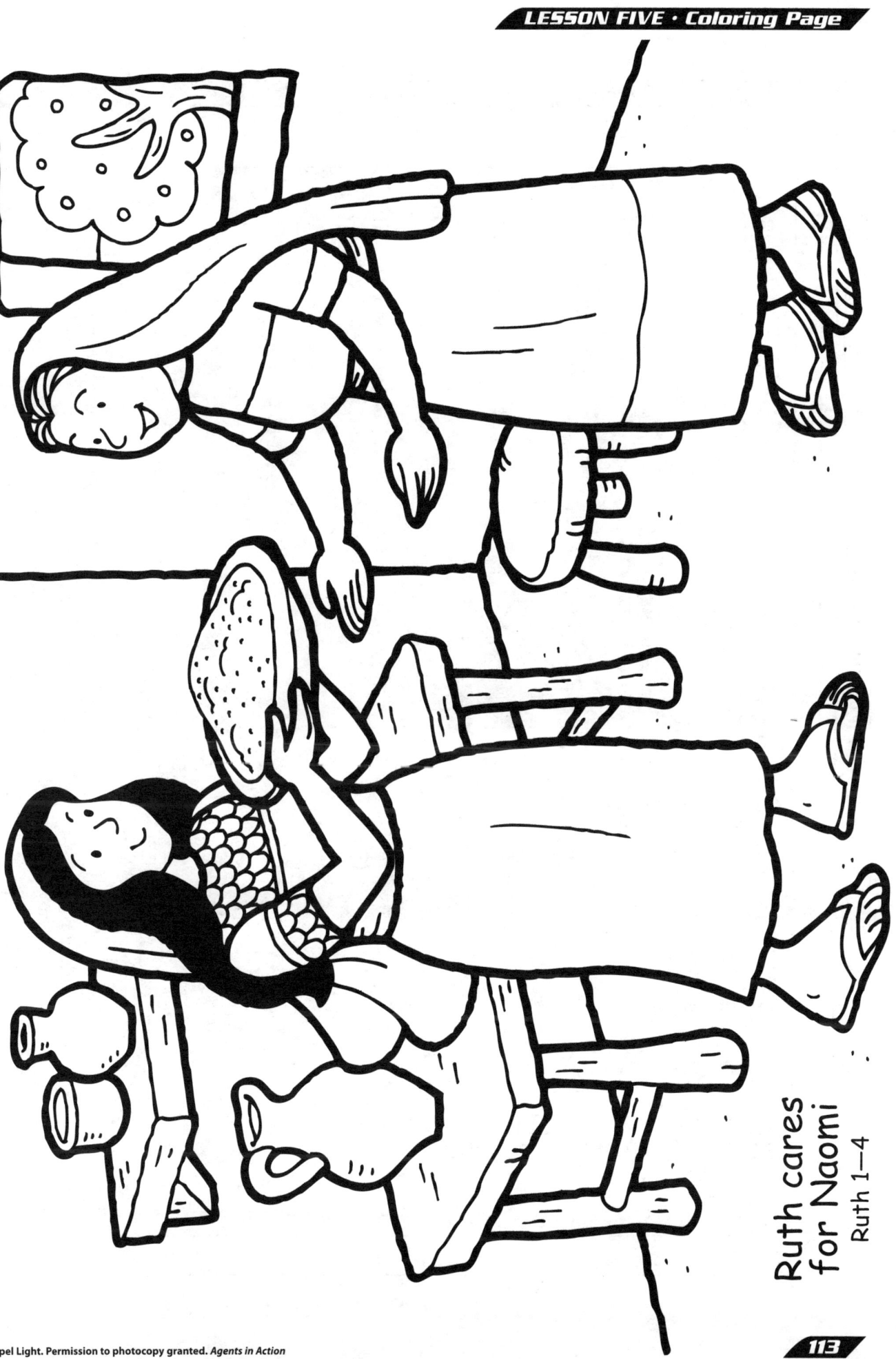

LESSON SIX

Temptation

Bible Story:
David Resists Temptation
1 Samuel 24:1-22; 26

Teacher's Devotional

Saul was set on murdering David! It didn't matter that David's music had given Saul such comfort. It didn't matter that David's courage had defeated Goliath and given Saul victory over the Philistines. Saul was insanely jealous and must have known that Samuel had already anointed David as king. He kept David on the run for months on end.

More than once, David watched and waited while Saul was unaware and undefended. Hadn't God provided this opportunity to do away with the hateful king? Shouldn't he kill his would-be murderer in self-defense? David's men certainly thought so. They urged David to take Saul's life. After all, God had already said David would rule as king—wouldn't he be justified to kill in self-defense and put himself on the throne?

David's attitude and response were almost shocking. Regardless of the danger to himself, David refused to kill Saul. No matter how he was urged, David called Saul the Lord's anointed. David was willing to remain in life-threatening danger, resist temptation and do what was right in order to preserve the life of the man who wanted to kill him!

The tempting situations your students face are probably unlike any faced by David, or even the temptations you struggled with as a child. It can be tough for children today to choose the right path—especially when others around them are urging them to give in to temptation! The conversations you have with children during this lesson may have a far-reaching impact. Use this lesson as an opportunity to share that the resources of our Lord are the same today as they were in Bible times.

God's Word

"Lead us not into temptation, but deliver us from the evil one." Matthew 6:13

For Younger Children:
"Help me to do what is right."

God's Word & Me

I can pray to God for help in saying no to temptation and living in right ways.

© 2007 Gospel Light. Permission to photocopy granted. *Agents in Action*

LESSON SIX

Planning Page

Choose which centers you will provide and the order in which children will participate in them (see pp. 14-18 for schedule tips and pp. 24-25 for guidelines in combining older and younger children). Also plan who will lead each center (for staffing tips see pp. 19-21). Use the reproducible planning sheet (p. 238) to record your plans.

Bible Story Center

Bible Story
David Resists Temptation • 1 Samuel 24:1-22; 26

Younger Child Option
Make expressive faces in a mirror to illustrate feelings of story characters

Older Child Option
Solve a flashlight code to discover the daily mission "say no to temptation"

Game Center

Younger Child Option
Play several balloon games, and talk about ways of doing what is right and obeying God

Materials
Bible, balloons

Older Child Option
Toss coins onto a bull's eye and identify how God can help them say no to temptation

Materials
Bible, large sheet of butcher paper, markers, index cards, coins

Art Center

Younger Child Option
Make and decorate crowns and talk about ways to do what is right, instead of disobeying God

Materials
Bible, poster board, scissors, markers, glue, stapler, colorful cereal (or similar snack)

Older Child Option
Make Bible-verse bookmarks and talk about situations in which God can help them say no to temptation

Materials
Bible, Lesson 6 Pattern Page (p. 126), markers, clear Contact paper, scissors, flat craft decorations (such as stickers, stick-on flat jewels, etc.)

Worship Center

For the Younger and Older Child
Participate in large-group activities to review Bible verse and to worship God together

Materials
Bibles, *Agent* Music CD and player, song charts (pp. 248, 252), construction paper in a variety of colors, scissors or paper cutter

Coloring/Puzzle Center

Younger Child Option
Review the Bible story while completing coloring page

Materials
Lesson 6 Coloring Page (p. 127) for each student, crayons

Older Child Option
Review ways of responding to temptation while completing puzzle page

Materials
Lesson 6 Puzzle Page (p. 128) for each student, pencils

LESSON SIX

Bonus Theme Ideas

Bonus Theme Ideas can be used at any time during this session: as an additional activity center, to extend the session for a longer time or for added theme excitement.

Special Agent Wacky Olympics

Plan one or more of these wacky games in which children may participate. (1) Javelin throw in which children use straws as javelins. (2) Shot put in which children use beanbags as shot puts. (3) Races in which children roll hula hoops or blow cotton balls. (4) Hurdles in which children jump over cardboard blocks or empty soda cans stacked at varying heights.

Mission of Love

Prepare a service project for children to complete. Give each child a solid-colored index card through which two holes have been punched (see sketch). Child decorates card and then inserts a lollipop through the punched holes. (Optional: Older children may write the words of Matthew 28:20 or John 14:1 on cards.) Collect and give to children who visit your church or to children at a community help organization.

Personalized Wraps

Give each child a small flour tortilla and plastic knife. Place softened cream cheese in one or more bowls. Set out a variety of fillings (thinly sliced deli meats, grated cheese, chopped tomatoes, shredded lettuce, raisins, sunflower seeds, etc.) on separate plates with plastic spoons. Child spreads cream cheese onto tortilla, adds several spoonfuls of fillings, rolls and eats!

Post a note alerting parents to the use of food. Also, check registration forms for possible food allergies.

© 2007 Gospel Light. Permission to photocopy granted. *Agents in Action*

LESSON SIX

Bible Story Center
for younger children
1 Samuel 24:1-22; 26

Collect

Bible.

Introduction

Cover your eyes and say "Ready or not" with me if you like to play hide and seek. Volunteers respond. **Today we're going to hear about a time in the Bible when a king was trying to find a man named David.**

Tell the Story

Step, step, step. King Saul and his men looked for David all day. King Saul was angry with David. King Saul wanted to find David and hurt him! Finally, King Saul and his men stopped for the night and set up their camp. King Saul slept on the ground. His men slept all around him.

Special Agent Option

In a box labeled "Top Secret," place a large hand mirror. At the beginning of the story, remove the mirror. At appropriate times in the story, invite children to make faces (angry, fearful, sleepy, shouting, happy, whispering) that illustrate the story action. Pause to show each child his or her face in the mirror. (Optional: If you have a large group, let several adult helpers use additional mirrors.)

While King Saul and his men were asleep, David and his men found King Saul's camp. Very quietly, David and his friend Abishai (AB-uh-shi) tiptoed up to King Saul.

"Here's our chance," whispered Abishai. "King Saul wants to hurt you. Let's hurt him!"

"No!" whispered David. "That would be wrong. Let's just take his spear and water jug." So David and Abishai picked up the king's spear and water jug.

They quietly ran to the top of a high hill. "Wake up!" David shouted. David held up King Saul's spear and jug. "See what happened while you slept!" King Saul and his men heard the shouting. They looked around and saw King Saul's spear and jug were gone.

"Is that you, David?" King Saul called out.

"Look!" David shouted. "I have your spear. Let one of your men come and get it. I could have hurt you, but I did not." Then King Saul was sorry for the way he had treated David.

David turned around and walked back to his men. He could have hurt King Saul, but he didn't. David's friend wanted him to hurt King Saul. But David wanted to do what was right.

God's Word & Me

David said no to doing what was wrong! It is not always easy to obey God when we feel like doing something wrong. But God wants to help us do what is right—all the time!

In the Bible, Jesus told us that we can pray to God and say, "Help me to do what is right." When we are playing with our friends, or doing things with our brothers and sisters, we can do what is right. God will help us obey Him.

LESSON SIX

Bible Story Center
for older children
1 Samuel 24:1-22; 26

Collect

Bible, story props (see below).

Introduction

What are some things you know about David in the Bible? (He was a famous king. He killed Goliath. He wrote many Psalms.) **Today we're going to hear about some difficult choices David had to make before he became king. Listen to see if you would have made the same choices as David did.** As you tell the Bible story, use the following props to illustrate story action: paper crown, knife, fabric, pillow or blanket, water jug, pretend spear or sword.

Special Agent Option

Before class, print the daily mission "say no to temptation" on a large sheet of paper, drawing blank lines for all the vowels. On another paper, print each vowel and number them from one to five. Place all items in a box labeled "Top Secret." At the end of the story, volunteers remove items from the box. Show papers to the group. For each blank line, turn the flashlight on and off the correct number of times to indicate which vowel belongs. Write vowels on paper.

Tell the Story

Many years had passed since David was a young boy in Israel. He had been chosen to be king and had killed the giant Goliath. He had come to work for King Saul and married King Saul's daughter. But after all this time, David was not yet the king. Saul was STILL the king of Israel. And Saul HATED David! He wanted to kill David. But David did NOT want to kill Saul. God had said David would be king someday. And David knew that GOD would decide when Saul should stop being king.

King Saul was so jealous of David and so angry at him, he took 3,000 men with him to the desert to chase and capture David! One time when Saul was chasing David, David and his men hid way back in a deep, dark cave. Then guess who walked right into the front of the cave? SAUL!

Saul was alone, away from his soldiers. One of David's men whispered, "Look! It's Saul! God has given you this chance to capture Saul, or even kill him!" As quiet as a shadow, David slipped to the front of the cave. He silently took his knife from his belt, but he didn't hurt Saul. He sliced a piece from Saul's clothes. David's men wanted to attack Saul, but David did not give in to the temptation to hurt him.

When Saul left the cave, he heard someone call, "My lord, the king!" It was DAVID! Saul whirled around. David lifted the piece of Saul's clothes high and said, "Why do you listen to people who tell you I am going to hurt you? Look! I cut this from your clothes! My men wanted me to kill you, but I said, 'I can't hurt Saul. He is God's chosen king.'" David knew that God's Word said to honor the ruler of God's people. (See Exodus 22:28.)

David continued, "King Saul, I will not hurt you, no matter what you do to me."

Saul felt SO ashamed! He said, "David, you have treated me kindly, but I have treated you badly. May God reward you for being kind to me today." Then Saul left safely. David made sure of that.

Even though King Saul was glad David had not killed him, it wasn't long before Saul was chasing David AGAIN! Saul took his 3,000 soldiers and went looking for David. They camped for the night near a hill. Saul lay down to sleep, right in the center of his soldiers. God put Saul and all his men into a deep sleep. Meanwhile, David and one of his men quietly made their way into Saul's camp.

© 2007 Gospel Light. Permission to photocopy granted. *Agents in Action*

LESSON SIX

David tiptoed past the sleeping men guarding Saul to where a spear and a water jug lay near Saul's head. David stood over the sleeping king who wanted so badly to kill him. He could have taken Saul's spear and killed Saul, right there and then! But David would not do it. Again, David chose to resist temptation. Instead, David picked up the jug and spear and climbed up the nearby hill.

At the top of the hill, David shouted out, "Who's guarding the king of Israel? Where are the water jug and the spear that were beside his head?"

Saul sat up! He saw David, holding up Saul's spear and water jug. David called, "Why are you chasing me? God put you into my hands again, but I would not hurt you." Saul promised not to try to hurt David again. But it didn't take long for Saul to forget his promise. In fact, Saul kept trying to kill David until the day Saul died! All those years, even though Saul was cruel to David, God gave David the courage to do what was right. David knew God would make him the king one day. And until then, he could love even his enemy Saul!

God's Word & Me

All through his life, David had to choose whether or not he was going to say no to temptation and obey God. David didn't always make the right choice. Sometimes he did disobey God. Sometimes we're tempted to disobey God, too.

When Jesus lived on Earth, He talked about being tempted to sin and do wrong things. Read Matthew 6:13. **Jesus said these words as part of a prayer that we call the Lord's Prayer. Jesus wanted His disciples, and us, to know that we can ask God for help in saying no to temptation—the wrong things Satan (the evil one) wants us to give in to. God will help us make the right choice. The step in receiving God's help is to become members of His family. God showed His great love to all of us when He sent His Son, Jesus, to die on the cross for our sins. Because Jesus is alive today, we can depend on Him.** (Talk with interested students about salvation. See "Leading a Child to Christ" on p. 12.)

>> **What are some of the most common temptations kids your age face at school? At home?** (Be honest. Treat others fairly. Not to make fun of others.)

>> **Why is saying no to temptation sometimes hard for kids your age?**

>> **How do we know what God wants us to do?** (He tells us in His Word. Parents and teachers help us know.)

>> **Think about a time when you found it hard to say no to temptation.** Pray with children, asking God's help to live in right ways.

LESSON SIX

Game Center
for younger children
1 Samuel 24:1-22; 26

Collect
Bible, balloons.

Prepare
Inflate and tie two balloons for each child in the class.

Do

1. **In our Bible story today, a man named David had to be very quiet. Let's see how quiet we can be as we play these balloon games.** (1) Give each child a balloon. Have each child try to tap it up in the air while you count to 10. Challenge children not to talk or make noise while keeping the balloon up in the air. (2) Children form pairs or trios. Each pair or trio tries to bat the balloon back and forth to each other without making noise. (3) Children form a circle and pass the balloon around the circle without making noise.

2. After children have experienced the challenge of trying to play the balloon game without making noise, let them play and make noise!

God's Word
"Lead us not into temptation, but deliver us from the evil one." Matthew 6:13

For Younger Children:
"Help me to do what is right."

God's Word & Me
I can pray to God for help in saying no to temptation and living in right ways.

Talk About

>> **In our Bible story today David had to be very quiet because King Saul was trying to capture him. David was tempted to do something very wrong. David was tempted to hurt his enemy King Saul. But David chose to obey God. David did not hurt King Saul.**

>> **Michaela, doing what your (dad) asks you to do is a way to obey God. What is something your (dad) asks you to do?** (Turn off the TV. Put away a toy.) **God will help us do what's right and obey Him.**

>> **I saw lots of you helping each other keep the balloons up in the air. Helping your friends is a way to obey God. Zoey, helping your friends is a way to obey God. What is one way you can help a friend?** (Share a snack. Let a friend choose which game to play.) **God will help us do what's right and obey Him.**

>> Pray briefly, **Dear God, we love You. Please help us do what's right, even when we want to disobey You. In Jesus' name, amen.**

For Older Children

Individuals, pairs, trios and the entire group try to keep multiple balloons up in the air without saying a word for longer and longer periods of time.

LESSON SIX

Game Center
for older children
1 Samuel 24:1-22; 26

Collect
Bible, large sheet of butcher paper, markers, index cards, coins.

Prepare
Draw a bull's-eye target on butcher paper.

Do
1. Brainstorm with children temptations often faced by kids their age. Each child writes a temptation on an index card. (Children may make more than one card.) Collect index cards.

2. Place the target on the floor. Place all index cards face down in the center of the target. Children stand around the target. Give each child a coin. Children take turns calling out "no" and pitching their coins, trying to get them to land on the target. Each time a coin lands on the bull's-eye, child removes card from target and reads the temptation aloud. Children take a step back before continuing with game. Repeat until all index cards have been removed from the target.

God's Word
"Lead us not into temptation, but deliver us from the evil one." Matthew 6:13

For Younger Children:
"Help me to do what is right."

God's Word & Me
I can pray to God for help in saying no to temptation and living in right ways.

Talk About

» **When do you think kids your age find it the hardest to say no to temptation—at school, at home, playing soccer? Why might it be hard for kids to say no to temptation?** (They're afraid of what will happen. Other kids might make fun of them.)

» **What might be the results of giving in to temptation?** (Feel bad. Know that you did wrong. Parents find out.)

» Read Matthew 6:13. **Satan, God's enemy, is the evil one this verse talks about. Satan wants us to disobey God by giving in to temptation. How can praying to God help us say no to temptation?** (Because when we ask God for help, He promises to answer our prayers.)

» **God understands when we are tempted to do wrong, but no matter how big the temptation is, we can pray to God for help in saying no to temptation.** Lead children in prayer, asking God to help us always say no to temptation.

For Younger Children
Instead of writing temptations on index cards, ask each child to say something right to do (share, tell the truth, help a baby sister, wait patiently at store, etc.) before taking a turn to toss the coin onto the target.

LESSON SIX

Art Center
for younger children
1 Samuel 24:1-22; 26

Collect
Bible, poster board, scissors, markers, glue, stapler, colorful cereal (or similar snack).

Prepare
Cut poster board into strips approximately 1x24 inch (2.5x61 cm) in size. (Optional: Instead of rectangular strips cut a crown-shape strip for each child.)

Do
1. Give each child a poster-board strip. Children decorate strips using markers. Children may also glue on cereal "jewels" to their crowns.
2. Measure and staple crowns to fit heads. Children eat leftover cereal after crown is completed.

God's Word
"Lead us not into temptation, but deliver us from the evil one." Matthew 6:13

For Younger Children:
"Help me to do what is right."

God's Word & Me
I can pray to God for help in saying no to temptation and living in right ways.

Talk About

>> **In our Bible story today, a king was trying to catch a man named David. David could have hurt the king, but he did not hurt the king. David did what was right. David obeyed God.**

>> **Every day we can say no to doing wrong. We can obey God. When we feel like doing wrong, we can ask God to help us obey Him.**

>> **Mei, one way to obey God is to say kind words. What are some kind words you can say to show that you want to obey God?** (Please. Thank you. I'll help you.)

>> **The Bible tells us that we can ask God for help to obey Him. We can say, "Help me to do what is right."** Pray briefly, **Dear God, help us to be like David and do what is right. In Jesus' name, amen.**

For Older Children
Give each child a sheet of paper. Children arrange and glue cereal to show a king wearing a crown.

© 2007 Gospel Light. Permission to photocopy granted. *Agents in Action*

Lesson Six

Art Center
for older children
1 Samuel 24:1-22; 26

Collect
Bible, Lesson 6 Pattern Page (p. 126), markers, clear Con-Tact paper, scissors, flat craft decorations (such as stickers, stick-on flat jewels, etc.).

Prepare
Make a copy of the Pattern Page for each child. Cut Con-Tact paper into strips that are a little larger than the bookmarks. Cut at least two strips for each child.

Do
1. Give each child a copy of the Pattern Page. Child cuts out bookmark(s) of his or her own choosing. Children decorate bookmarks with markers and the craft decorations provided. (Optional: On the blank side of the bookmark, each child writes a prayer asking God's help to say no to temptation.)

2. Help children peel off the backing from Con-Tact paper and cover both sides of the bookmark. Trim Con-Tact paper as needed, leaving 1/4-inch (.6 cm) border beyond the edge of the bookmark.

God's Word
"Lead us not into temptation, but deliver us from the evil one." Matthew 6:13

For Younger Children:
"Help me to do what is right."

God's Word & Me
I can pray to God for help in saying no to temptation and living in right ways.

Talk About

>> **There will always be times when we are tempted to disobey God. The Bible tells us that even Jesus, God's Son, was tempted to do wrong. But Jesus also told us that we can ask God to help us say no to temptation. What else can we do to avoid or say no to temptation?** (Plan what to do when tempted. Remember God's promise of help. Spend time with people who want to do what's right.)

>> Read Matthew 6:13. **"The evil one" means Satan, God's enemy, who wants us to give in to temptations. When we pray, how can God help us with those temptations?** (He can give us the strength to say no. He can help us know right things to do.)

>> **What kinds of temptations do kids face when they are with their friends? With brothers and sisters? Saying no to temptation is something we need God's help to do.** Lead children in prayer, asking God's help to avoid temptation.

For Younger Children
Precut bookmarks with the appropriate Bible verse. Each child chooses a bookmark and decorates it. Attach Con-Tact paper, letting children help to smooth down the paper. Trim as needed.

LESSON SIX

Worship Center
for younger and older children
1 Samuel 24:1-22; 26

Collect

Bibles, *Agent* Music CD and player, song charts (pp. 248, 252), construction paper in a variety of colors, scissors or paper cutter.

Preparation

Cut construction paper into small squares, making eight of each color for each student. Hide at least two Bibles in the room (one for each group in the Bible Verse Game), and tell location of Bibles to leaders.

Team Game

Distribute squares of construction paper randomly to students, making sure that each student receives a mix of colors. (In a large group, walk among the group tossing handfuls of squares into the air. Each student picks up eight squares.) **Today we're going to see how fast you can help each other get eight squares of the same color.** At your signal, students begin trading squares with each other. Squares may also be picked up from the floor, but student must place an equal number of squares on the floor. As soon as a student has eight squares, he or she sits down. (Optional: Pair younger children with older children for this game.) Continue until all students are seated.

God's Word

"Lead us not into temptation, but deliver us from the evil one." Matthew 6:13

For Younger Children:
"Help me to do what is right."

God's Word & Me

I can pray to God for help in saying no to temptation and living in right ways.

Bible Verse Game

Repeat Matthew 6:13 aloud with children. Then form two or more groups. Assign a leader to each group. Students in each group form a line with the leader first in line. Students place hands on shoulders of person in front of them. At your signal, children begin saying words of Matthew 6:13 aloud while leader leads the group around the room in a random pattern. After at least three or four repetitions, each leader leads his or her group to one of the hidden Bibles. **Knowing what is in God's Word helps us know right ways to live and helps us say no to temptation.**

Song

Lead children in singing "Smart Choices." Add motions and/or clapping if desired.

Prayer

God is so great that He promises to help us resist temptation, and He also promises to forgive us when we disobey Him. Let's ask His help in living in right ways. Invite volunteers to take turns saying Matthew 6:13 as a prayer.

Song

Lead children in singing "Be Strong and Courageous." Add motions and/or clapping if desired.

© 2007 Gospel Light. Permission to photocopy granted. *Agents in Action*

LESSON SIX · Pattern Page

"Lead us not into temptation, but deliver us from the evil one." Matthew 6:13

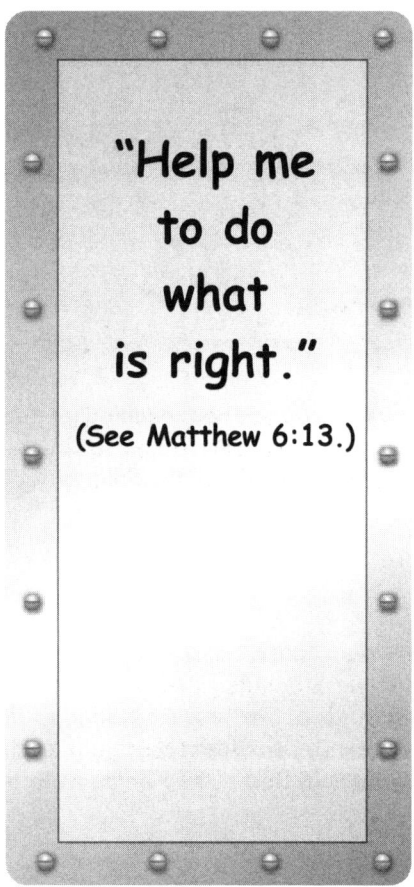

"Help me to do what is right."

(See Matthew 6:13.)

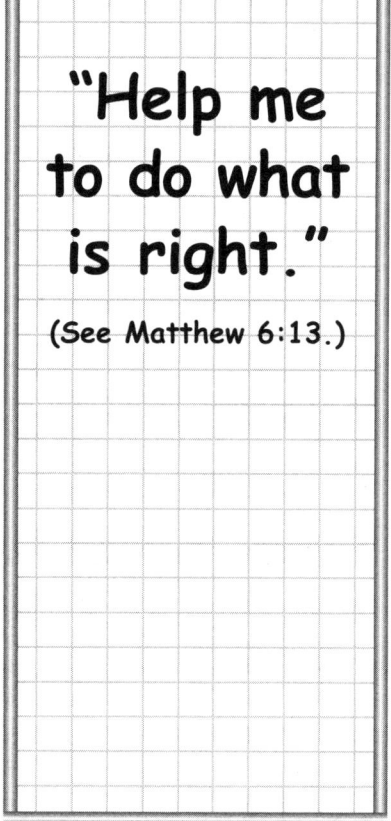

"Help me to do what is right."

(See Matthew 6:13.)

"Lead us not into temptation, but deliver us from the evil one." Matthew 6:13

LESSON SIX • Puzzle Page

RHYME TIME

Rhyme Time

In each row, circle the word that does not rhyme with the other words.

wonder thunder temptation under
giraffe opportunity half calf
tart heart something smart
you sing thing ring
star far know car
hello toe wrong go

Write the words you circled in order on the blank lines:

_____ is the _____ that _____ is _____ to do _____ .

When have you been tempted to do wrong? What did you do?

What can you do to say no to temptation?

LESSON SEVEN

Bullies

Bible Story:
Elisha's Surprise
2 Kings 6:8-23

Teacher's Devotional

Bullies—we've all known a few! Did bullies punch you in the school hallway? Take your lunch money? Call you names? Make fun of you? Human nature wants to hurt bullies in return. But there are powerful supernatural ways to overcome the bullies of the world—by showing genuine kindness! Elisha gave us a delightfully ironic example.

Aramean soldiers were camped around Elisha's home. When his terrified servant reported what he saw, Elisha asked God to make the servant able to see God's army around the enemy. He then asked God to blind the enemy soldiers. Elisha could have easily killed every blind Aramean and given God praise for delivering the enemy into his hands. Instead, he gave them a creative object lesson! He marched them into the city of Samaria. Once the gate was locked behind them, he asked God to restore their sight! They had time to take stock of the situation as the king of Israel debated about ways to kill them! But Elisha told the king no. He instructed the people to prepare food for these soldiers instead! A meal was not only a stunning act of kindness; eating together also symbolized being at peace. Even though he could have taken revenge, Elisha gave everyone a hands-on (and tasty!) lesson in active kindness.

Kids today all know what it's like to be "picked on." They have all wanted to hurt in return for cruelty. And some children may need to first consider the question, Am I a bully? Point out through this amazing story that God can help them solve bully problems—when they ask for His help! Give children suggestions for actions and words that will help them stay safe. If appropriate, help them evaluate their own actions and words. Above all, remind them that God promises to be with them just as when His army camped around Elisha's house. He promises wisdom (see James 1:5) so that they and the parents and teachers who care for them can see solutions, even while demonstrating God's kindness and forgiveness. God will give them power and protection so that they do not have to feel alone when facing bullies.

God's Word

"I tell you: Love your enemies and pray for those who persecute you."
Matthew 5:44

For Younger Children:
"Love others and pray for them."

God's Word & Me

Treating others kindly, even while protecting myself, helps me show God's love to others.

Planning Page

LESSON SEVEN

Choose which centers you will provide and the order in which children will participate in them (see pp. 14-18 for schedule tips and pp. 24-25 for guidelines in combining older and younger children). Also plan who will lead each center (for staffing tips see pp. 19-21). Use the reproducible planning sheet (p. 238) to record your plans.

Bible Story Center

Bible Story
Elisha's Surprise • 2 Kings 6:8-23

Younger Child Option
Move stand-up cards to show story action

Older Child Option
Children fold and assemble papers to discover the daily mission "love your enemies"

Game Center

Younger Child Option
Play a helping game, and talk about showing God's love when others are mean

Materials
Bible, *Agent* Music CD and player, paper, tape

Older Child Option
Play a relay jumping game, saying the words of Matthew 5:44, and talk about God's help when facing bullies

Materials
Bible, masking tape, paper, markers

Art Center

Younger Child Option
Create string-art paintings on paper hearts and name people to show God's love to

Materials
Bible, newspaper, tempera paint, shallow baking pans, white construction paper, scissors, clothespins, yarn

Older Child Option
Make and decorate glasses and discuss ways of "seeing" enemies so that we can show God's love to them

Materials
Bible, Lesson 7 Pattern Page (p. 140), white card stock, acetate, scissors, card stock, pencils, markers, decorating materials, glue stick, several staplers

Worship Center

For the Younger and Older Child
Participate in large-group activities to review Bible verse and to worship God together

Materials
Bibles, *Agent* Music CD and player, song charts (pp. 246, 250), inflated balloons

Coloring/Puzzle Center

Younger Child Option
Review the Bible story while completing coloring page

Materials
Lesson 7 Coloring Page (p. 141) for each student, crayons

Older Child Option
Compare Bible verses about loving enemies while completing puzzle page

Materials
Lesson 7 Puzzle Page (p. 142) for each student, pencils

LESSON SEVEN

Bonus Theme Ideas

Bonus Theme Ideas can be used at any time during this session: as an additional activity center, to extend the session for a longer time or for added theme excitement.

Agent Discovery

Prepare a large sheet of butcher paper by using a white crayon to write each child's name. (For a large group, write each child's name on a separate sheet of paper.) Challenge children to discover each other's names. Set out the prepared butcher paper (or give each child a separate sheet). Give each child a watercolor marker to color over the paper and discover the name of an agent.

Special Agent Information

Caught in the Act

Throughout today's lesson, give prize tickets or stickers to children caught acting like a special agent serving God (sharing, caring, forgiving, etc.). Prize tickets may be exchanged for prizes.

Special Agent Information

Mystery Salad

Prepare salad ahead of time (see recipe below). Gather children together and ask for several volunteers who will try to identify the items in the Mystery Salad. One at a time, blindfold each volunteer and let each sample one of the salad ingredients, alternating easy- and hard-to-guess items. Children identify the ingredients. Give help as needed. Then serve the Mystery Salad to children in small disposable cups or bowls. **Ingredients:** 1 dozen apples, sliced; 2 cups halved seedless grapes, 1 cup raisins, 1 cut chopped walnuts, 1/3 cup brown sugar, 1 tablespoon cinnamon, 1 teaspoon nutmeg. **Instructions:** Place sliced apples in large bowl, add raisins, walnuts, brown sugar, cinnamon and nutmeg and stir. Add grapes. Refrigerate until ready to serve.

Special Agent Information

Post a note alerting parents to the use of food. Also, check registration forms for possible food allergies.

LESSON SEVEN

Bible Story Center
for younger children
2 Kings 6:8-23

Collect

Bible.

Introduction

Hold up three fingers. **How many fingers am I holding up?** Volunteers answer. Hold up seven fingers for children to count. **Now let's close our eyes.** Hold up five fingers. **Can you see how many fingers I am holding up?** Children open eyes. **We need to see to do lots of things. Listen to hear about some men who had to walk far without being able to see!**

Tell the Story

The Arameans were enemies of God's people, the Israelites. Elisha loved and obeyed God. And Elisha was making the king of the Arameans very angry! Every time the king made a secret plan, God told Elisha what was going to happen. So when the Arameans came to fight the Israelites, the Israelites were always ready for them! Finally, the king of the Arameans was so angry at Elisha that he sent an army to capture Elisha!

At night, the army surrounded the town where Elisha was. In the morning, Elisha's helper saw the army. He told Elisha, "Oh, no! There is an army waiting outside! What will we do?"

Elisha said, "Don't be afraid." Elisha prayed that God would show his helper how God was protecting them. The helper looked again and all around the enemy army he saw horses and chariots that looked like fire! God was protecting Elisha and his helper.

Then Elisha prayed again. He prayed that God would make the enemy army blind. God did! So Elisha led the army of blind men to the city where the king of Israel was. The people shut the gates so the army could not get away. Then Elisha prayed again. He prayed that God would let the army see again. God did! The soldiers looked around. Uh-oh—they were trapped!

The king of Israel wanted to hurt these enemy soldiers. But Elijah told him, "We will not hurt them. Give these soldiers food and water and then let them go back home." So the people made a big dinner for the enemy soldiers. They were kind to the enemies who had come to capture Elisha! Then they let the enemy soldiers go home.

The Arameans must have been surprised by such kindness. They stopped trying to fight Elisha and the Israelites for a while.

Special Agent Option

Fold five small index cards in half to make stand-up cards. On separate cards, draw one of the following: stick figure with "Elisha" printed below, crown shape colored blue with "king" printed below to represent the Aramean king, stick figure with "helper" printed below, five stick figures with "army" printed below, crown shape colored red with "king" printed below to represent the Israelite king. (Optional: Make a set of cards for each child.) Place cards in a box labeled "Top Secret." At the appropriate times in the story, remove items from box. Move cards to show story action.

God's Word & Me

Elisha could have decided to fight against the mean soldiers. But instead, he prayed to God and asked God's help. Then when God protected him, Elisha was kind to the soldiers. In the Bible, Jesus said, "Love others and pray for them." That's just what Elisha did! And that's what we can do, too.

Sometimes other kids might be mean to us. We can pray and ask God to help us and protect us. God has given us people like moms and dads and teachers who will help us know how to stay safe. We can show God's love to others, too. God will help us!

LESSON SEVEN

Bible Story Center
for older children
2 Kings 6:8-23

Collect
Bible, five large sheets of paper, markers, tape.

Prepare
Print one of these questions at the top of separate sheets of paper: "Who?" "What?" "When?" "Where?" "Why?" Number each question from one to five. Attach papers to classroom walls.

Introduction

When has someone done something kind to surprise you? (Friend gave me a present. Grandparent took me on a trip. Teacher said there wasn't any homework.) **Today in our Bible story, we'll find out how a man named Elisha surprised a whole army of soldiers.** As you tell the Bible story, invite children to hold up the appropriate number of fingers when they first hear an answer to one of the questions on the sheets of paper. Write, or ask a helper, to write answers to the questions on the sheets of paper.

Tell the Story

Elisha was a prophet of God who lived in Israel. Elisha told God's messages to the people of Israel and their king. God also gave Elisha power to do amazing things.

At this time, some people called the Arameans were at war with Israel. But the king of the Arameans was getting very upset. The Israelite army always KNEW what he was going to do before he did it! Was there a spy in his army? No. It was just that God kept telling Elisha all of the Arameans' battle plans! And Elisha told the king of Israel everything God said!

Special Agent Option
Before class, on two large sheets of paper, print letters as shown in sketch a. Place papers in a box labeled "Top Secret". At the end of the story, volunteers remove items and show to group. Children suggest ways of folding and placing papers together until the daily mission "love your enemy" is discovered (see sketch b).

a.

b.

Finally, one officer in the Aramean army told the king that Elisha the prophet was the one who was finding out and telling all the king's plans. "Elisha even tells the king of Israel what you say in your bedroom!" he added.

The king of the Arameans was FURIOUS! He sent out spies to find out where Elisha was. When he found out that Elisha was at a city called Dothan, the king sent soldiers to CAPTURE Elisha.

When Elisha's servant got up early the next morning, there were Aramean soldiers all around the city! Elisha's servant was AFRAID! But Elisha knew God had armies of His own! Elisha asked God to show his servant that the hills all around them were full of soldiers and horses and chariots of FIRE! God's army was ready to protect them!

As the enemy soldiers came to capture him, Elisha asked God to make them blind. Suddenly, the whole army of Aramean soldiers couldn't see! Elisha came to the leader and told him that the army was on the wrong road. He invited them to follow him. What else could the soldiers DO? They had to trust this man they couldn't see! So the whole Aramean army followed Elisha. He led them on a long walk, all the way into the Israelite city of Samaria!

Once the soldiers were inside and the city gates were closed, Elisha asked God to take away the soldiers' blindness. God did! NOW the Arameans looked around. They could see they were in big trouble—shut inside an Israelite city! There was no way to escape! *Will we all be KILLED?* they wondered.

Even the king of Israel thought this was the perfect time to get rid of these bullies. He was ready to kill the Aramean soldiers! But Elisha told the king God's very SURPRISING plan: They were to feed the soldiers and send them safely HOME!

So the people of Samaria prepared a big feast for the enemy soldiers. The soldiers may have wondered why the Israelites were being so kind! But they were hungry, so they ate. When they were full, the whole army was allowed to go home unharmed. No one had hurt them. Instead, the Israelites had been very GOOD to them! And for a very long time, the Arameans didn't fight with the Israelites at all!

Elisha had shown God's love to the very same enemies who didn't deserve kindness. His actions helped change the situation so that the Israelites stayed safe for a time.

God's Word & Me

The Bible doesn't tell us if Elisha was afraid of the army when he first heard they were gathered around his house. But we do know what Elisha did: He prayed for God's protection. And God did protect him. Then, however, when most people would have thought about trying to get even with their enemies or bullies, Elisha showed God's love.

Elisha's action are a good example of how to obey a command that Jesus gave His followers. Read Matthew 5:44. **Jesus knew that there will always be times when others or even ourselves treat others in mean ways—like bullies. So first, we can make sure we choose to be fair and kind to others, and then we can ask God's help in knowing what to do when someone acts like a bully toward us. God gives us people, like our parents and teachers, who can help us plan what to do when someone is mean or unfair to us or wants to fight us. We can remember that God's help and protection is for us, too—just like it was for Elisha. God will help us stay safe and show His love to others.**

>> **When are some times that kids your age act in mean and unfair ways—like bullies?** (Cut in front of others in line. Push kids out of the way. Take something that belongs to others.)

>> **What are some ways that God can help you know how to protect yourself from a bully?** (Answers my prayers to know what to do. Gives me friends to stay with at school or in the neighborhood. Gives me parents or teachers who can help me.)

>> **What makes it so hard for kids your age to show God's love and kindness to a bully?** (The bully doesn't deserve to be treated kindly. Kids might feel afraid of the bully.) **It can be hard to remember that God loves each person—no matter how wrong their actions are. God understands how we feel. God doesn't expect us to become best friends with a bully, but if we ask Him, He can help us be kind to someone who may not deserve our kindness.** Pray with children, asking God's help in knowing what to do when others are mean and unfair, and that others may come to know God's love through our actions.

LESSON SEVEN

Game Center
for younger children
2 Kings 6:8-23

Collect
Bible, *Agent* Music CD and player, paper, tape.

Prepare
Tape sheets of paper, one for each pair of children, in a circle on the floor.

Do

1. Play "God's Kids" while children walk in a circle around the papers. After 10-15 seconds stop the music. Each child finds a paper on which to place a foot, with two children sharing each paper. Encourage children to help each other find papers on which to stand.

2. Repeat activity as time and interest permit. For each round, name a different body part which children place on papers (hands, elbows, knees, etc.).

God's Word
"I tell you: Love your enemies and pray for those who persecute you."
Matthew 5:44

For Younger Children:
"Love others and pray for them."

God's Word & Me
Treating others kindly, even while protecting myself, helps me show God's love to others.

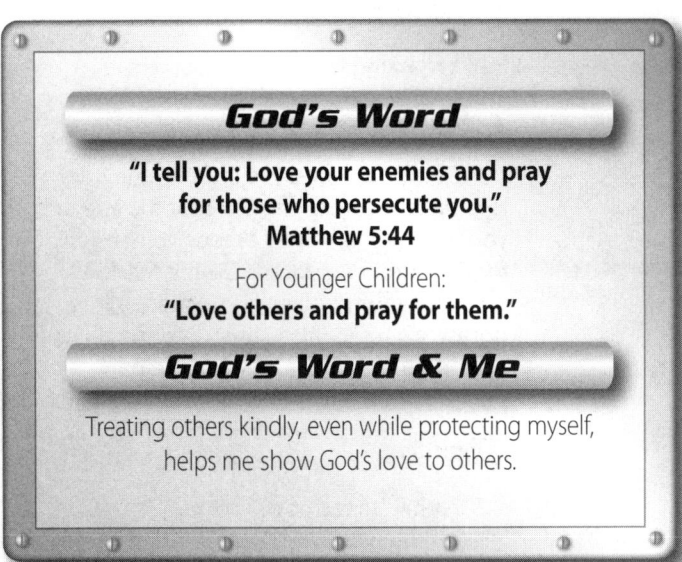

Talk About

>> **We're having fun playing this game with each other. How are we helping each other and showing God's love?** (Helping each other find a paper to stand on.)

>> **What would happen if kids playing this game did not want to let someone stand on the papers with them?** (Not everyone could play. It wouldn't be fun. Kids might say mean things.) **When we are kind and helpful, it helps everyone get along and have more fun.**

>> **Damon, when might kids your age not want to share or take turns? When kids don't take turns, we might feel like being mean to them. God can help us know what to do so that everyone can have a turn. We can say, "Everyone needs a turn."**

>> **In the Bible, Jesus said, "Love others and pray for them." Even when people are mean to us, we can pray for them. We can ask God's help to show love to them.** Pray briefly, **Dear God, help us to show love to others. And when someone is mean to us, help us know how to be kind. In Jesus' name, amen.**

For Older Children

Begin game by placing a paper on the floor for each child. After each round of the game, remove one sheet of paper until there is only one sheet left. Children work together to see how many can stand on or touch one sheet of paper.

© 2007 Gospel Light. Permission to photocopy granted. *Agents in Action*

LESSON SEVEN

Game Center
for older children
2 Kings 6:8-23

Collect
Bible, masking tape, paper, markers.

Prepare
Make four masking-tape lines on the floor (see sketch). Adjust distances for the age of your group. Make lines as long as needed for the number of teams. Divide Matthew 5:44 into four phrases and write each phrase on a separate sheet of paper. Arrange papers in order with one paper in the middle of each line.

> **God's Word**
> "I tell you: Love your enemies and pray for those who persecute you."
> Matthew 5:44
>
> For Younger Children:
> "Love others and pray for them."
>
> **God's Word & Me**
> Treating others kindly, even while protecting myself, helps me show God's love to others.

Do

1. Form two teams of no more than six children. Children in each team line up behind the first masking-tape line. **Some of the things God asks us to do are easy. But some of the things God asks us to do might be hard. Today we're going to play a game that has both easy and hard things to do.**

2. At your signal, first child in each team jumps from one line to the next, saying the phrases aloud as they jump. After jumping to all the lines and saying the verse aloud, player returns to his or her team. Team whose players complete the relay first is the winner.

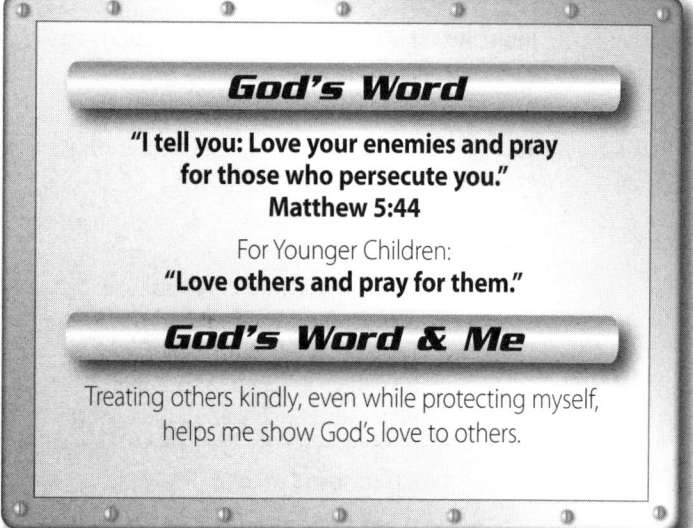

Talk About

>> **Which was the easiest line to jump to? Which was the hardest? When is it easy to be kind and show God's love to other kids?** (When they are friends. When they have been kind to you.) **When would it be hard for kids to show God's love to others?** (When they are bullies. When they try to start a fight.) **When others are mean or hurt us in some way, it's natural to think about wanting to get revenge. God understands how we feel, and He will help us know what to do so that we can be safe.**

>> Read Matthew 5:44. **What might be the results of obeying this command from Jesus? Why should we pray for people who are mean to us?** (God loves them. God tells us to. We can pray for everyone, and praying for them can help us not be mad at them.)

>> **We can ask God's help to make sure we don't act as bullies, and we can ask His help in knowing how to stay safe and show His love when others are mean to us.** Lead children in prayer, thanking God for His help and protection, and asking for His help in showing His love.

For Younger Children

Make three large masking-tape squares. Children take turns jumping into each square as they say "Love others," "and pray," "for them."

LESSON SEVEN

Art Center
for younger children
2 Kings 6:8-23

Collect

Bible, newspaper, tempera paint, shallow baking pans, white construction paper, scissors, clothespins, yarn.

Prepare

Cover table with newspaper. Pour ½-inch of (1.3 cm) paint into baking pans and set on newspaper. For each child, cut from construction paper a heart shape approximately 8 inches (20.5 cm) in width. Clip 4-inch (10-cm) lengths of yarn onto clothespins and set several next to each paint pan.

God's Word

"I tell you: Love your enemies and pray for those who persecute you."
Matthew 5:44

For Younger Children:
"Love others and pray for them."

God's Word & Me

Treating others kindly, even while protecting myself, helps me show God's love to others.

Do

1. Give each child a paper heart. Demonstrate how to hold on to clothespin, dip yarn into paint and drag the yarn around on the paper heart to make swirls and designs.

2. Children decorate their hearts with string painting. Remind children to use each piece of yarn for only one color.

Talk About

>> **Jesse, who do you love? These hearts remind us to show love to others.**

>> **Show me a mad face. When others are mean to us, we might make mad faces. We can ask God to help us and protect us when others are mean. God can help us be kind, even when others are mean. What would your kind face look like?**

>> **In the Bible Jesus said, "Love others and pray for them." We can pray for people who aren't friendly to us. We can also show God's love to them.** Pray briefly, **Dear God, help us show love to people who are mean and pray for them. In Jesus' name, amen.**

For Older Children

Provide a variety of papers (construction paper, card stock, neon copier paper, etc.) in various sizes. Children choose to make "string art" bookmarks or posters. Children write Matthew 5:44 on the bookmarks or posters before painting.

© 2007 Gospel Light. Permission to photocopy granted. *Agents in Action*

LESSON SEVEN

Art Center
for older children
2 Kings 6:8-23

Collect

Bible, Lesson 7 Pattern Page (p. 140), white card stock, acetate (available as report covers in office supply stores), scissors, card stock, pencils, markers, decorating materials (small stickers, puffy paint, glitter paint, etc.), glue stick, several staplers.

Prepare

For each child, make a copy of Pattern Page onto card stock and cut two 2-inch (5-cm) squares of acetate.

Do

1. Pass out a Pattern Page and scissors to each child. Each child cuts out an eyeglasses pattern. Children decorate glasses.

2. Child places eyeglasses under acetate squares, traces the openings and cuts out, leaving a ¼-inch (.6 cm) edge (see sketch). Child glues acetate to inside of glasses.

3. Children staple sides to front of glasses.

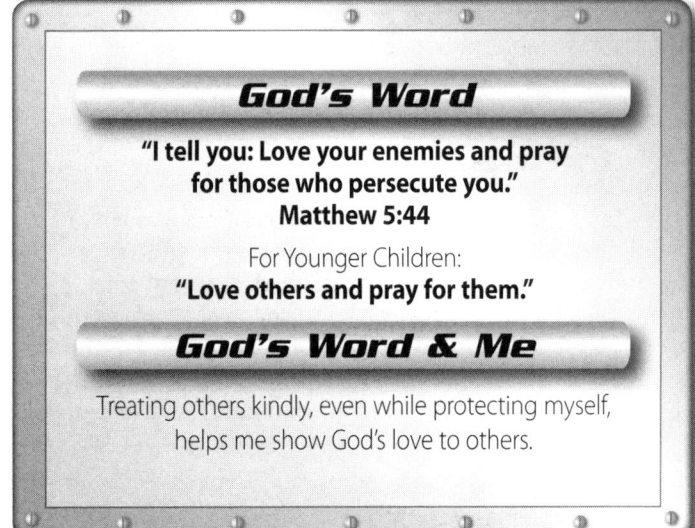

Talk About

>> **Why do people wear eyeglasses?** (To see better.) **How can understanding, or "seeing," other kids who are mean help us love them?** (When we understand God's love for everyone, it helps us remember to ask God's help in showing His love.)

>> **What are some ways to show love to an enemy?** (Pray for them. Help them. Get help in figuring out a way to get along.)

>> **Why does God want us to love everyone, including people like bullies and enemies?** (Because God loves everyone and He wants us to show His love to others.)

>> Read Matthew 6:13. **According to this verse, what is one way we can love our enemies?**

>> **When we are able to "see" our enemies as God sees them, it makes it easier to be able to pray for them. God wants us to love everyone, even people like bullies and enemies, because when we do, we share His love. Let's ask God to help us love our enemies, and let's pray for them right now.** Pray, asking God to help us love others. Also include a short silent time for students to silently pray.

For Younger Children

Ahead of time, cut out and staple together the glasses pattern for each child. Children color and decorate glasses, without gluing on the acetate. Invite children to wear decorated glasses. **Julie, who do you see? We can love (Gabriel) and pray for him.** Continue, until each child has been named.

God's Word

"I tell you: Love your enemies and pray for those who persecute you."
Matthew 5:44

For Younger Children:
"Love others and pray for them."

God's Word & Me

Treating others kindly, even while protecting myself, helps me show God's love to others.

LESSON SEVEN

Worship Center
for younger and older children
2 Kings 6:8-23

Collect

Bibles, *Agent* Music CD and player, song charts (pp. 246, 250), inflated balloons.

Team Game

Divide group into two or more teams. Ask six players from each team to form a line in an open area of the room. Players in each line stand at least 2 feet (.6 m) apart from each other. Give an inflated balloon to the first player in each line. At your signal, first player taps balloon to next player in line, and so on until balloon reaches the last player in line. Last player holds balloon, runs to front of line and begins activity again. Children cheer for their teams. First team to finish is the winner. (Optional: Designate a different body part [hands, elbows, heads, knees, wrists, feet] that must be used for each round of the game.)

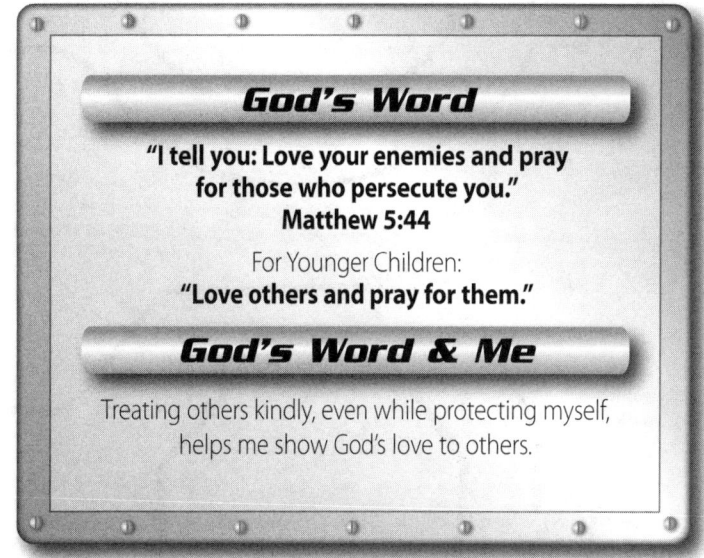

God's Word

"I tell you: Love your enemies and pray for those who persecute you."
Matthew 5:44

For Younger Children:
"Love others and pray for them."

God's Word & Me

Treating others kindly, even while protecting myself, helps me show God's love to others.

Bible Verse Game

Lead children in a game of Charades to guess words of the verse. Volunteer comes forward. Whisper a word from Matthew 5:44 to volunteer, who demonstrates one or more motions until children in audience guess the word. Continue as time and interest allow. Repeat verse together after all words have been guessed. (Optional: Lead children to silently demonstrate all motions in verse order.)

Song

Lead children in singing "Mission of Love." Add motions and/or clapping if desired.

Prayer

Today we've been talking about loving our enemies—people who are bullies and who are mean and unfair. Show me how hard you think it is to be kind to an enemy. When I call out "Love your enemy," hold up one finger if you think it's easy, five fingers if you think it's sort of hard and ten fingers if you think it's really hard. Lead children to complete activity. **Loving our enemies can be hard to do without God's help. Let's ask Him now.** Lead children in prayer.

Song

Lead children in singing "God's Kids." Add motions and/or clapping if desired.

© 2007 Gospel Light. Permission to photocopy granted. *Agents in Action*

LESSON SEVEN · Pattern Page

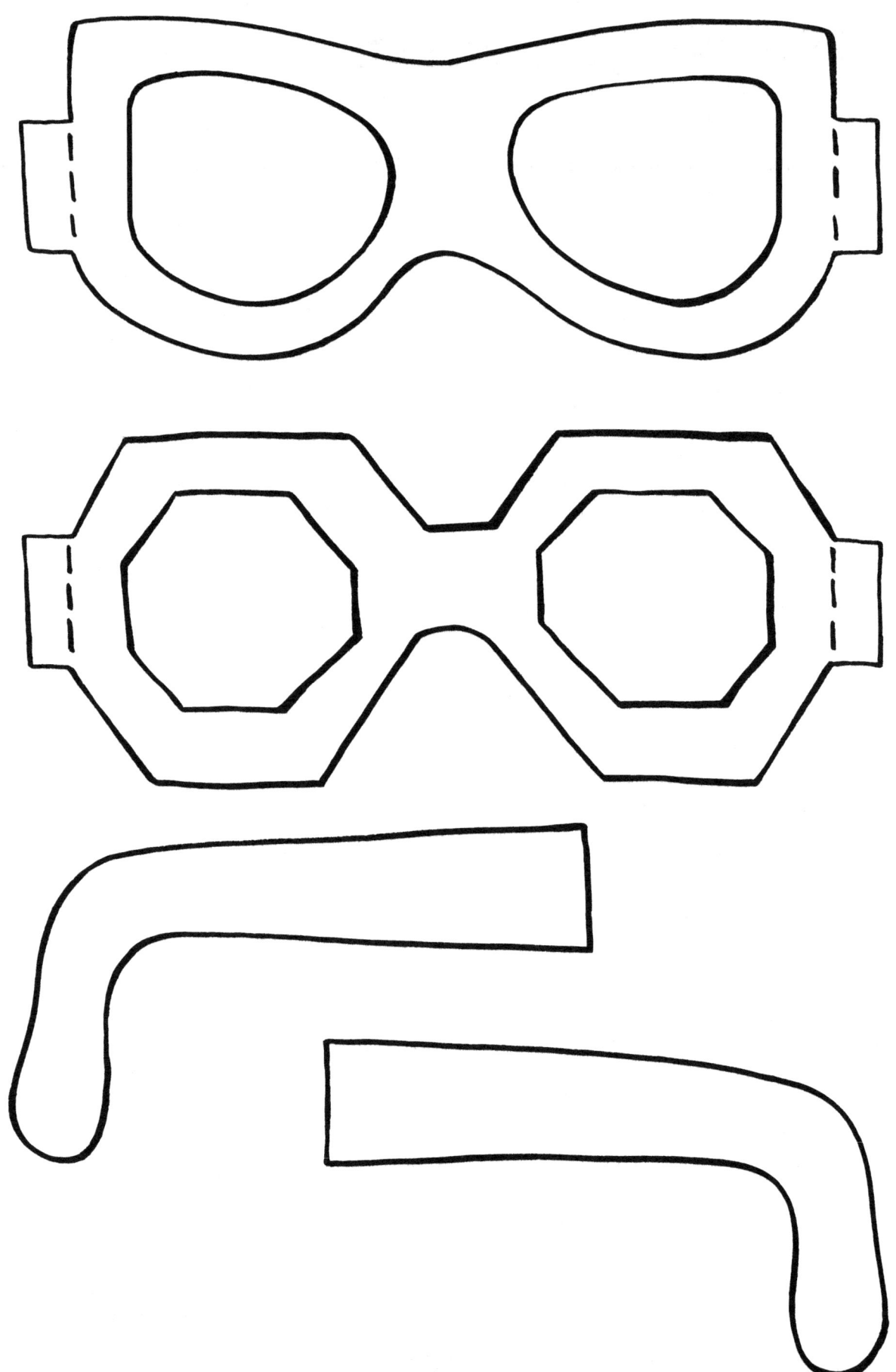

LESSON SEVEN • Puzzle Page

VIDEO VERSE

These kids are trying to discover the hidden message on the wall. Fill in the clues. Decipher the message by writing on the blank lines only the letters in the squares.

Compare this verse from Luke 6:27 to Matthew 5:44. What is the same? What is different?

The opposite of hate	A popular toy	Animal covering	The number after nine
☐☐☐☐	YO - ☐☐	F ☐☐	T ☐☐

Another name for a jewel	Tells a fib	Not a cat but a	The opposite of bad
G ☐☐	L ☐☐☐	☐☐ G	☐☐☐☐

The number after one	The planet we live on	A fragrant flower	Two halves equal a
☐ W ☐	EAR ☐☐	R ☐☐☐	☐☐ LE

The opposite of love	Not me but		
☐☐☐☐	☐☐☐		

_____

_____

_____

LESSON EIGHT

Choices

Bible Story:
Sow and Grow
Mark 4:1-20

Teacher's Devotional

There is no thrill for a parent like seeing his or her child actually reading the Bible with interest or acting in a way that shows God's work in that child's heart! However, such good things don't happen by accident—if they are regular occurrences, they are likely to be the result of regular, intentional efforts, fueled by the Holy Spirit. While we all would love to see our kids grow good habits and be free of the distractions of the world, our fast-paced lives seem to keep such focused intentionality just beyond our frenzied grasp!

As we retell Jesus' familiar parable about the four soils, the story may be so familiar that we might not notice its powerful portrayals. Of course we are not like the first, stony soil. We've received the good news with joy—and we haven't given up, or we wouldn't be teaching this lesson! But when Jesus describes the third soil, it's easy to breeze by the disturbing details on the way to the cheery description of the soil with the great fruit-bearing potential!

In each of our lives, there are areas where those creeping "weeds" of time crunch, financial worry, overcommitment and other worldly concerns may begin to sprout. We often don't notice their choke hold until these cares of the world have us in a tight grip! Because we prove what we value by the choices we make, we are teaching our kids moment by moment what really matters to us. We don't want our lives to fail at communicating the real importance of God's kingdom. Take time today to ask God's Spirit to show you the spots in your "garden" where the cares of the world may be sprouting. Then choose to take time with God so that you can teach by your own choices how fruitful soil looks—daily more and more free of those choking weeds of worldly concerns! The habits you build will offer a model to the children you teach of how to let God's Word motivate lifelong choices of obedience to God.

God's Word

"If you love me, you will obey what I command."
John 14:15

For Younger Children:
"Love God and obey His commands."

God's Word & Me

God's Word can help me make right choices and build good habits.

© 2007 Gospel Light. Permission to photocopy granted. *Agents in Action*

LESSON EIGHT

Planning Page

Choose which centers you will provide and the order in which children will participate in them (see pp. 14-18 for schedule tips and pp. 24-25 for guidelines in combining older and younger children). Also plan who will lead each center (for staffing tips see pp. 19-21). Use the reproducible planning sheet (p. 238) to record your plans.

Bible Story Center

Bible Story
Sow and Grow • Mark 4:1-20

Younger Child Option
Observe and touch items used in the story

Older Child Option
Use grape-juice concentrate to discover the daily mission "make right choices"

Game Center

Younger Child Option
Play a game pretending to be farmers or seeds, and talk about people who help them learn about God's Word

Materials
Bible

Older Child Option
Play a game of Human Concentration, and discuss choices and habits that show love for God

Materials
Bible

Art Center

Younger Child Option
Make a minibook about the story Jesus told, and talk about making right choices in different places children like to go

Materials
Bible, Lesson 8 Pattern Page (p. 154), scissors, tape, stapler, crayons or markers

Older Child Option
Make paper-plate art displays and talk about making choices that help to build good habits and show love for God

Materials
Bible, a large white thin paper plate for each child, markers, stapler

Worship Center

For the Younger and Older Child
Participate in large-group activities to review Bible verse and to worship God together

Materials
Bibles, *Agent* Music CD and player, song charts (pp. 252, 254), masking tape, at least two Frisbees and two hula hoops

Coloring/Puzzle Center

Younger Child Option
Review the Bible story while completing coloring page

Materials
Lesson 8 Coloring Page (p. 155) for each student, crayons

Older Child Option
Review ways of learning to make wise choices while completing puzzle page

Materials
Lesson 8 Puzzle Page (p. 156) for each student, pencils

> LESSON EIGHT

Bonus Theme Ideas

Bonus Theme Ideas can be used at any time during this session: as an additional activity center, to extend the session for a longer time or for added theme excitement.

SPECIAL AGENT DAY

Special Agent Practice

Listening is an important skill for agents to practice. Let's play a game where you find your team of agents by listening. Children line up. Whisper a number to each child, repeating numbers at least twice. (If you have a large group of children, repeat numbers more often.) Do not give out the numbers in order. At your signal, children walk around the playing area and clap the number you whispered to them. Children may not talk to each other; they listen to the number of claps to figure out what number a child was given. Children assigned the same number form teams. Give a small prize to the first team to gather. As time and interest permit, repeat game, assigning different numbers to children.

Special Agent Information

Special Agent Day

Send home an announcement inviting children to wear one or more elements of a special-agent costume at the next session of *Agents in Action*. (Optional: For fun, write the announcement in backwards letters that have to be held up to a mirror to read.) Children may wear sunglasses, wristbands, hats, suit jackets, black T-shirts, etc. If desired, give each child who participates a small prize (special-agent gadget such as toy camera, pen, decoder ring, etc). Take pictures of children and display at church or on your church's website (with parent permission).

Special Agent Information

Agents on the Go S'more Mix

Gather 2 cups honey graham cereal, 1 cup minimarshmallows, ½ cup semi-sweet chocolate chips, ½ cup raisins. Thoroughly mix ingredients together and place in one or more large bowls. Children use large spoons to place several spoonfuls into disposable cups. Eat and enjoy!

Post a note alerting parents to the use of food. Also, check registration forms for possible food allergies.

Special Agent Information

© 2007 Gospel Light. Permission to photocopy granted. *Agents in Action*

LESSON EIGHT

Bible Story Center
for younger children
Mark 4:1-20

Collect

Bible.

Introduction

Let's pretend to be seeds that grow up into tall plants. Invite children to follow your actions as you crouch down on the floor and then gradually stand up and spread out your arms. **Listen to find out what happened to some plants in a story Jesus told.**

Special Agent Option

Collect seeds, dry dirt, several small rocks, weeds, small plant. Place each item into a resealable plastic bag. Place the bags into a box labeled "Top Secret." At the appropriate times in the story, remove bags from box and show items to children. (If group is small enough, children may also touch each item.)

Tell the Story

One day, Jesus told a crowd this story: "A farmer went out to his field to plant some seeds. The farmer tossed seeds onto the ground. Some seeds fell on the hard dirt. The birds ate these seeds.

"Other seeds fell on rocky ground. The plants grew for a little while. But there wasn't enough water, and the plants soon died. Other seeds fell near thorny weeds. The weeds grew faster and stronger than the plants. The plants couldn't grow! These plants died, too."

Finally Jesus said that some of the seed fell on good soil. Those seeds grew and became tall and strong plants. Jesus' friends wondered, *What does this story mean?*

Jesus said, "The seeds are like God's Word. People who hear God's Word but never believe it are like the hard dirt where birds ate the seeds. Some people are glad to hear the Word of God. They believe it, but later it's too hard to do what God wants. They stop believing God's Word. They are like the rocky soil."

One of the friends asked, "What kind of people are like the thorny soil?"

Jesus said, "Some people hear and believe God's Word. They begin to love and obey God, but then their worries keep them from obeying God. Soon they forget about God's Word.

"The good soil is like people who hear and believe God's Word. They are glad to always love and obey God."

Jesus told this story to teach His helpers to obey God's Word and choose to do what's right.

God's Word & Me

In this story, Jesus said that when we love and obey God, it's like we are plants growing tall and strong. Hold up your Bible. **God's Word helps us choose to do what's right. Every day we can choose to obey the commands we read in God's Word.**

In the Bible, Jesus said, "Love God and obey His commands." Some of God's commands are to be kind, to help others and to play fair. Each time we choose to obey one of God's commands, we show that we know what it means to love and obey God.

LESSON EIGHT

Bible Story Center
for older children
Mark 4:1-20

Collect
Bible, index cards, marker.

Prepare
Print each of the following words on separate index cards: farmer, seed, bird, rock, dried-up plant, thorny weed, choked plant, healthy plant.

Introduction
When have you planted some seeds? What were the results? What would you do differently the next time you planted some seeds? Volunteers respond. **Today we're going to hear one of Jesus' most famous stories—the parable of the soil. Listen to hear which kind of soil you are most like.** Before telling the story, give prepared index cards to volunteers. Ask each volunteer to stand in front of the group and make a motion to demonstrate his or her assigned item at the appropriate times in the story Jesus told.

Special Agent Option
Before class, place purple grape-juice concentrate into a cup. Mix equal parts water and baking soda in a bowl. Dip cotton swab into mixture and print the daily mission "make right choices" on several sheets of paper. Allow to dry. Place sheets and several paintbrushes in a box labeled "Top Secret." At the end of the story, cover table or floor with plastic tablecloth. Volunteers remove the papers and lightly paint over them with juice concentrate to read the daily mission.

Tell the Story
One day, a big crowd of people gathered to see Jesus. Shopkeepers closed their stores for the day; farmers left their fields, and women and children left their cooking and gardening and playing to come and hear Jesus. After all, Jesus healed sick people and made crippled people walk. Everyone wanted to see and hear Jesus! The people settled down and waited to hear Jesus' every word.

Jesus began His story: "A farmer went out to his field to plant a crop. He scattered handfuls of seeds from his seed pouch onto the ground. Some of the seeds fell on a pathway where the dirt was packed down as hard and smooth as rock. NO seed could put down roots and grow in such rock-hard soil!"

Jesus continued, "The seeds lay there until birds swooped down and snatched up the seeds."

Everyone nodded. They had all planted gardens and sown seeds themselves. And they all knew that a seed on hard ground NEVER becomes a plant that produces grain! Those seeds just become food for hungry birds!

Jesus went on. "Other seeds fell in a spot where the soil was very shallow. The soil was soft on top, but there was hard rock under it. These seeds sprang up quickly because the soil was warm there. But as the plants grew, their roots hit the rock and could go no farther. The shallow soil didn't hold much water, either. Soon, the little plants dried up and died."

Everyone had seen those kind of plants, too. They sprang up but soon dried out and died because the soil was shallow.

Jesus said, "Some of the seeds that the farmer scattered landed in good soil, but the soil was full of weeds. At first, those thorny weeds shaded the young plants as they began to grow. But as the thorny weeds grew bigger, they took the water and light the young plants needed. Soon, the weeds had taken everything. The young plants had all the life choked out of them. They could never bear fruit."

Some people began to wonder if the farmer would have any crop at all! But Jesus wasn't finished.

He said, "The rest of the seeds fell on soft, rich soil. They grew into an ENORMOUS crop of healthy plants. Some plants had produced 30 times what the farmer had planted, some grew 60 times as much, and some produced even 100 times more! The farmer was delighted when he saw the crop!"

The disciples looked at each other, puzzled. "What does this story mean?" they asked Jesus.

He answered, "The seed is like the Word of God. Any person who hears God's Word is like one of those kinds of soil. Some people never believe the Word of God at all. They are like the hard dirt where the seeds were snatched up and eaten by birds. Other people are like the shallow soil. These people hear and gladly believe God's Word at first! But when it becomes too hard to do what God wants, they forget all about God and His Word. The truth they heard dries right up and dies. People who are like the soil full of weeds are people who become very, very busy with anything and everything," Jesus continued. "The truth they heard is choked by their busyness. They soon forget all about God."

Then Jesus said, "But people who hear and believe God's Word are like the GOOD soil. They grow when they learn from it." Jesus meant that as these people grow, their choices and habits show what they've learned about God. People who are like the good soil love and obey God every day!

God's Word & Me

The people who listened to Jesus' story must have thought about what kind of soil they were. We can think about that, too. Jesus' story helps us know that God's Word can help us know how to be good soil. Read John 14:15. **The commands we read in the Bible help us know what kind of choices to make. Every day, the choices we make and the things we make a habit of doing can show if we are like good soil—people who love and obey God.**

>> **What are some things you think kids your age could do every day to show that they are like good soil?** (Pray to God. Ask His help to love and obey Him. Pay attention to God's commands in the Bible. Pray for others.)

>> **Knowing God's commands can make a difference in the way we act. For example, how might a kid your age act if he or she wants to obey God's command to be honest and fair?** (Tell parent the truth about doing homework. Not cheat in a game or on a test.)

>> **Why might kids your age find it hard to make right choices?** (They are worried about something that might happen. Their friends are making wrong choices.) **Let's thank God that His Word helps us build good habits and make right choices.** Pray with children, thanking God for the Bible and asking His help in making right choices and building good habits.

LESSON EIGHT

Game Center
for younger children
Mark 4:1-20

Collect
Bible.

Do
Our Bible story today is about a farmer. In Bible times, farmers planted seeds by tossing them onto the ground. Let's pretend to be farmers today. Children walk in a circle. When you call out "farmers," children stop walking and pretend to toss seeds onto the ground. When you call out "seeds," children stop walking, crouch down and pretend to slowly grow into tall plants. Repeat activity as time and interest allow.

God's Word
"If you love me, you will obey what I command."
John 14:15

For Younger Children:
"Love God and obey His commands."

God's Word & Me
God's Word can help me make right choices and build good habits.

Talk About

>> In the Bible, Jesus told us, "Love God and obey His commands." God's commands are the good and right things we can choose to do. We find out about God's commands by listening to Bible stories.

>> Jesus told a story about a farmer. Some of the seeds the farmer planted grew to be tall, healthy plants. Jesus said that when we choose to obey the commands we read in the Bible, we are like tall, healthy plants. Max, who helps you learn the good things in the Bible? Joshua, who tells you Bible stories?

>> One good thing the Bible tells us to do is to help our friends. Jessica, who is a friend you can help? What can you help (Kenna) do?

>> **The Bible helps us learn to make good choices that show how much we love God.** Pray briefly, **Dear God, thank You for the Bible. Help us choose to obey Your commands. We love You. In Jesus' name, amen.**

For Older Children
Play Plant Tag. When a child is tagged, he or she freezes and poses like a plant. Other children free frozen children by touching them and saying the words of John 14:15.

LESSON EIGHT

Game Center
for older children
Mark 4:1-20

Collect
Bible.

Do

1. Whisper a word in each child's ear that has to do with situations in which they make choices (TV, movies, school, friends, soccer, money, church, etc.). Make sure to give the same word to two children and instruct children not to tell their words to anyone. Have all children except one volunteer sit on the floor in a circle. (Make sure volunteer has been given a word.)

2. Ask the volunteer to stand in the middle of the circle and choose two people to reveal their words. If the words match, those two people leave the circle and sit together as a "match." If the words do not match, volunteer continues choosing people until he or she finds a match. Then the volunteer trades places with someone in the circle who then stands in the middle of the circle and tries to make a match. Continue to play until all the matches are made.

God's Word
"If you love me, you will obey what I command."
John 14:15

For Younger Children:
"Love God and obey His commands."

God's Word & Me
God's Word can help me make right choices and build good habits.

Talk About

>> **What's one of the words we used in our game? What are some of the right and wrong choices kids your age have to make at (school)?**

>> Read John 14:15. **What do you know about the Bible that makes you think it's a good place to find help for making right choices?** (It's God's messages to us. Verses in the Bible have helped me and my family before. The Bible is true.)

>> **What's something you are in the habit of doing?** Making choices that show we love and obey God is something we can get in the habit of doing.

>> **What kinds of choices to show love for God can kids your age get in the habit of doing?** (Choose to read the Bible. Choose to obey God's command to tell the truth. Choose to pray to God.) Lead children in prayer, thanking God for the Bible and asking God to help us always know the right choices to make.

For Younger Children

Find magazine pictures of things and people and glue them onto index cards. (Note: Either find two similar pictures [soccer ball, toy, baby, television, etc.], or else use a color photocopier to make two identical pictures.) Lead children to play Concentration, placing cards facedown and letting children take turns turning over two cards at a time to find a match. Talk with children about the choices represented by the pictures.

LESSON EIGHT

Art Center
for younger children
Mark 4:1-20

Collect
Bible, Lesson 8 Pattern Page (p. 154), scissors, tape, crayons or markers, stapler.

Prepare
Make one copy of the Pattern Page for each child. Cut apart book pages and flaps for each child. Make a sample book.

Do
1. Show and read your sample book.
2. Give each child pages and flaps for one book. Help children tape the top of one flap onto the bottom of each page.
3. Children color the pages. Help children staple pages together in order to form books. Invite children to show the pages, lift the flaps on their books and tell story action.

God's Word
"If you love me, you will obey what I command."
John 14:15

For Younger Children:
"Love God and obey His commands."

God's Word & Me
God's Word can help me make right choices and build good habits.

Talk About

>> The pictures in our books help us learn about a story Jesus told. In this story, Jesus said that when we choose to love and obey God, we are like plants that grow tall and strong.

>> We can learn how to love and obey God by hearing stories from the Bible. One thing the Bible helps us learn is to say kind words. Charis, who says kind words to you? Who can you say kind words to?

>> Every day we can choose to do good things. Caleb, where is some place you like to go? You can choose to do good when you are at the (park). Obeying God's commands in the Bible helps us make right choices. Pray briefly, **Dear God, thank You for giving us the Bible. Please help us make right choices. In Jesus' name, amen.**

For Older Children
Children cut and assemble books on their own.

© 2007 Gospel Light. Permission to photocopy granted. *Agents in Action*

Art Center
for older children
Mark 4:1-20

LESSON EIGHT

Collect

Bible, a large white thin paper plate for each child, markers, stapler.

Prepare

Make a sample paper-plate picture display.

Do

1. Show children the sample paper-plate display you made.

2. Give each child a paper plate. In the center of his or her plate, each child draws a picture that represents a choice he or she has to make (TV to represent choosing what to watch, stick figure person to represent choosing a friend to spend time with, sports ball to represent choosing which sport to play, dish to represent choosing to do a chore, etc.). Children may also add designs to their paper plates.

3. Children form trios and staple their paper plates together at sides to form stand-up paper-plate displays.

God's Word

"If you love me, you will obey what I command."
John 14:15

For Younger Children:
"Love God and obey His commands."

God's Word & Me

God's Word can help me make right choices and build good habits.

Talk About

>> **I see a lot of you have made pictures of (friends). What are some of the choices kids your age have to make about friends?** (Which friends to spend time with. What to do with friends. How to treat friends.) **What choices related to friends are hardest for kids your age?**

>> **What are some of the things kids can do when they are trying to make choices that show their love and obedience for God?** (Ask God for help. Remember Bible verses about loving and obeying God. Think about the positive results that take place from making right choices.)

>> **What kind of habits help you make right choices?** (Remembering to pray. Reading God's Word. Spending time with kids who want to show their love for God.)

>> Read John 14:15. **Who are some people kids obey? Why? What might help a kid choose to obey God?** (Remembering God's love. Trusting that God's ways are the best way to live.)

>> **The choices you make today might seem like they don't matter very much. But every time we make a good choice, it helps us build a habit of doing what's right and showing our love for God.** Pray, thanking God for His Word and asking His help in making right choices and building good habits.

For Younger Children

After children draw pictures, staple plates together for them. Talk with children about how the Bible helps us know good and right things to do.

LESSON EIGHT

Worship Center
for younger and older children
Mark 4:1-20

Collect

Bibles, *Agent* Music CD and player, song charts (pp. 252, 254), masking tape, at least two Frisbees and two hula hoops.

Preparation

Make a masking-tape line at one side of an open area of the room. Place hula hoops 10 to 20 feet (3 to 6 m) from the masking-tape line.

Team Game

Divide group into two or more teams. Four volunteers from each team line up behind the masking-tape line. Another volunteer from each team stands 10 to 20 feet (3 to 6 m) from the masking-tape line and holds a hula hoop vertically up in the air. At your signal, one at a time, the players on each team try to throw a Frisbee through the hula hoop while standing at the line, retrieving the Frisbee after each throw. (Optional: Players say one word of Bible verse each time they attempt to toss the Frisbee through the hula hoop.) The first team on which all players throw Frisbee through hula hoop is the winner. Members of each team cheer for their teams.

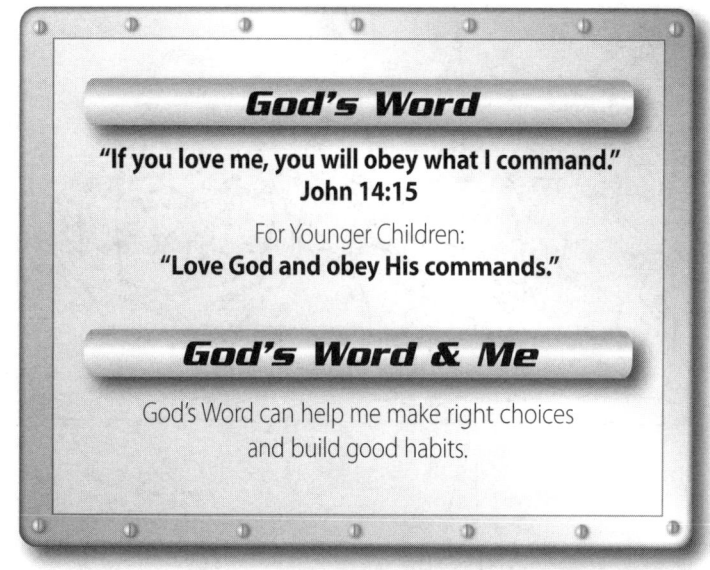

God's Word

"If you love me, you will obey what I command."
John 14:15

For Younger Children:
"Love God and obey His commands."

God's Word & Me

God's Word can help me make right choices and build good habits.

Bible Verse Game

Repeat John 14:15 aloud with children. Then count off to divide group into teams of 10 players each. Each team stands and forms a line. Players repeat verse with each player saying one word of the verse and all children saying the reference. When you begin playing "God's Kids," children move randomly around the room. When the music stops, teams see how fast they can line up in verse order, say the verse and reference and then sit down. Repeat game as time and interest permit.

Song

Lead children in singing "Train Me Up." Add motions and/or clapping if desired.

Prayer

Let's see how many Bible commands we can list. Volunteers call out commands. **Remembering these commands will help us make wise choices. One of God's commands is to pray to Him. Let's obey that command right now and ask His help in making right choices and building good habits.** Lead children in prayer.

Song

Play "Smart Choices." Lead children in singing and doing suggested motions.

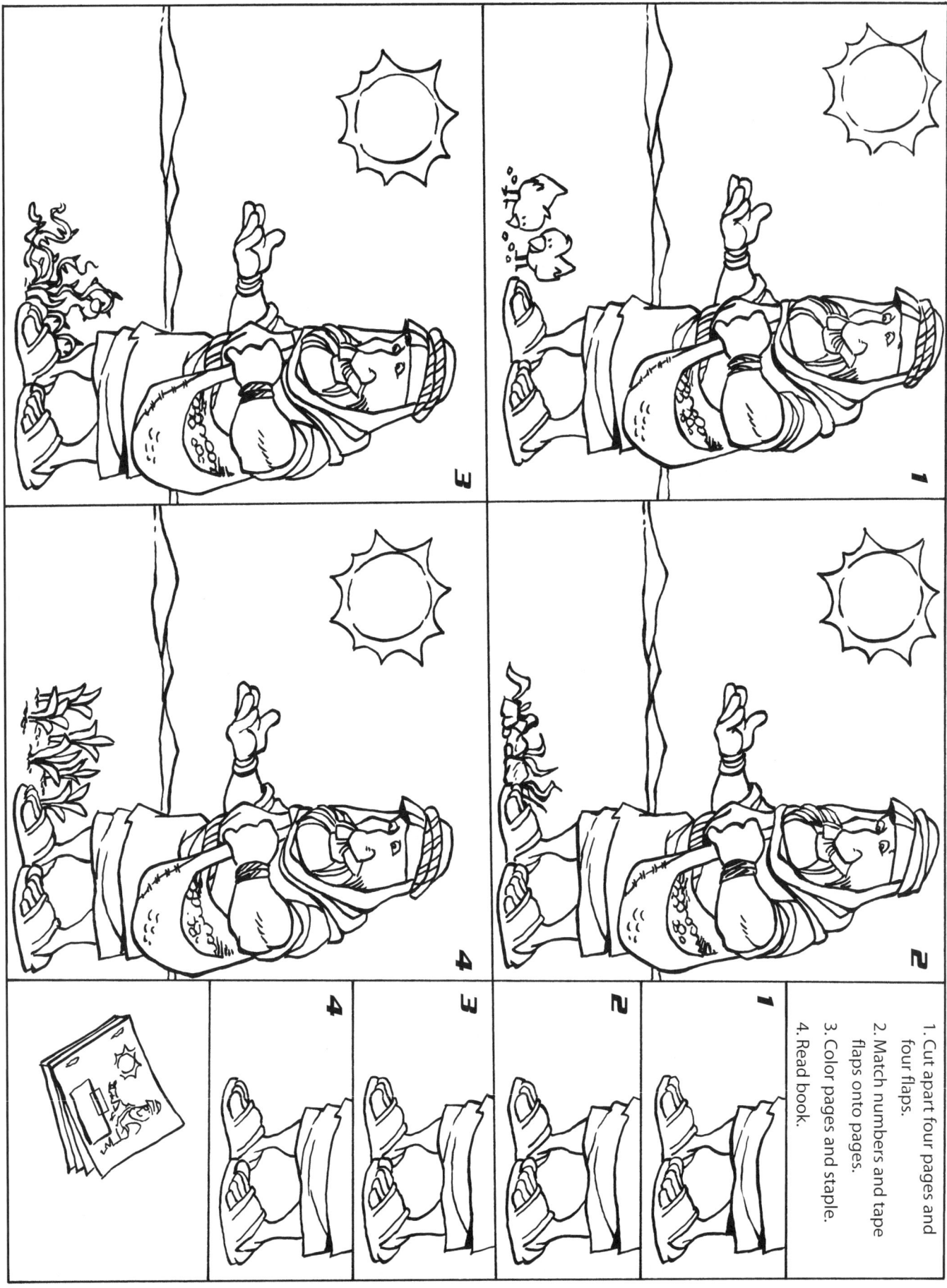

LESSON EIGHT · Coloring Page

Jesus tells a story about a farmer planting seed. Mark 4:1-20

Jesus' story reminds us to obey God's Word, the Bible. When do you learn Bible verses?

© 2007 Gospel Light. Permission to photocopy granted. *Agents in Action*

LESSON EIGHT · Puzzle Page

WHAT IS IT?

What Is It?
Complete the rhymes to find four ways to learn and remember God's instructions for us.

1. It has four letters,
It rhymes with ring,
It needs some music,
The way is _____.

2. It has four letters,
It rhymes with bead,
It needs a book,
The way is _____.

3. It has four letters,
It rhymes with walk,
It needs a friend,
The way is _____.

4. It has eight letters,
It rhymes with exercise,
It needs some practice,
The way is _____.

memorize talk bring read chalk fries sing seed

Lost in a Maze

Andrew and Danielle need God's Word to make right choices each day! Help them find their way to the Bible.

DRAW YOUR LINE THROUGH ALL THE BOXES. THERE MAY BE MORE THAN ONE PATH.

START — FINISH

156

© 2007 Gospel Light. Permission to photocopy granted. *Agents in Action*

LESSON NINE

Money

Bible Story:
Bigger, Better Barns
Luke 12:13-21

Teacher's Devotional

We often hear of our kids' desire for designer clothing or the latest gaming equipment—they are often convinced that these expensive items are things they need and that these things will make them happy. Millions of dollars in advertising are spent bombarding all of us—especially children—with messages that we'll be happier if we buy the right products. Saturated with such messages, our kids can easily become confused about what really matters!

People in Jesus' time struggled with priorities, too. Jesus often reminded His listeners that material wealth is a gift from God that should be used to honor Him. He told about a foolish farmer who hoarded grain and got great pleasure out of planning to build bigger barns. But God warned the farmer that he would die that night; even though he possessed all the stuff that he expected would make him happy, he left it all behind when he died! Jesus consistently reminded His hearers that life is not just about the physical, material world—it's about eternal things, too. What we can buy, touch and use will break, wear out or be left behind.

Kids (and adults) need to hear the truth that counteracts society's materialistic message. Even though it may seem difficult for kids to get a handle on things that cannot be seen or touched, remember that they do understand the value of genuine love that motivates the sharing of a possession or the gift of a kind word. Tell your own stories of how you discovered that real happiness comes from nothing we buy. (For example, briefly describe the value of a friendship.) As we all learn to live as Jesus taught, we'll discover the only kind of happiness that lasts—forever!

God's Word

"Freely you have received, freely give."
Matthew 10:8

For Younger Children:
"Be glad to give to others."

God's Word & Me

I can be generous with my money and possessions to show my thankfulness for God's gifts to me.

© 2007 Gospel Light. Permission to photocopy granted. *Agents in Action*

LESSON NINE

Planning Page

Choose which centers you will provide and the order in which children will participate in them (see pp. 14-18 for schedule tips and pp. 24-25 for guidelines in combining older and younger children). Also plan who will lead each center (for staffing tips see pp. 19-21). Use the reproducible planning sheet (p. 238) to record your plans.

Bible Story Center

Bible Story
Bigger, Better Barns • Luke 12:13-21

Younger Child Option
Use blocks to build a barn to illustrate story action

Older Child Option
Assemble hidden papers to discover the daily mission "be generous and thankful"

Game Center

Younger Child Option
Build block barns in a relay race, and name people with whom to share the good things God helps them have

Materials
Bible, wooden or cardboard blocks

Older Child Option
Participate in a Money Scramble, making sure everyone gets the same amount, and then talk about what it means to be generous in sharing God's gifts

Materials
Bible, paper, scissors

Art Center

Younger Child Option
Make and decorate gift boxes drawn on paper, and talk about ways of sharing the good things God helps us have

Materials
Bible, ribbon, scissors, one large sheet of paper for each child, markers, pre-cut magazine pictures of items children are likely to have, glue, gift bows

Older Child Option
Make banks to use in collecting money for an offering, and talk about what it means to freely give the good things God has given us

Materials
Bible, Lesson 9 Pattern Page (p. 168), card stock, scissors, tape, craft decorations (such as stickers, jewel stickers, glitter, etc.), markers

Worship Center

For the Younger and Older Child
Participate in large-group activities to review Bible verse and to worship God together

Materials
Bibles, *Agent* Music CD and player, song charts (pp. 249, 253), yarn in a variety of colors, scissors, several coins

Coloring/Puzzle Center

Younger Child Option
Review the Bible story while completing coloring page

Materials
Lesson 9 Coloring Page (p. 169) for each student, crayons

Older Child Option
Review what it means to be thankful for their possessions while completing puzzle page

Materials
Lesson 9 Puzzle Page (p. 170) for each student, pencils

© 2007 Gospel Light. Permission to photocopy granted. *Agents in Action*

LESSON NINE

Bonus Theme Ideas

Bonus Theme Ideas can be used at any time during this session: as an additional activity center, to extend the session for a longer time or for added theme excitement.

Special Agent Says

Play a game like Simon Says but with an *Agents in Action* twist. Replace "Simon Says" with "Special Agent Says" to indicate when children are to follow one of your instructions. Give instructions that are active such as, "Shake the hand of a friend," "Salute a friend," "Jump as high as you can," "Spin in a circle one time," "Do a sit-up," "Link arms with (two) friends," "Run in place while counting to five."

Special Agent Information

Mission of Love

Invite children to help you assemble one or more Birthday Boxes to be used for children at a community help organization. Purchase (or ask parents to donate) inexpensive birthday party plates, napkins, cups, tablecloth, party favors, etc. Provide length of butcher paper, markers, ribbon, scissors and glue. Children letter and decorate Happy Birthday banners. Children place enough birthday party items for 8 to 10 people in small boxes. Give boxes to organizations who provide aid for children.

Special Agent Information

Agent Thirst Quencher

Combine and stir thoroughly 2 12-oz cans lemon-lime soft drink, 1 32-oz bottle cranberry juice cocktail, 1 cup white grape juice and ½ cup lime juice. (Makes enough for 2 quarts.) Serve over ice cubes. (Optional: Add a lime slice to each cup.)

Special Agent Information

Post a note alerting parents to the use of food. Also, check registration forms for possible food allergies.

© 2007 Gospel Light. Permission to photocopy granted. *Agents in Action*

159

LESSON NINE

Bible Story Center
for younger children
Luke 12:13-21

Collect

Bible.

Introduction

Make the sound of a cow if you can tell me an animal that usually lives in a barn. Volunteers respond. **Today we're going to hear a story about a man who kept grain in his barn. The grain was used to make food like bread. Listen to what happened.**

Special Agent Option

In a box labeled "Top Secret," place several dozen wooden blocks. At the appropriate times in the story, remove blocks from box. Build a small barn, and then a larger barn to show story action.

Tell the Story

One day Jesus was teaching a big crowd of people. Jesus wanted the people to know that loving and obeying God is more important than collecting lots of money and things. So Jesus told the people a story to help them understand. This is the story Jesus told:

"There was a farmer whose fields grew a lot of grain. In fact, the farmer had so much extra grain that his barns could not hold anymore. So he decided to tear down his barns and build bigger barns. The farmer decided that he would collect more and more and MORE grain and put all his grain in his BIG barns. Then he would have so much grain, that he could sell it and always have lots of money! The farmer thought he would have so much money that he would not have to work anymore. He decided he would just eat and drink and have fun! The farmer was so happy about all the money he would have!

"But God knew the farmer's life would end soon. God said to him, 'You fool! You will die tonight. Then who will get all your money?'"

Jesus wanted the crowd to know why the farmer was foolish. The farmer only thought about his fields full of grain. The farmer only thought about his big barns and all the money he would get for his grain! He didn't even THINK about loving and obeying God. He didn't thank God for all the good things he had. Jesus told this story to help us know that loving and obeying God is more important than having lots of money or getting lots of things.

God's Word & Me

The farmer really wanted to have lots of money. And when he got a lot of money, he wanted to keep it for himself. He didn't want to use it to help others or show that he cared about them.

Sometimes kids your age like to have a lot of toys. Kids who are older than you might want to have lots of money. Having toys and money is not wrong. But God wants us to know that we should thank Him for the good things we have. And we can always share what we have with others. In the Bible, Jesus said, "Be glad to give to others." When we have lots of good things or even when we don't, Jesus wants us to thank God and show His love to others.

LESSON NINE

Bible Story Center
for older children
Luke 12:13-21

Collect

Bible, highlighter, pen.

Prepare

Make six copies of this Bible story. On each copy, use a highlighter to mark each sentence (indicated by quote marks) spoken by the story characters. Number the copies in order.

Introduction

What would you do if you had as much money as you wanted? Volunteers respond. **It's fun to think about what we would do with lots of money. Today we're going to hear a story Jesus told about a man who had plenty of money. We'll find out what happened to this man and his money.** Before telling the story, distribute prepared copies of the story to volunteers. Ask volunteers to stand in number order. As you tell the story, volunteers read highlighted sentences or thoughts at the appropriate times.

Special Agent Option

Purchase six minicandy tubes and remove the candy, or collect six film canisters. Print each word of the daily mission "be generous and thankful" on separate small strips of paper. Print the words "soccer" and "summer" on two additional strips of paper. Insert each strip of paper into a tube or canister. Place items into a box labeled "Top Secret." At the end of the story, volunteers remove tubes or canisters and remove the strips of paper. Volunteers assemble strips in order to discover the daily mission, discarding the two extra words.

Tell the Story

One day, as Jesus was speaking to His disciples on a hillside, people began to gather around them. Before long there were thousands of people pushing and crowding together, almost trampling each other. They were all trying to see Jesus.

One young man pushed his way through the crowd to Jesus. When he finally reached Jesus, he blurted out his problem. "Teacher, my father died recently and left all his money and possessions to my brother and me. My brother hasn't paid me my fair share. Tell him to pay me my part of the inheritance!"

Jesus turned toward the man. "Why are you asking Me to solve your problem?" Jesus cared about the young man's problem, but Jesus knew more about this man than the man knew about himself. Jesus knew this man had a problem that was a much bigger problem than getting his share of the inheritance!

Jesus knew that the man was paying too much attention to how much money he had. This man loved money so much that all he could think of was how to get his hands on his father's wealth!

So this is what Jesus told the man, and all the people listening. "Watch out! Don't be greedy! There's more to life than getting lots of money and possessions!" Jesus wanted the people to know that money and possessions are not the most important things in life. To help people understand what He had said, Jesus told this story:

There was a farmer whose fields produced very well one year. He had many more baskets of grain than he usually had at harvesttime. In fact, he had SO MUCH grain that his barns could hold no more!

Now the farmer might have done something with his extra grain. He could have left some of the grain in the fields so that there would be something for the poor people to harvest. He could have given his extra grain away. He could even have started a bakery with all that grain so that other people could buy bread.

LESSON NINE

But the farmer didn't think for a minute about any of those things. No, he thought about himself. "I'm going to build new and BIGGER barns," the farmer said. "Then I'll have lots of space for all my grain!"

The farmer was so excited by his great crop that he thought of nothing else. He laid down in bed at night and dreamed about how much wealth this crop meant. He dreamed of his riches and was certain he had all he needed for the rest of his life.

"I think I will just take life easy," said the farmer. "I'll eat, drink and just have FUN all the time. I won't worry about anyone or anything—after all, I have EVERYTHING I need and PLENTY of wealth stored up to last me the rest of my life."

But this rich farmer was in for a big surprise. God knew the farmer's life would end soon. God said to him, "You FOOL! Tonight you will die. Then who will get those things you have stored away for yourself?"

God's Word & Me

The rich farmer had thought only about HIS plans, HIS money, HIS future. He thought all he needed was plenty of money. He didn't take time to thank God for the good crop God had given him. He didn't think about how he could help someone else with all his riches.

Listen to what Jesus said about the good things we have. Read Matthew 10:8. **Jesus said these words to His disciples. Jesus wanted His disciples and us to know that it's because of God's love for us that we have the things we need. And we can show God's love to others by generously giving and sharing our money and possessions. When we're generous, it doesn't mean that we have to give away everything that we have. Being generous means that we care about the needs of others and help them as much as we can.**

>> **What are some of the things kids your age might have?** (Games. Books. Money. Clothes. Toys.)

>> **How might a kid your age act like the rich farmer?** (Spend lots of time thinking about how they can get more money or things. Think that having lots of things is more important than loving or obeying God. Act in greedy ways—try to get the most of everything.)

>> **How might a kid show he or she is thankful for money or things?** (Remember to thank God for His love and things He provides. Be ready to share with others.)

>> **What are some ways kids can use what they have to care about the needs of others?** (Take turns using things with friends. Talk to parent or teacher about ways to help needy kids.) Pray with children, thanking God for His love and the good things He helps us have. Ask His help in being generous with money and the things we have.

LESSON NINE

Game Center
for younger children
Luke 12:13-21

Collect

Bible, wooden or cardboard blocks.

Do

1. Help children form at least two lines. Place blocks near children. Play a relay where children take turns picking up blocks, running across the room and arranging blocks to build barns. Continue until each child has had a turn adding a block or until the barns fall down. Repeat as long as children are interested.

2. As time permits, children play with blocks, building blocks or other structures.

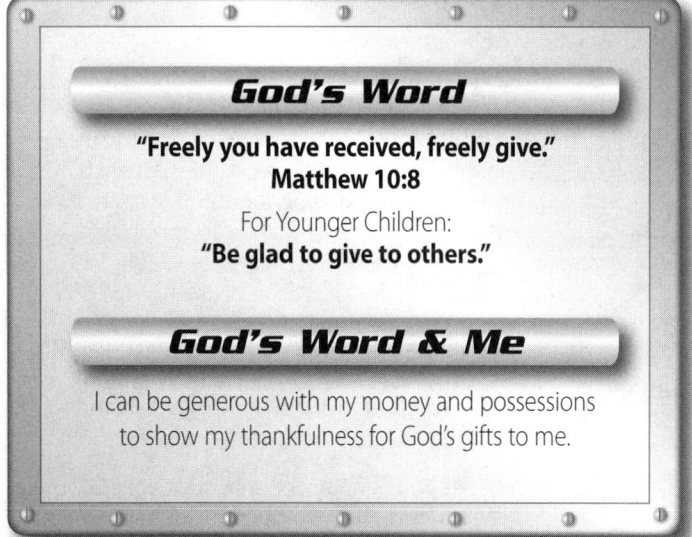

God's Word

"Freely you have received, freely give."
Matthew 10:8

For Younger Children:
"Be glad to give to others."

God's Word & Me

I can be generous with my money and possessions to show my thankfulness for God's gifts to me.

Talk About

>> **In today's Bible story, a rich man built some big barns. He built the barns to keep his grain. Grain is used to make bread. The rich man didn't thank God for all his grain. The rich man didn't share his grain with anyone!**

>> **Jesus said, "Be glad to give to others." Micah, who do you like giving gifts to? God has given us good things. We can share those good things with others.**

>> **Hailey, who is someone who shares with you? What does (Jaden) share with you? We're glad that God helps us have good things. We can thank God for the good things He gives us.** Invite children to thank God, or pray briefly, **Dear God, thank You for the good things You give us. Help us share with others. In Jesus' name, amen.**

For Older Children

Provide large Post-it Notes. Children write items God has given them on separate notes and attach one to each block before adding it to the barns. After the barns are built, let each child choose a block. Lead children in a prayer to thank God for the good things He has given them. Children read items on the notes as part of the prayer.

LESSON NINE

Game Center
for older children
Luke 12:13-21

Collect
Bible, paper, scissors.

Prepare
Cut rectangles out of paper to look like money. Cut four to six rectangles for each child, making an even amount for each child.

Do
1. Students stand in a large circle around the room. Stand in the middle of the circle and toss the "money" up in the air.
2. At your signal, children start collecting the money. After five to ten seconds, count down from 10 to 1, challenging children to be sure everyone has the same amount of money by the time you get to 1. Repeat activity as time and interest permit.

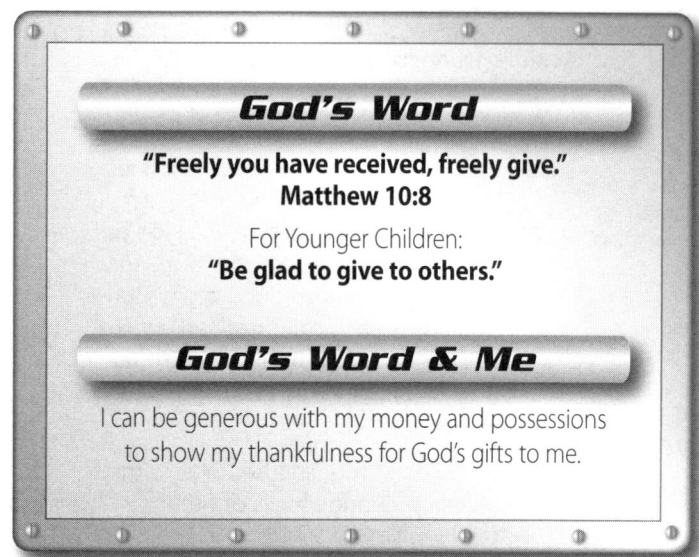

God's Word
"Freely you have received, freely give."
Matthew 10:8

For Younger Children:
"Be glad to give to others."

God's Word & Me
I can be generous with my money and possessions to show my thankfulness for God's gifts to me.

Talk About

>> **What was hard about this game? What was easy? How did it feel to give away some "money" so that everyone could have the same amount?** (It was hard to get money before someone else got it. It was hard to give away some of my money. It was easy to give away my money if someone really needed it.)

>> **What are some things kids your age find it easy to share with others? Hard to share?**

>> Read Matthew 10:8. **Why does this verse say God wants us to generously share with others?** (Because God has generously shared His love and help with us.) **What does it mean to be generous?** (Give more than is expected. Give a lot.)

>> **What are some times in which kids at your school can share generously with others? In your neighborhood?** Lead children in prayer, thanking God for the good things He helps them have and asking His help in sharing generously with others. In your prayer, refer to children's responses.

For Younger Children
Use four different colors of paper for the paper money. After children have gathered money, ask them to share money with each other so that each child has one paper of each color. Be ready to help children share as needed.

© 2007 Gospel Light. Permission to photocopy granted. *Agents in Action*

LESSON NINE

Art Center
for younger children
Luke 12:13-21

Collect

Bible, ribbon, scissors, one large sheet of paper for each child, markers, pre-cut magazine pictures of items children are likely to have (toys, bikes, sports items, favorite foods, pets, etc.), glue, gift bows.

Prepare

Cut ribbon in varying lengths. Draw a rectangle shape to represent a gift box on each sheet of paper.

Do

1. Children glue pre-cut magazine pictures inside the gift-box outline.
2. Children decorate gift boxes, attach bows at the top and glue ribbon pieces on the gift box.

God's Word

"Freely you have received, freely give."
Matthew 10:8

For Younger Children:
"Be glad to give to others."

God's Word & Me

I can be generous with my money and possessions to show my thankfulness for God's gifts to me.

Talk About

>> **Sam, what do you like to get at a birthday party? What birthday gift have you given a friend? We all like to get presents. We can be thankful for the good things God helps us have.**

>> **Jesus said, "Be glad to give to others." Hannah, who shares toys with you? Who shares food with you? What toys can you share? What food can you share? I'm glad that we have friends who share with us. I'm thankful for the good things God helps us have.**

>> **Braden, I see that you are sharing the pieces of ribbon. Thank you. God helps us have all the good things we have. We can share the good things we have. We can thank God for them, too.** Pray briefly, **Dear God, thank You for what You help us have. Help us be glad to share with others. In Jesus' name, amen.**

For Older Children

Children draw their own gift boxes and draw pictures of things they can give to others. Decorate as described above. (Optional: Instead of drawing gift boxes, children glue pre-cut magazine pictures onto several large wrapped gift boxes.)

© 2007 Gospel Light. Permission to photocopy granted. *Agents in Action*

LESSON NINE

Art Center
for older children
Luke 12:13-21

Collect
Bible, Lesson 9 Pattern Page (p. 168), card stock, scissors, tape, craft decorations (stickers, jewel stickers, glitter, etc.), markers.

Prepare
Make a copy of the Pattern Page on card stock for each child. Make a sample bank and insert several coins. Talk to your pastor or missions coordinator to determine a project for which children can collect money.

God's Word
"Freely you have received, freely give."
Matthew 10:8

For Younger Children:
"Be glad to give to others."

God's Word & Me
I can be generous with my money and possessions to show my thankfulness for God's gifts to me.

Do

1. Show sample bank. Give each child a Pattern Page. Demonstrate how to fold page to make a bank and tape edges securely. Help each child cut a slit in the bank.

2. Children color banks and decorate them with craft decorations you have provided. Children take home banks to collect money. Ask children to return banks to give as an offering at church. (Note: You may wish to send home a note to parents explaining how the money will be used and when the banks should be returned.)

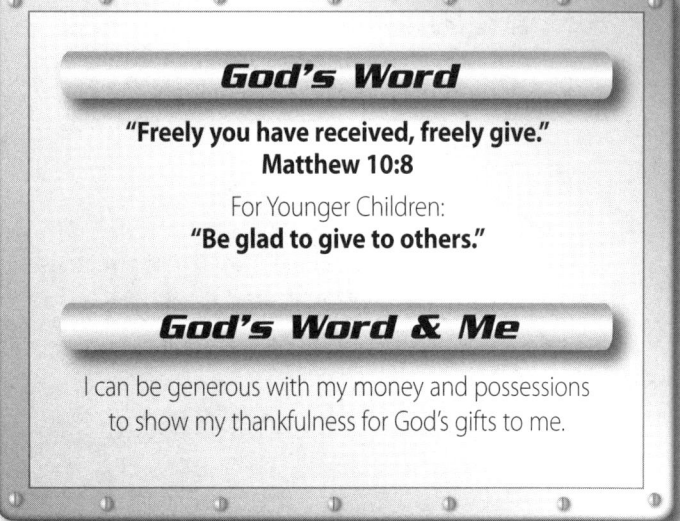

Talk About

>> **What are some of the ways our church uses money to help others?** (Give to mission projects. Sponsor a child in a third-world country. Give to a local homeless shelter.) **The money we collect in our banks will be given to others in need.** Explain the giving project you have selected.

>> Read Matthew 10:8. **Why does God want us to give?** (Because He has given us a lot and we should do the same.) **What do you think it means to "freely give"?** (To give or share without holding back or worrying about how much. To be glad to share with others.)

>> **What's something a friend or family member has freely given to you? What are some of the good things God has helped you have that you can freely give to someone else?** Pray, thanking God for His gifts to us, and asking His help in freely giving to others.

For Younger Children
Prefold banks for children and then unfold them. Children color banks before folding and assembling them. Be available to help as needed.

LESSON NINE

Worship Center
for younger and older children
Luke 12:13-21

Collect

Bibles, *Agent* Music CD and player, song charts (pp. 249, 253), yarn in a variety of colors, scissors, several coins.

Preparation

Cut yarn into a variety of lengths from 6 inches (15 cm) to 2 feet (1.2 m). Make at least one length for each child.

Team Game

Divide group into two or more teams of special agents. (Optional: Teams choose names.) **Your team's mission is to collect as many pieces of yarn as you can find and tie them together. We'll find out which team's yarn is the longest.** Toss prepared lengths of yarn among children or around the room. (Optional: Hide yarn ahead of time.) At your signal, children quickly pick up pieces of yarn and work together with team members to tie pieces together. Teams lay out yarn and compare lengths.

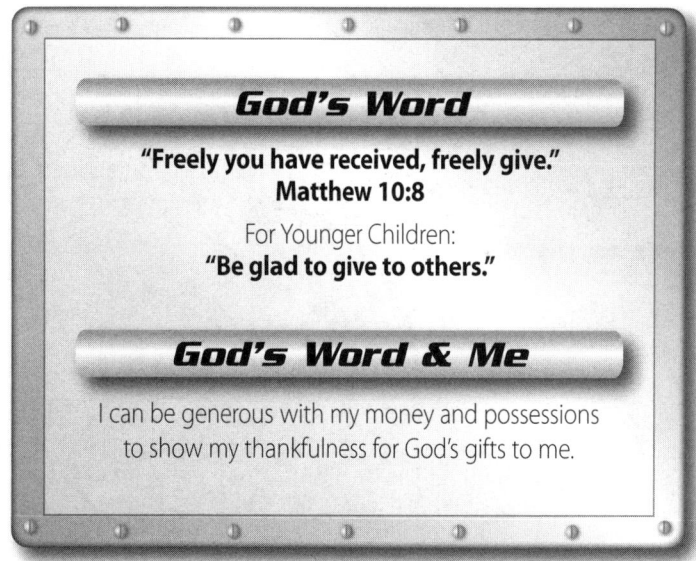

God's Word

"Freely you have received, freely give."
Matthew 10:8

For Younger Children:
"Be glad to give to others."

God's Word & Me

I can be generous with my money and possessions to show my thankfulness for God's gifts to me.

Bible Verse Game

Repeat Matthew 10:8 aloud with children. Give coins to several children. While you play "Mission of Love," children pass coins around the room. After 20 seconds or so, stop the music. Children holding coins stand up, say words of verse in unison and give the coins to others in the group. Repeat activity as time and interest permit.

Song

Lead children in singing "Gotta Give It Up!" Add motions and/or clapping if desired.

Prayer

Ask children to each silently think of something they are glad they have. At your signal, ask children to call out the items for which they are thankful. (You may need to repeat several times if children need encouragement to speak items aloud.) Then lead children in a closing prayer, thanking God for His love and asking His help in showing love to others by generously sharing and giving to them. (Optional: Ask children to list needs for shelter, food or medical care that people in your community may have. Encourage children to pray regularly for people with these needs and, as possible, provide opportunities for children to serve needy people through service projects.)

Song

Lead children in singing "That's What I'm Gonna Do." Add motions and/or clapping if desired.

© 2007 Gospel Light. Permission to photocopy granted. *Agents in Action*

LESSON NINE • Pattern Page

1. Cut along the solid lines.

2. Fold the paper inward along all the dotted lines, making creases. Make one fold and crease at a time, opening the paper back up before making the next fold and crease.

3. Bring the side flaps in to meet each other; then bring the notched flaps in and connect the notches to form a box. Tape edges securely.

168

© 2007 Gospel Light. Permission to photocopy granted. *Agents in Action*

LESSON NINE · Coloring Page

Jesus talks about a rich man who did not thank God.
Luke 12:13-21

What can you thank God for?

LESSON NINE • Puzzle Page

What do you want to thank God for today?
What can you do to be generous and care for someone else?

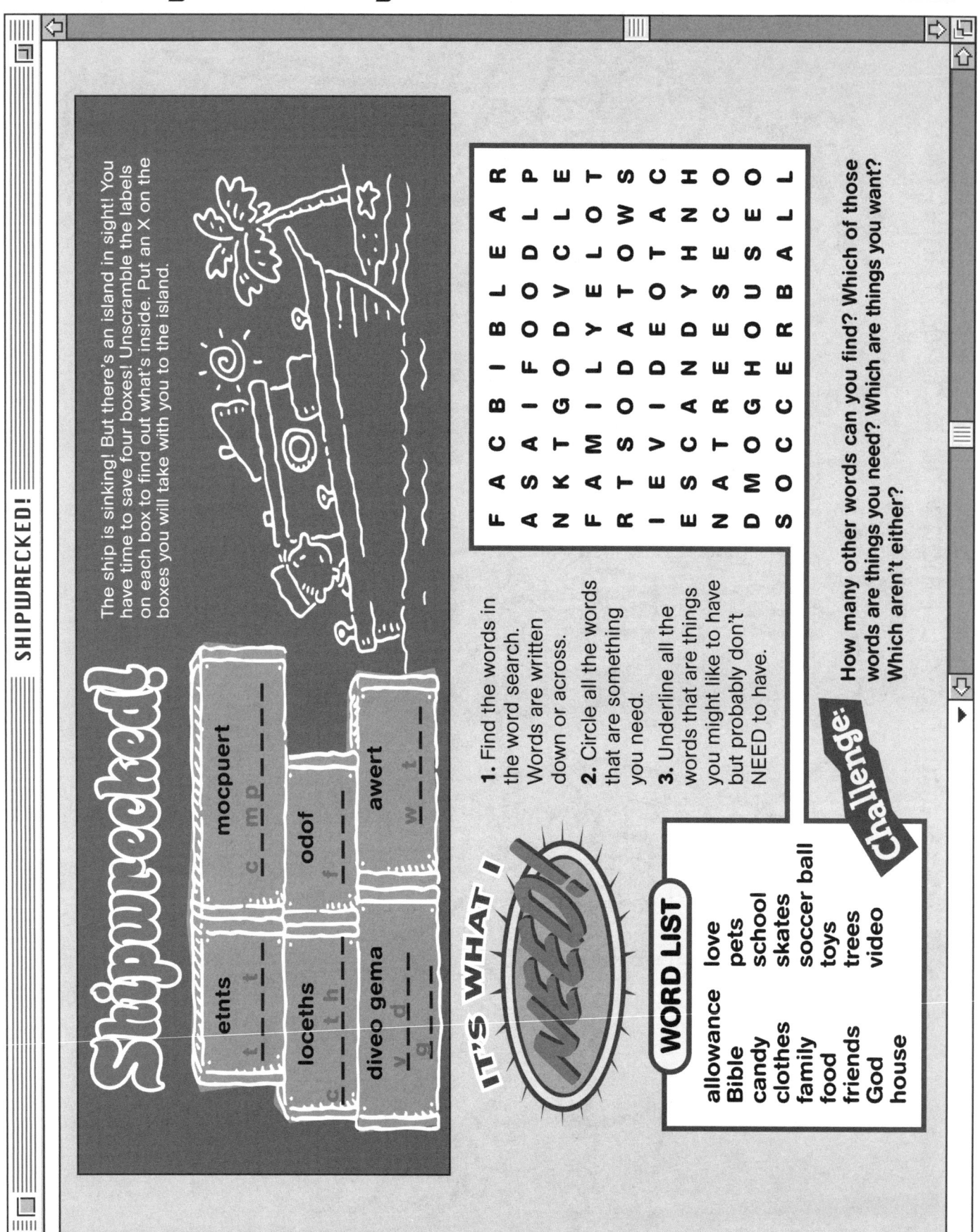

SHIPWRECKED!

Shipwrecked!

The ship is sinking! But there's an island in sight! You have time to save four boxes! Unscramble the labels on each box to find out what's inside. Put an X on the boxes you will take with you to the island.

- etnts → t _ _ t _
- mocpuert → c _ mp _ _ _ _
- loceths → c _ _ t h _ _
- odof → f _ _ _
- diveo gema → v _ d _ _   g _ _ _
- awert → w _ t _ _

IT'S WHAT I NEED!

1. Find the words in the word search. Words are written down or across.
2. Circle all the words that are something you need.
3. Underline all the words that are things you might like to have but probably don't NEED to have.

```
F A C B I B L E A R
A S A I F O O D L P
N K T G O D V C L E
F A M I L Y E L O T
R T S O D A T O W S
I E V I D E O T A C
E S C A N D Y H N H
N A T R E E S E C O
D M O G H O U S E O
S O C C E R B A L L
```

WORD LIST
- allowance
- Bible
- candy
- clothes
- family
- food
- friends
- God
- house
- love
- pets
- school
- skates
- soccer ball
- toys
- trees
- video

Challenge: How many other words can you find? Which of those words are things you need? Which are things you want? Which aren't either?

LESSON TEN

Friends

Bible Story:
Widows in Need
Acts 6:1-7

Teacher's Devotional

A real friend is someone who knows you—even your faults—and loves you anyway. A good friendship refreshes you and helps you enjoy even the small things in life. A hard or tedious task is made easier when done with a friend. But friendship is not something we do once and then we're done. It requires careful cultivation to grow better and better over time.

The kids you teach are ready to be friends, and they want to have good friends. These formative years are the perfect time for children to begin learning how to be true friends. Learning skills for treating others the way in which they want to be treated is a significant way for friendship building to occur.

The Bible tells about a time when God's family faced a crisis that brought up the issue of how to treat others. The Hebrew widows seemed to be getting more food than the Greek widows. Although their apparent need was for equal food, there was a deeper need for God's family to show equal love and respect—the foundation for true friendship. To be sure that no one fell through the cracks, the church chose ministers whose sole purpose would be to show love equally by meeting the physical needs of all, regardless of background or culture. In this way, the obvious need for food and the deeper and more important need for love and respect were both met.

In our lives, we can sometimes forget that in the midst of the "stuff" of teaching (the need for more helpers or equipment or space) it is God's friendship, His power and love that we need most! Just as the widows needed both outer and inner needs met, so also do we—and so do our children. Take time this week to think about each child you teach. Ask God for His power and love to help you teach that child about friendship in effective ways. The best way to teach it is, of course, to live it out. As you give each child respect and love, you show your class practical ways of making and keeping friends. Your genuine friendship to each child will speak volumes to them about how to treat others, and how to know God's love and friendship!

God's Word

"So in everything, do to others what you would have them do to you." Matthew 7:12

For Younger Children:
"Treat others the same way you want to be treated."

God's Word & Me

Obeying God's command to treat others like I want to be treated will help me make and keep friends.

LESSON TEN

Planning Page

Choose which centers you will provide and the order in which children will participate in them (see pp. 14-18 for schedule tips and pp. 24-25 for guidelines in combining older and younger children). Also plan who will lead each center (for staffing tips see pp. 19-21). Use the reproducible planning sheet (p. 238) to record your plans.

Bible Story Center

Bible Story
Widows in Need • Acts 6:1-7

Younger Child Option
Cut out magazine pictures of food or toy food to show story action

Older Child Option
Solve a pinprick code to discover the daily mission "make and keep friends"

Game Center

Younger Child Option
Hide and then find toy people, and talk about ways of treating friends in good ways as a way of obeying Matthew 7:12

Materials
Bible, a toy person for each child, large container, filling material

Older Child Option
Play a basketball game like HORSE to collect the letters of the word "friend," and discuss what it means to obey Jesus' words in Matthew 7:12

Materials
Bible, Lesson 10 Pattern Page (p. 182), scissors, toy basketball hoop or container, ball

Art Center

Younger Child Option
Make Pretzel Pals to eat and to give away, naming friends and talking about how Jesus said to treat friends

Materials
Bible, paper plates, minimarshmallows, stick pretzels, disposable wipes, resealable plastic bags, stickers, paper cut to fit inside bags, markers

Older Child Option
Work with friends to build structures, and identify results of obeying Jesus' words to treat others the way we want to be treated

Materials
Bible, one or more kinds of building materials

Worship Center

For the Younger and Older Child
Participate in large-group activities to review Bible verse and to worship God together

Materials
Bibles, *Agent* Music CD and player, song charts (pp. 246, 253), large balloons, permanent marker

Coloring/Puzzle Center

Younger Child Option
Review the Bible story while completing coloring page

Materials
Lesson 10 Coloring Page (p. 183) for each student, crayons

Older Child Option
Review ways of treating friends while completing puzzle page

Materials
Lesson 10 Puzzle Page (p. 184) for each student, pencils

Lesson Ten

Bonus Theme Ideas

Bonus Theme Ideas can be used at any time during this session: as an additional activity center, to extend the session for a longer time or for added theme excitement.

Mystery Friend

Give each child a large index card. Ask each child to number his or her card from one to four and answer each of these questions (be available to write answers for children who need help): What is your favorite food? What is your favorite game? How old are you? What letter does your first name start with? Collect cards. Choose one card and read questions and answers aloud, encouraging volunteers to guess the identity of the Mystery Friend. Repeat as time and interest allow. (Optional: Repeat guessing activity each of the remaining weeks of *Agents in Action*.)

Special Agent Information

Mission Possible: Families

Send invitations to families (see p. 233 for a sample that can be modified) to join together for a fun party of movie watching and snacks. Show a family film that relates to the theme of *Agents in Action* (courageous kids, detective or special-agent kids, etc.). Ask families to bring blankets or beach chairs on which to sit and a favorite snack to share with others. Provide beverages. (Optional: Give each child a party favor bag to take home. Fill bags with inexpensive stickers, gum, bite-size candy, etc.)

Special Agent Information

Cookie Crumb Roll-Ups

Prepare dough ahead of time following the recipe below. Each child washes hands, rolls small portions of dough into several small balls and then rolls balls in powdered sugar before eating.

Recipe: Crush 1 box (10 oz) of shortbread cookies. Mix cookie crumbs, 1 cup shredded coconut and 2/3 cup sifted powdered sugar in a large bowl. Add 1/2 cup thawed, frozen orange or lemonade concentrate. Mix thoroughly.

Special Agent Information

Post a note alerting parents to the use of food. Also, check registration forms for possible food allergies.

© 2007 Gospel Light. Permission to photocopy granted. *Agents in Action*

LESSON TEN

Bible Story Center
for younger children
Acts 6:1-7

Collect

Bible.

Introduction

Pretend to throw a ball if you can think of something you like to do with your friends. Volunteers respond. **Now cross your arms and make a mad face if you can think of something friends sometimes argue about. Most of the time we have fun with our friends. But sometimes friends don't want to take turns, or they don't want to share. Listen to our Bible story to hear about some friends who could have had a big argument.**

Special Agent Option

In a box labeled "Top Secret," place at least a dozen pre-cut magazine pictures of food or toy food. During the story, remove items from box and use them to show story action. (For example, when talking about the women who did not have enough food, move all the food pictures or toy food to one side. Then later in the story, count out the food pictures or toy food evenly into sets of two or three to show that the women were being treated fairly.)

Tell the Story

Every day more and more people heard the good news that Jesus loved them. More and more people learned to love Jesus. And every day these people were sharing their food and clothing with people who had none. These friends were very happy.

However, one group of women whose husbands had died was not happy. These women said, "No one is sharing food with us. We are not getting enough to eat!" This was a problem!

When the people who were friends of the women heard about this problem, they felt sad. They could have gotten angry. They could have grumbled and argued and caused lots of trouble, but they didn't. They wanted everyone to have enough food to eat. They wanted to be kind to all their friends.

The friends called everyone together. "We know it isn't fair that some people don't get enough food to eat." The people listened quietly.

"This is what we will do," the friends said. "Choose seven special helpers. These special helpers will make sure everyone gets enough food." So the people chose one, two, three, four, five, six, seven men to be special helpers. Then the friends prayed and asked God to help the seven men do their best work.

These special helpers did a good job. Now the women had enough food eat, just like everyone else. Everyone worked together to treat their friends in the same kind and loving way they would want to be treated.

God's Word & Me

The women in this story must have been glad for their friends. They were glad that their friends wanted to help them and show God's love to them.

In the Bible, Jesus said, "Treat others the same way you want to be treated." That's just what the friends in our story did! We can obey these words of Jesus, too. We can treat others in helpful and loving ways just like we want to be treated. We know how good it feels when a friend helps us and shows God's love to us. Pray, **Dear God, thank You for our friends. Please help us be kind and loving to our friends. In Jesus' name, amen.**

LESSON TEN

Bible Story Center
for older children
Acts 6:1-7

Collect

Bible.

Introduction

Why do kids your age like having friends? What's your favorite thing to do with a friend? Volunteers respond. **We all like to have friends—but sometimes things happen that cause problems with friends. In our Bible story today, we're going to hear about some people who had a lot of friends and they had to figure out a way to KEEP their friends.** Before you tell the Bible story, invite volunteers to take the part of several people in God's family, Jesus' disciples, two groups of widows and the helpers (seven volunteers if possible). Ask these volunteers to stand in front of the group. As you tell the story, volunteers show facial expressions and pantomime actions to illustrate story action.

Special Agent Option

Before class, collect several pages of comic strips. On each page, use a straight pin to poke holes in titles or large letters that spell out the daily mission "make and keep friends." (To simplify for younger children, cut off unused comic strips.) Place pages, blank paper and markers in a box labeled "Top Secret." At the end of the story, volunteers remove pages and hold them up to the light to see the pinpricks and identify the letters. Volunteers write letters on blank paper and unscramble as needed to read the daily mission.

Tell the Story

In the days after Jesus went back to heaven, God's family was growing! Many people heard the good news about Jesus. People believed that Jesus is the Son of God and asked God to forgive their sins. Thousands of people became part of God's family.

But the best thing about the growing family of God was that they loved each other. Their love was so obvious that even people who didn't know them were watching them to see how they loved each other. They cared about each other so much that they didn't want anyone to be hungry or cold or not have the things they needed. All the people in God's church shared the things they owned. Out of the money they had, Jesus' disciples bought food and things people needed. Jesus had said that everyone would know members of His family by the way they showed love. That's just what they were doing!

Even in that big, loving group of friends, there were some widows who had a need. (A widow is a woman whose husband has died. In Bible times, women did not go out and get jobs. So that meant widows often had no way to earn enough money to live on.) People in the church were sharing what they had with others, but these needy widows weren't getting as much food as some of the other widows.

Now, these widows COULD have gotten angry and quit meeting with others in their church family. They COULD have decided that they would not talk to the other people. But INSTEAD, they told Jesus' disciples about their need.

"We're not getting as much food as the other widows," they said. "We're not being treated fairly."

Jesus' disciples didn't want ANYONE to be without enough food. They did NOT want these widows to think the other people in God's family didn't care about them! So Jesus' disciples called a meeting with God's people to solve the problem.

© 2007 Gospel Light. Permission to photocopy granted. *Agents in Action*

They said, "We need someone to make sure no one goes hungry. We want to be sure everyone in God's family is shown love in the same way. Let's choose some people who can make sure everyone gets enough food."

Everyone listened carefully to what the disciples said. They thought about what they said and agreed that having more people to help with the sharing of food was a good way to take care of this need. They chose seven men and prayed for them, asking God to help them do this important job.

After that, we never hear again about ANYONE in the first church family who was needy! God's family talked about the need. They listened to each other and then obeyed God so that they took care of the need in a way that everyone felt loved and cared for. That's one way they showed they loved Jesus!

God's Word & Me

These friends could have let this little problem become a BIG problem. And if they did let this problem continue, they might have even stopped being friends. But they chose a different way to act. Read Matthew 7:12. **Jesus thought this command about how to treat others was so important that He told them to a HUGE crowd of people. Sometimes this command is called the Golden Rule to show how important it is.**

These words are also important for us to pay attention to. We all want to have good friends and one of the best ways to make and keep friends is to treat them the way we want to be treated. We want our friends to help and care for us—so that's what Jesus told us to do, too.

>> **When do kids your age have a hard time getting along with friends?** (When kids are selfish or mean. When kids make fun or tease.)

>> **Why might it be hard for kids to make friends?** (They are shy. They move to a new class or join a new team. Other kids don't talk to them or are mean. They have been mean to others.) **What is an example of a time a new kid could make a friend by helping someone?** (Help do a task at school. Offer to share a snack or dessert.)

>> **How do kids feel when another kid helps them or does something kind? What difference would it make at your school or on your (baseball) team if kids treated others in the same helpful and kind ways they want to be treated? Who is someone you know who doesn't have many friends?** Pray with children, thanking God for friends and asking His help in obeying Jesus' command. Encourage each child to ask God to help him or her think of ways to be a friend to someone who is lonely.

LESSON TEN

Game Center
for younger children
Acts 6:1-7

Collect

Bible, a toy person for each child, large container (box, plastic tub, etc.), filling material (sand, rice, beans, confetti, crumpled tissue paper, etc.); optional—index cards, scissors, marker.

Prepare

Put filling in container. (Optional: If toy person for each child is not available, cut cards into small strips and letter each child's name on a separate strip.)

Do

1. Children line up on one side of open area in classroom. Place filled container on other side of the open area. Give each child a toy person. (Optional: Give each child a prepared strip.)

2. At your signal, each child takes a turn to run across the room, bury a toy person (or strip) in the container and run back to the group. Then repeat the relay, with each child taking a turn to find one of the hidden "friends." Repeat as time allows.

God's Word

"So in everything, do to others what you would have them do to you." Matthew 7:12

For Younger Children:
"Treat others the same way you want to be treated."

God's Word & Me

Obeying God's command to treat others like I want to be treated will help me make and keep friends.

Talk About

>> Tanya, tell us the name of one of your friends. What is something you like to do with your friend? You can treat your friend (Cade) in good ways when you take turns.

>> Jesus said, "Treat others the same way you want to be treated." Nikki, what is something a friend can help you with? When you and a friend help each other (pick up toys), you are treating each other in good ways.

>> Gabriel, what do you like to do with your friends? How can you be kind to your friends when you are playing with (dinosaur toys)? Let's thank God for our friends. Renee, what friend do you want to thank God for? Help each child complete the following prayer. **Dear God, thank You for** (child says a friend's name). **In Jesus' name, amen.**

For Older Children

Before class, write the letters of the word "friend" on separate pieces of paper, making a set of letters for each pair of children. Mix up the letters and bury them in the container. In class, children form pairs. After completing the relay to find all the buried letters, children work in pairs to spell the word "friend," trading with other pairs to collect the letters they need.

© 2007 Gospel Light. Permission to photocopy granted. *Agents in Action*

LESSON TEN

Game Center
for older children
Acts 6:1-7

Collect

Bible, Lesson 10 Pattern Page (p. 182), scissor, toy basketball hoop or container (bucket, trash can, etc.), ball.

Prepare

Make a copy of the Pattern Page for each team of six players. Cut apart the picture cards. (Note: Set up a hoop or container for every two teams.)

Do

1. Set out the basketball hoop or container. Children form teams of no more than six players. Teams line up about 6 feet (1.8 m) away from the hoop or container. (Adjust distance according to age level and ability.) Place each team's set of picture cards in a stack by the hoop or container.

2. Players on each team take turns trying to toss the ball into the hoop or container, with the next player on the team rebounding the ball before taking his or her turn. If player makes the basket, he or she collects a card. Continue until one team has collected all six cards to spell the word "friend." Player from winning team shows one of the cards. Volunteers tell ways to treat the person in good ways.

God's Word

"So in everything, do to others what you would have them do to you." Matthew 7:12

For Younger Children:
"Treat others the same way you want to be treated."

God's Word & Me

Obeying God's command to treat others like I want to be treated will help me make and keep friends.

Talk About

>> **What are some times kids your age are glad they have friends? What might happen to cause a kid your age to be angry at a friend?** (Friend is bossy. Gets you in trouble at school. Makes fun of you.)

>> **What are some of the ways we expect good friends to treat us?** (Stand up for you. Want to play with you. Let you choose what to play.) **When is a time you can treat a friend in one of these good ways?**

>> Read Matthew 7:12. **What do you think would happen if kids obeyed these words of Jesus?** (Kids would have more friends and more fun. There would be fewer arguments.)

>> **We're glad for our friends, but sometimes it can be hard to make and keep friends. Let's ask God to help us to always treat others the way we want to be treated.** Invite volunteers to pray or lead children in prayer, thanking God for friends and asking His help in treating friends in good ways.

For Younger Children

Make a copy of the Pattern Page for each child. Children stand close enough to hoop or basket so that they can succeed at making baskets. Before each turn, child names a friend he or she can treat in good ways. After making a basket, child collects a card, trying to collect all six cards.

LESSON TEN

Art Center
for younger children
Acts 6:1-7

Collect

Bible, paper plates, minimarshmallows, stick pretzels, disposable wipes, resealable plastic bags, stickers, paper cut to fit inside bags, markers.

Prepare

Place marshmallows and pretzels on separate paper plates.

Do

1. Each child washes or cleans hands and then makes a Pretzel Pal by pushing a marshmallow on one end of a pretzel stick. Allow time for each child to make 10 to 12 pretzel pals.

2. Give each child two bags. Help children divide pretzel pals evenly and place into bags. Children decorate the bags with stickers.

3. Ask each child to tell name of friend to whom he or she plans to give a bag of pretzel pals. Write name on prepared paper. Child decorates paper and places it into bag. Children take home bags, giving one bag to a friend and keeping a bag.

God's Word

"So in everything, do to others what you would have them do to you." Matthew 7:12

For Younger Children:
"Treat others the same way you want to be treated."

God's Word & Me

Obeying God's command to treat others like I want to be treated will help me make and keep friends.

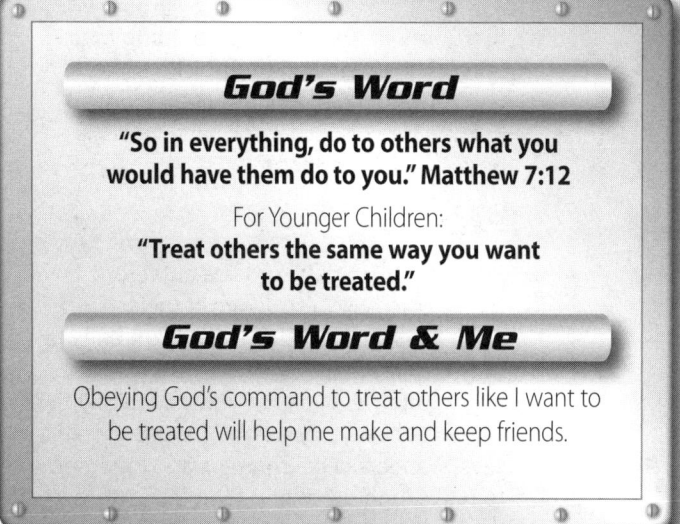

Talk About

>> We're making pretzel pals today. I heard Micah say "thank-you" when Terah handed him the plate of pretzels. Saying thank-you is a good way to treat our friends.

>> Jesus said, "Treat others the same way you want to be treated." Taking turns is a good way to treat a friend. Aidan, what is something you and a friend take turns playing with?

>> Colin, what is the name of one of your friends? What do you like to play with (Damon)? When you and (Damon) take turns (going down the slide), you are treating each other in good ways. I'm glad that you and Damon are good friends. Pray briefly, **Dear God, thank You for our friends. Help us treat our friends the way we want to be treated. In Jesus' name, amen.**

For Older Children

Children make pretzel pals with arms and legs by breaking pretzel sticks and using minimarshmallows in creative ways to secure the pieces. Children complete this sentence on papers they place in bags to give away: "To (name of child), thank you for being a good friend by (describe action)."

LESSON TEN

Art Center
для older children
Acts 6:1-7

Collect

Bible, one or more kinds of building materials (play dough and toothpicks; toilet-paper tubes, hole punches and string; Legos; straws, scissors and tape; newspapers and masking tape).

Do

Students form pairs or trios and work together to build a structure of their choice (insert toothpicks into play-dough balls; punch holes in tubes, insert string and tie tubes together in creative ways; build with Legos; cut and tape straws together; roll several sheets of newspaper, tape together to make long tubes and then tape tubes together). When everyone is finished, take some time to admire all the different creations.

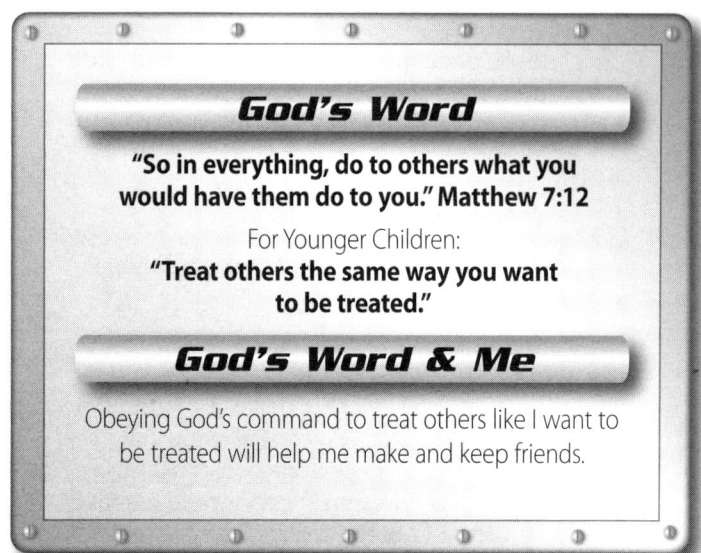

God's Word

"So in everything, do to others what you would have them do to you." Matthew 7:12

For Younger Children:
"Treat others the same way you want to be treated."

God's Word & Me

Obeying God's command to treat others like I want to be treated will help me make and keep friends.

Talk About

>> **How did you and your friends help each other build together today?** (We talked about ideas of what and how to build. We helped each other roll up the tubes of newspaper.)

>> **How would you describe someone who is a really great friend? How would a really great friend treat others?** (Listen to what people say. Invite them to play. Share things with them.)

>> Read Matthew 7:12. **How would you say this verse in your own words? Why do you think this verse is sometimes called the Golden Rule? When is a time you can obey these words of Jesus?**

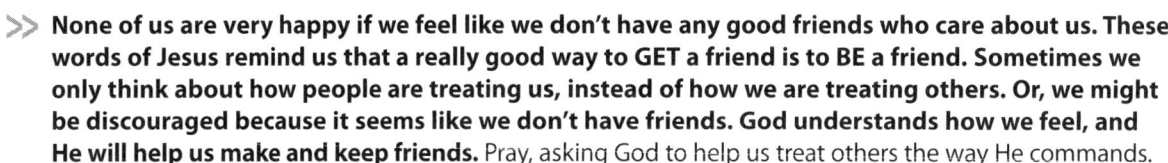

>> **None of us are very happy if we feel like we don't have any good friends who care about us. These words of Jesus remind us that a really good way to GET a friend is to BE a friend. Sometimes we only think about how people are treating us, instead of how we are treating others. Or, we might be discouraged because it seems like we don't have friends. God understands how we feel, and He will help us make and keep friends.** Pray, asking God to help us treat others the way He commands.

For Younger Children

Children will enjoy playing with the building materials you have provided. As they play, look for opportunities to talk about examples of children showing friendship (taking turns using the hole punch, picking up something that has fallen on the floor, sharing something, etc.).

LESSON TEN

Worship Center
for younger and older children
Acts 6:1-7

Collect

Bibles, *Agent* Music CD and player, song charts (pp. 246, 253), large balloons, permanent marker.

Preparation

Blow up at least four balloons. Use marker to print each of these words on each balloon: game, TV show, place, pizza.

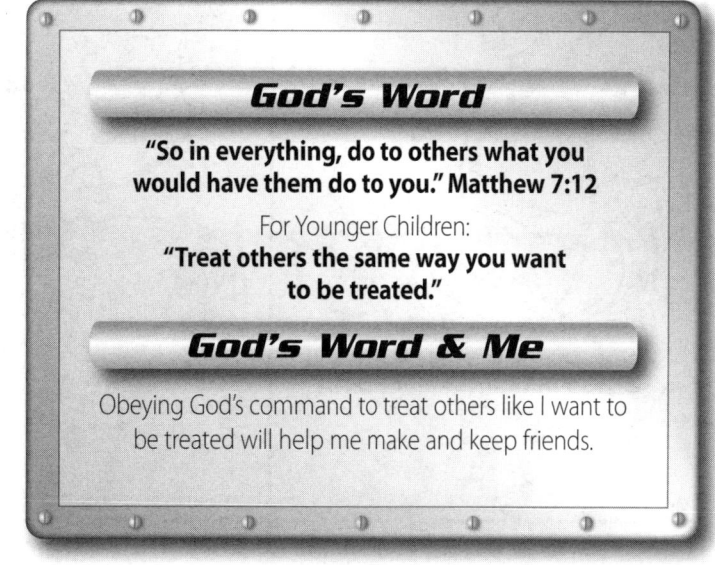

God's Word

"So in everything, do to others what you would have them do to you." Matthew 7:12

For Younger Children:
"Treat others the same way you want to be treated."

God's Word & Me

Obeying God's command to treat others like I want to be treated will help me make and keep friends.

Team Game

Let's play a game to find out what favorites we have in common. Play "Gotta Give It Up!" while children tap balloons around the room. After 20 seconds, stop the music. Whoever catches each balloon, freezes in place and looks to see which word is closest to his or her right thumb. Each child holding a balloon tells what his or her favorite (pizza) is. As each answer is given, ask anyone who agrees to cheer.

Bible Verse Game

Repeat Matthew 7:12 aloud with children. Ask an adult helper to stand facing you. As you both slowly repeat the words of the verse in unison, make motions with your hands, arms, feet and/or legs. Adult helper mirrors your actions. Then invite children to form pairs (assist as needed) and stand facing each other. Each pair decides who will make the motions and who will mirror the motions. Lead all children in repeating verse while doing the motions. Repeat, with children changing roles. Continue with new pairs as time permits. (Optional: Leader faces group. Children mirror actions of leader.)

Song

Lead children in singing "That's What I'm Gonna Do." Add motions and/or clapping if desired.

Prayer

Let's see if we can list a friend's name for every letter of the alphabet. Call out "A". One child or more children call out a friend's name that begins with the letter A. Continue through the alphabet. (Optional: For younger children, write letters and names on large sheet of paper.) Lead children in prayer, thanking God for friends and asking His help in making and keeping friends.

Song

Lead children in singing "God's Kids." Add motions and/or clapping if desired.

© 2007 Gospel Light. Permission to photocopy granted. *Agents in Action*

LESSON TEN • Pattern Page

182

LESSON TEN · Coloring Page

Hungry widows are given food.
Acts 6:1-7

What can you share with a friend?

LESSON TEN · Puzzle Page

RUNAWAY VOWELS

Help! The vowels are running away! Fill in the missing vowels to find actions that sometimes cause arguments!

1. br_g
2. l_ _
3. _gn_r_
4. ch__t
5. l_ _gh _t
6. _nk_nd w_rds

Make Your Own Cartoon!

Draw a cartoon about two friends who get in an argument. What did these two friends argue about? How else could they have ended their argument to obey Matthew 7:12?

| Where are the friends? | What do they argue about? | What happens next? | How does it end? |

184

© 2007 Gospel Light. Permission to photocopy granted. *Agents in Action*

LESSON ELEVEN

Evangelism

Bible Story:
Lydia Hears Good News
Acts 16:6-15

Teacher's Devotional

Our world has rapidly shrunk in recent years. People now travel from country to country the way they used to go from one state to another. Yet, we don't even have to go anywhere to encounter other cultures: Through the Internet, we can contact anyone in the world without delay! The classrooms, the neighborhoods and the sports teams in which children live often include friends from a variety of cultures. In such a world, how can we help children develop a respect for other cultures and yet still tell the uncompromised truth about Jesus?

Paul's life gives us an excellent example. Paul had a clear mission from God: to focus on telling non-Jews about Jesus, although he himself was a Jew. Paul also gave us a clear model for how to approach people who have no understanding of the gospel. Rather than criticize them for wrong beliefs, Paul understood Greek and Roman culture and used their interests and beliefs to prepare them to hear about Jesus. Because Paul understood what they worshiped, read what they read and listened to their philosophies, he was able to use what they understood and valued to help make the story of Jesus clear to them.

We would do well to imitate Paul! As we learn about the cultures of the world and even the cultures (music, movies, books, religions and philosophies) of the people in our own hometowns, we gain a greater understanding of the values and interests of others. This knowledge helps us prepare as we ask God to show us how to help nonbelievers understand what Jesus did for them. Use the discussion in this lesson to help children recognize opportunities they may have to express or demonstrate Christian truth in ways that will open doors to becoming witnesses for Jesus. Our actions and words will demonstrate how to become all things to all people, so that by all possible means we might help some come to know Jesus (see 1 Corinthians 9:22)! Ask God to help you give children the motivation to be witnesses for Him.

God's Word

"Let your light shine before men, that they may see your good deeds and praise your Father in heaven." Matthew 5:16

For Younger Children:
"Your good actions help others learn about God."

God's Word & Me

My actions and words can be a witness for Jesus, helping others see and understand what it means to be a Christian.

LESSON ELEVEN

Planning Page

Choose which centers you will provide and the order in which children will participate in them (see pp. 14-18 for schedule tips and pp. 24-25 for guidelines in combining older and younger children). Also plan who will lead each center (for staffing tips see pp. 19-21). Use the reproducible planning sheet (p. 238) to record your plans.

Bible Story Center

Bible Story
Lydia Hears Good News • Acts 16:6-15

Younger Child Option
Touch and feel fabric pieces that represent story action

Older Child Option
Follow a pattern to solve a code and discover the daily mission "be a witness about Jesus"

Game Center

Younger Child Option
Play a game to tell the names of friends who Jesus loves

Materials
Bible, *Agent* Music CD and player, index cards, marker

Older Child Option
Play a flashlight game and talk about what the words "let our light shine" mean and ways of witnessing for Jesus

Materials
Bible, flashlight

Art Center

Younger Child Option
Color in the letters of Jesus' name with a variety of colors and patterns, and talk about the good news of Jesus' love

Materials
Bible, Lesson 11 Pattern Page (p. 196), markers

Older Child Option
Make bead candles as reminders of what it means to obey Matthew 5:16

Materials
Bible, chenille wires (one for each child), yellow plastic tapered beads (one for each child), large interlocking plastic beads in at least two colors (ten for each child)

Worship Center

For the Younger and Older Child
Participate in large-group activities to review Bible verse and to worship God together

Materials
Bibles, *Agent* Music CD and player, song charts (pp. 248, 250), at least two rolls of crepe paper

Coloring/Puzzle Center

Younger Child Option
Review the Bible story while completing coloring page

Materials
Lesson 11 Coloring Page (p. 197) for each student, crayons

Older Child Option
Review ways of witnessing about Jesus while completing puzzle page

Materials
Lesson 11 Puzzle Page (p. 198) for each student, pencils

LESSON ELEVEN

Bonus Theme Ideas

Bonus Theme Ideas can be used at any time during this session: as an additional activity center, to extend the session for a longer time or for added theme excitement.

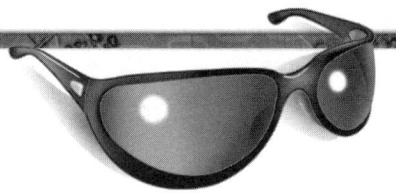

Mission of Love

Contact your church staff to find out projects children can help raise money to support. Explain to children how the money students raise will benefit others. Give each child a clean baby food jar or other small container. Children decorate jars or containers by writing or drawing with permanent markers, adding stickers, etc. Children fold construction-paper squares in half to make stand-up cards and print "Coins for Change" on the front of their cards. Children take home jars or containers and stand-up cards. Send a letter to parents explaining the project. You may also place one or more jars in a well-traveled place at your church. Be sure to report the results to the congregation!

Special Agent Information

Top-Secret Talk

Announce to children that today they will have a top-secret method of saying certain words. For example, tell children to tap one time on someone's back for "no," two taps for "yes" and three taps for "let's go." Children may also enjoy using their fingers to trace letters of words on the backs of friends. (Optional: Assign each group of children a different way of talking: say "log" in front of every vowel, say "so" in front of every word, etc.) Throughout the session, use the top-secret talk yourself and encourage children to do the same.

Special Agent Information

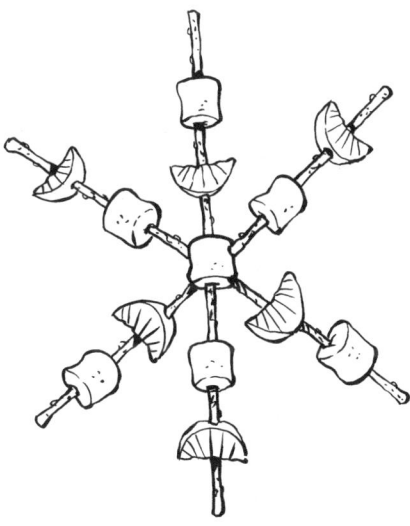

Build-a-Snack

Collect the following ingredients and set them out on separate plates: large marshmallows, a variety of fruits cut into small pieces, minimarshmallows, and coffee-stirring sticks. Children build snacks by skewering marshmallows, minimarshmallows and pieces of fruit onto one or more sticks (see sketch). (Optional: Provide purple napkins and explain that in today's Bible story, children will hear about a woman who made expensive purple cloth.)

Special Agent Information

> Post a note alerting parents to the use of food. Also, check registration forms for possible food allergies.

© 2007 Gospel Light. Permission to photocopy granted. *Agents in Action*

LESSON ELEVEN

Bible Story Center
for younger children
Acts 16:6-15

Collect

Bible.

Introduction

Make a pillow with your hands and pretend to rest your head on it if you can tell about a dream you've had. Volunteers answer. **Listen to hear what Paul, a man in the Bible, dreamed about.**

Tell the Story

Paul was a man who loved God very much. Paul wanted everyone to know about Jesus, God's Son. Up and down the dusty roads Paul would walk. He would stop in towns and tell the good news: "God loves you, and Jesus is His Son."

Special Agent Option

In a box labeled "Top Secret," place small pieces of three kinds of fabric: flannel to represent the time when Paul was asleep, blue to represent water and purple to represent the cloth Lydia sold. Cut enough pieces so that each child has one piece of each fabric. At the appropriate times in the story, remove fabric pieces from box and give to children.

One night, Paul had a dream. In the dream, a man asked him to please come to his country. After Paul woke up, he and his friends got into a boat. They sailed to a big town in that country.

The big town was called Philippi. It was near the ocean. Many people came there to buy and sell things. One thing people bought and sold in Philippi was cloth dyed a beautiful purple color.

Paul and his friends walked alongside a river. They found a group of women. The women had come together to pray. These women loved God. They wanted to hear all about Jesus and His love. Paul told them that Jesus is God's Son. Paul's words were good news!

Many women believed Paul's words. One woman named Lydia believed the good news about Jesus. Lydia sold purple cloth. She probably sold the cloth to rich people. She may have even had a big house. Lydia was baptized. So was everyone in her house! They all showed they believed that Jesus was God's Son.

Now Lydia was part of God's family, so she wanted to share! Lydia asked Paul and his friends to stay at her house. She wanted to help them. Paul and his friends stayed at Lydia's house. Paul and his friends had come a long, long way to tell people in Philippi the good news about Jesus!

God's Word & Me

Lydia must have been very glad to know that Jesus loved her. And Paul must have been very glad to be the one who told Lydia about Jesus' love.

We can help other people learn about Jesus, too. In the Bible, Jesus said, "Your good actions help others learn about God." When we say and do good things, our friends learn how people who love Jesus act. We can show Jesus' love to people. And we can tell others that Jesus loves them!

LESSON ELEVEN

Bible Story Center
for older children
Acts 16:6-15

Collect
Bible.

Prepare
Print one of these questions at the top of separate sheets of paper: "Who?" "What?" "When?" "Where?" "Why?" Number each question from one to five. Attach papers to classroom walls.

Introduction

What's the most important thing you think someone should know about Jesus? What would you tell someone who had never heard about Jesus? Volunteers respond. **Today in our Bible story we're going to hear what Paul told about Jesus.** Several times during the story or at the end of the story, invite volunteers to answer interview questions as if they were characters in the story. (Optional: Videotape questions and answers.) For example, ask, "Paul, how did you feel about the dream you had?" A student might answer, "At first I was afraid, but then I realized it was a message from God."

Special Agent Option
Before class, prepare several copies of each of the papers shown in the sketch. Place papers and pencils in a box labeled "Top Secret." At the end of the story, volunteers remove items, match each puzzle to a pattern and then follow the patterns to discover the daily mission "be a witness about Jesus."

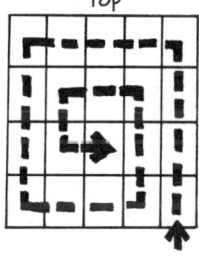
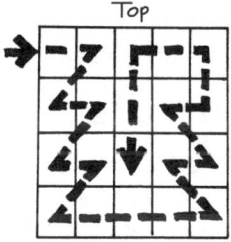

Tell the Story

Paul and his friends Silas and Timothy started out on a trip. Now, they had no idea how long this trip would last. They didn't even know exactly where they would be going! But they did know why they were taking this trip: They wanted to keep spreading the good news about Jesus. And they knew that God's Holy Spirit would guide them and be with them everywhere they went.

After leaving the country of Galatia, Paul and Silas traveled toward an area called Mysia (MISH-ee-uh). We don't know how God did it, but the Bible tells us that the Holy Spirit directed them past Mysia and on to another town called Troas. Paul and his friends were ready to follow God wherever He wanted them to go!

One night when they were in Troas, perhaps when Paul was trying to sleep, he suddenly saw a vision of a man in front of him! Paul must have rubbed his eyes in surprise! Paul could tell that this man was from Macedonia across the sea in the northern part of Greece. "Come over to Macedonia and help us," the man said.

Right away, Paul knew that this was the direction he'd been waiting for! God wanted them to take His good news across the Aegean Sea to Macedonia. Paul woke his friends and they went out early, searching for any boat that would take them to Macedonia.

© 2007 Gospel Light. Permission to photocopy granted. *Agents in Action*

Two days later they landed in Macedonia. They began to travel along the Egnatian Way, the famous highway the Romans had built all the way across Macedonia. They walked about 10 miles (16 km) and came to Philippi, the most important city in the area.

Whenever he entered a new city, Paul usually went to the local synagogue as a place to begin sharing the exciting news about Jesus. But in Philippi there was no synagogue. That means there weren't even 10 Jewish men in the city. According to Jewish law, it took at least that many to start a synagogue.

So instead of going to the synagogue Paul and his friends went to the river. They knew that if there weren't enough Jews to start a synagogue, the custom was to meet for prayer near running water. Sure enough, a group of women had come to the river for prayer. Paul and his friends began talking to them about Jesus.

One well-dressed woman was especially interested in what Paul had to say. This woman's name was Lydia, and she had a business selling expensive purple cloth. Lydia worshiped God, even though she wasn't Jewish.

Lydia paid close attention to Paul as he told how Jesus died for the sins of everyone in the world and that He came back to life again. She knew that no one but God had the power to bring anyone back to life. Now she had to decide whether or not she believed that Jesus is the Son of the one true God who has power over death and life. God's Holy Spirit helped Lydia understand that Paul's message about Jesus was true! Jesus had died to pay for her sin so that she could be forgiven and live forever with God. Not only did Lydia become the first person in Philippi to believe this good news about Jesus, but her whole household, probably including servants and their families, also came to know Him!

Paul asked Lydia if she would like to be baptized. All through the New Testament the followers of Jesus baptized new believers with water to show that their sins were forgiven and that they were members of God's family. What a great day for Lydia and her new friends!

After Lydia and everyone in her household was baptized, Lydia wanted to help Paul and his friends. She knew that they needed a place to sleep and food to eat, so she invited them to stay at her house! Paul and his friends were glad for Lydia's willingness to share her home with them. And Lydia was glad that Paul had shared the good news about Jesus.

God's Word & Me

The good news that Paul preached is the same good news that we can help others learn about. Every day we have opportunities to talk with lots of different people. As we get to know them, we might find out that they believe different things than we believe about God and Jesus. Even when we disagree, however, we can always show respect. Because God loves every person, all people deserve our respect. Our words and actions can always help others learn about God's love.

Listen to these words that Jesus said when He was teaching us how to live. Read Matthew 5:16. **Jesus said these words because He wanted us to know that our words and actions can make a difference in the lives of others. Our right actions show our love for God, and might result in an opportunity to witness or talk about what it means to be a Christian.**

>> **What are some ways of acting that show others what it means to be a Christian?** (Being honest. Treating others fairly.)

>> **What kinds of things can kids your age say to witness about what it means to be a Christian?** (Being a Christian means I believe that God loves me and helps me know what to do. Being a Christian means that I believe the Bible is true.)

>> **Why might someone not believe that Jesus is God's Son?** (Haven't heard about Jesus. Their parents have taught them to believe something else.)

>> **What might stop a kid your age from witnessing about Jesus?** (Don't know what to say. Afraid someone will make fun of him or her. Don't think others want to know about Jesus.) Pray with children, asking God's help in being witnesses about Jesus and showing children times their actions and words can help others learn about God.

LESSON ELEVEN

Game Center
for younger children
Acts 16:6-15

Collect

Bible, *Agent* Music CD and player, index cards, marker.

Prepare

Write the numbers 1 and 2 on an equal number of separate index cards. Place one card for each child facedown in a circle on the floor.

Do

1. As you play "God's Kids," children walk around the cards. After 10 to 15 seconds stop the music. Children stop walking. Each child picks up the card closest to him or her and says the number on the card.

2. Volunteers take turns completing the sentence, "Jesus loves (saying the names of the appropriate number of friends)." Repeat as time permits, changing the way children move around the circle (slowly, clapping hands, pretending to fly, waving hands in the air, hopping).

Talk About

>> In today's Bible story, Paul and his friends told a woman named Lydia the good news about Jesus. You can tell your friends the good news about Jesus' love.

>> Cole, I see a number one on the card you picked up. What is the name of one of your friends? Let's say this sentence together: "Jesus loves (Gabriel)."

>> Quentin, what friend do you like to play with? It's good news to know that Jesus loves (Niki). You can tell Niki about Jesus' love.

>> Pray briefly, **Dear God, thank You that Jesus loves us. Help us tell our friends about Jesus' love. In Jesus' name, amen.**

For Older Children

Draw several hearts of varying sizes on a sheet of butcher paper. Print "Jesus loves . . ." on the butcher paper. Instead of index cards, place different colored markers on floor in circle. When music stops, each child picks up the nearest marker, runs to the butcher paper and writes the name of a friend in one of the hearts. Children arrange markers in a new path (curvy, zigzag, etc.) and play again. Continue as time allows, trying to fill up each heart with names of children who need to know the good news about Jesus' love. (Optional: If appropriate in your situation, provide completed paper to prayer team in your church who will pray for each of the named children.)

God's Word

"Let your light shine before men, that they may see your good deeds and praise your Father in heaven." Matthew 5:16

For Younger Children:
"Your good actions help others learn about God."

God's Word & Me

My actions and words can be a witness for Jesus, helping others see and understand what it means to be a Christian.

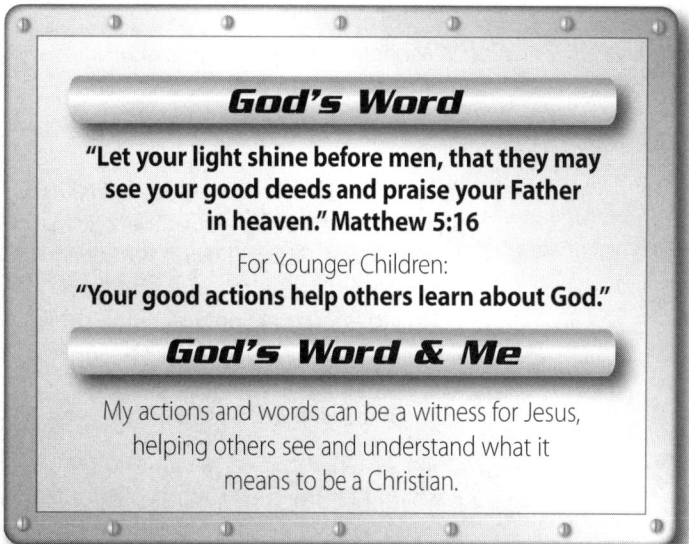

© 2007 Gospel Light. Permission to photocopy granted. *Agents in Action*

Game Center
for older children
Acts 16:6-15

Collect
Bible, flashlight (such as mini Maglite®).

Do
1. Children stand in a circle around a table or on hard surface. Place a flashlight in the middle and turn it on. Spin the flashlight. (Note: If using flashlight with protruding switch, spin the flashlight with switch facing up.) When the flashlight stops spinning, look to see on whom the light is shining. Child says (or reads) Matthew 5:16.

2. Child who said the verse spins the flashlight for the next round. Continue as time permits. (Variation: Instead of having the child on whom the light is shining say the verse, ask another child to read the verse leaving out one or more words for the child to fill in.)

God's Word
"Let your light shine before men, that they may see your good deeds and praise your Father in heaven." Matthew 5:16

For Younger Children:
"Your good actions help others learn about God."

God's Word & Me
My actions and words can be a witness for Jesus, helping others see and understand what it means to be a Christian.

Talk About

>> Read Matthew 5:16. **What do the words "let our light shine" mean?** (We show others by our actions and by our words that we love and obey Jesus.)

>> **When has someone helped you learn the good news about Jesus? Why is it important to witness or tell about Jesus' love to others?** (Other people might never know that Jesus loves them. Jesus commanded us to witness about Him. We shouldn't keep good news to ourselves.) Briefly tell children about a time you witnessed about Jesus' love.

>> **What might make it hard to tell the good news about Jesus?** (We don't know if the person believes in Jesus. Others might not understand what we're talking about.)

>> **What are some times that kids your age might want to know about Jesus' love and the ways that Jesus helps His followers?** (When they have problems or bad things happen. When they think no one cares about them.) **When we show Jesus' love by our actions and words, we are witnessing about Him.** Lead children in prayer, asking God to show us times to witness about Jesus.

For Younger Children
Instead of saying or reading Matthew 5:16 when the light shines on a child, he or she says the name of a friend or family member who Jesus loves. Make sure that every child has a chance to tell a name.

LESSON ELEVEN

Art Center
for younger children
Acts 16:6-15

Collect

Bible, Lesson 11 Pattern Page (p. 196), markers.

Prepare

Make a copy of the Pattern Page for each child.

Do

1. Give each child a copy of the Pattern Page. Say each letter on the page as you point to it so that children are able to "read" the name of Jesus.

2. Children color the letters with different colors. Encourage children to fill letters with different patterns (stripes, circles, dots, curvy lines, etc.).

God's Word

"Let your light shine before men, that they may see your good deeds and praise your Father in heaven." Matthew 5:16

For Younger Children:
"Your good actions help others learn about God."

God's Word & Me

My actions and words can be a witness for Jesus, helping others see and understand what it means to be a Christian.

Talk About

>> **What letter does Jesus' name start with? When we see Jesus' name, it reminds us that He loves us. It's good news to know that Jesus loves all of us. We can tell our friends about Jesus' love.**

>> **Put your finger on each letter and say the letters with me. Jesus loves (Gage). Jesus loves (Vincent).** Continue, naming each child in the group.

>> **Casey, who is one of your friends? Jesus loves (Jaden). You can tell the good news that Jesus loves us.** Pray briefly, **Thank You, Jesus, for loving each person. Please help us tell the good news that You love us. Amen.**

For Older Children

In addition to a copy of the Pattern Page for each child, provide black construction paper and glue. Children color Jesus' name, using a variety of colors and patterns. Children cut out letters. Collect all letters and mix them up. Place letters face down. Then let children take turns turning over letters and collecting them until they have all the letters for Jesus' name. Children glue letters onto black construction paper.

© 2007 Gospel Light. Permission to photocopy granted. *Agents in Action*

LESSON ELEVEN

Art Center
for older children
Acts 16:6-15

Collect
Bible, chenille wires (one for each child), yellow plastic tapered beads (one for each child), large interlocking plastic beads in two colors (10 for each child).

Prepare
Make a sample candle.

Do
1. Give each child a chenille wire, one tapered bead and 10 interlocking beads (two different colors). Each child bends wire about 3 inches (7.5 cm) from one end (demonstrate as you give directions).
2. Each child then threads the 10 interlocking beads onto the chenille wire, alternating two colors, to the bend topping it off with the tapered bead (see sketches a and b).
3. To make the candle stand, child bends the remaining wire 1½ inches (4 cm) from the base of the candle and back to the base (see sketch c). Repeat for each leg of the candle stand. Adjust position of wires as needed to make the candle stand up straight.

God's Word
"Let your light shine before men, that they may see your good deeds and praise your Father in heaven." Matthew 5:16

For Younger Children:
"Your good actions help others learn about God."

God's Word & Me
My actions and words can be a witness for Jesus, helping others see and understand what it means to be a Christian.

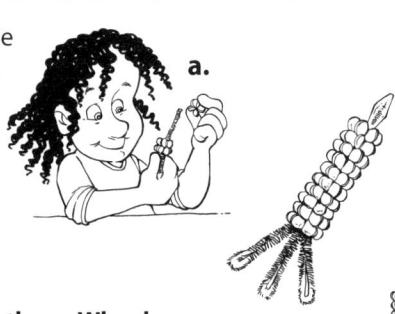

a.
b.
c.

Talk About

>> Read Matthew 5:16. **Jesus told us to let our light shine before others. Why does He want us to do that?** (So others will come to know the good news of Jesus' love.)

>> **How do you usually hear about good news? What are some ways we can witness or tell others the good news about Jesus?** (Talk to friends about Jesus' love when we're spending time with them. Invite people to church. Show Jesus' love by our actions.)

>> **When we are making right choices and showing that we want to love and obey God, how is that like telling others about Jesus?** (People see the way we live and it helps them learn what God has planned for people.)

>> **What are some of the ways you've seen others witness about Jesus' love? What are some things you can tell others about Jesus?** (The stories about Jesus in the Bible are true. Jesus showed people the right way to live. Jesus died and is alive now so that everyone can know God's love.)

>> **Our candles can remind us to always "let our light shine" so that others learn about Jesus.** Pray, thanking God for Jesus and asking God to show us times we can witness about Jesus.

For Younger Children
Ahead of time, make the candle stands. Children thread the beads onto the stands.

LESSON ELEVEN

Worship Center
for younger and older children
Acts 16:6-15

Collect

Bibles, *Agent* Music CD and player, song charts (pp. 248, 250), at least two rolls of crepe paper.

Team Game

Divide group into two or more teams. (Optional: Volunteers from each team choose names for their teams.) Invite at least four or five children from each team to stand together in a group. Give a roll of crepe paper to one child in each group. At your signal, child wraps crepe paper around his or her waist two times (so that the end is anchored securely) and then passes the crepe paper to another child in the group. Child wraps crepe paper around his or her waist and passes on the roll. When all children in the group have been connected, the group reverses the process. The first group to get unwrapped is the winner. Team members cheer for their team. Repeat as time permits.

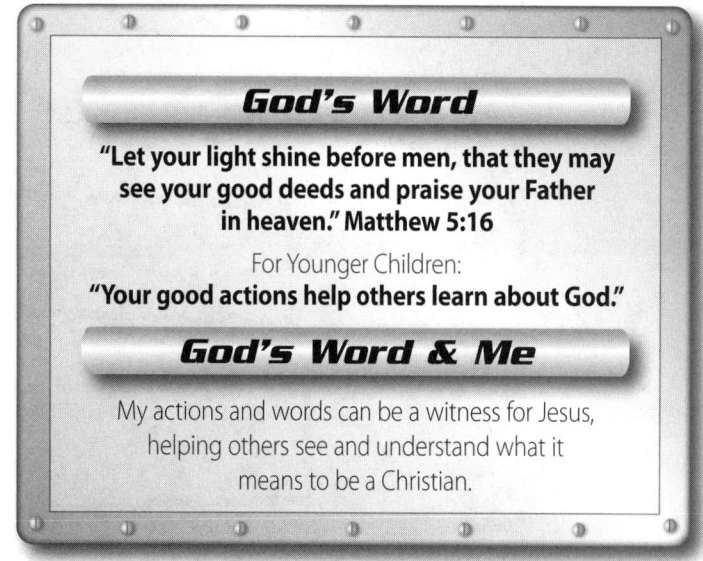

God's Word

"Let your light shine before men, that they may see your good deeds and praise your Father in heaven." Matthew 5:16

For Younger Children:
"Your good actions help others learn about God."

God's Word & Me

My actions and words can be a witness for Jesus, helping others see and understand what it means to be a Christian.

Bible Verse Game

Repeat Matthew 5:16 aloud with children. Then ask a volunteer to be your partner. Ask your partner to choose "odd" or "even." Each of you puts a hand behind your back and together count "one-two-three." On "three," both of you put a hand in front of you with one to five fingers showing. If the total number of fingers is odd, the person who chose "odd" says the verse aloud. If the total is even, the other player says the verse. Then invite children to form pairs. (Give help as needed.) Lead pairs in this activity several times.

Song

Lead children in singing "Mission of Love." Add motions and/or clapping if desired.

Prayer

How many words can you think of that describe Jesus? Volunteers respond. **These words remind us of the things we want to help others learn when we witness about Jesus. Let's ask God to help us see opportunities to share about Jesus with others.** Lead children in prayer.

Song

Lead children in singing "Be Strong and Courageous." Add motions and/or clapping if desired.

© 2007 Gospel Light. Permission to photocopy granted. *Agents in Action*

LESSON ELEVEN • Pattern Page

LESSON ELEVEN • Puzzle Page

BIBLE CHARACTERS—NEW TESTAMENT
Puzzling Words

Find the Bible verses and fill in the names of these people from the book of Acts who witnessed about Jesus.

Choose one or two clues and rewrite them to describe ways you can witness about Jesus.

ACROSS
1. He preached about Jesus to a large crowd in Jerusalem. (Acts 2:14)
2. She lived in Philippi and became a Christian after listening to Paul tell about Jesus. (Acts 16:14)
5. The Bible describes this man as so full of God's power that he was able to do many miracles. Later, he was killed because of his faith in God. (Acts 6:8)

DOWN
1. After he believed that Jesus is God's Son, this man traveled to many places telling about Jesus. (Acts 17:2,3)
3. She was known for helping poor widows. (Acts 9:36)
4. This man wrote five books of the New Testament. Four of these books are named after him.
6. He explained the Scriptures to an Ethiopian (Acts 8:26,27,35)

LESSON TWELVE

Getting Even

Bible Story:
Philemon's Choice
Philemon

Teacher's Devotional

For many, forgiveness is a foreign concept. Revenge is often an accepted way of life and an excuse for many cruel acts. According to the Bible, there is only one antidote to revenge: the kind of forgiveness that leaves the consequences of a situation and the desire for revenge to God Himself. But as we look around, we see that the number of people who live biblical forgiveness is small.

Even within the Church, people often passively avoid both forgiveness and revenge. While this approach may seem better than open revenge, it's still only a poor substitute for true forgiveness. The anger remains, and instead of being healed, we Christians may instead suppress our pain and bitterness. This often results in a lifelong crippling of our abilities to grow in relationship with God and with others. It also leaves us self-focused and less able to reach out to those whom we need to love and to forgive.

One of the reasons we lack forgiveness so often is that we easily forget the truth that forgiveness springs from God's grace. We can't produce forgiveness by our own efforts—it's truly God's supernatural gift. We can trust Jesus Christ to help us truly forgive others—even when in the midst of wounded emotions it feels impossible. And as we forgive, we are then able to show mercy to others, teaching forgiveness by our own living example! Children experience real and imagined hurts every day. They are just beginning to grasp what it means to forgive, to stop being angry or to let another person off the hook of

God's Word

"Be merciful, just as your Father is merciful."
Luke 6:36

For Younger Children:
"Be merciful."

God's Word & Me

Because God forgives me, I can show mercy and forgive others who have treated me wrongly.

our own anger and hurt feelings. As we talk patiently with them about forgiving in everyday life and as we genuinely forgive kids again and again, the living truth of what forgiveness is all about will be planted in their hearts!

LESSON TWELVE

Planning Page

Choose which centers you will provide and the order in which children will participate in them (see pp. 14-18 for schedule tips and pp. 24-25 for guidelines in combining older and younger children). Also plan who will lead each center (for staffing tips see pp. 19-21). Use the reproducible planning sheet (p. 238) to record your plans.

Bible Story Center

Bible Story
Philemon's Choice • Philemon

Younger Child Option
Call out letters while looking at Paul's words written to Philemon

Older Child Option
Discover the daily mission "show mercy" written in candle wax

Game Center

Younger Child Option
Play a game to place names on heart drawings, and talk about ways of showing God's love and mercy to others

Materials
Bible, Post-it Notes, markers in three or four colors, large sheet of paper, tape, blindfolds

Older Child Option
Play a game like Fruit Basket Upset, and talk about times when it is hard to show God's love and mercy

Materials
Bible, chairs

Art Center

Younger Child Option
Make paper-chain loops showing names of children, and talk about ways of showing God's love and forgiveness to each other

Materials
Bible, construction paper, scissors, crayons or markers, stickers, stapler or tape

Older Child Option
Make Mercy Posters as reminders to show God's mercy to others, and talk about how children act who are merciful

Materials
Bible, Lesson 12 Pattern Page (p. 210), construction paper in a variety of colors, scissors, markers, glue, (decorating supplies such as stickers, glitter, etc.)

Worship Center

For the Younger and Older Child
Participate in large-group activities to review Bible verse and to worship God together

Materials
Bibles, *Agent* Music CD and player, song charts (pp. 246, 252), at least two inflated and tied balloons, several beanbags

Coloring/Puzzle Center

Younger Child Option
Review the Bible story while completing coloring page

Materials
Lesson 12 Coloring Page (p. 211) for each student, crayons

Older Child Option
Review what Jesus said about forgiveness while completing puzzle page

Materials
Lesson 12 Puzzle Page (p. 212) for each student, pencils

© 2007 Gospel Light. Permission to photocopy granted. *Agents in Action*

LESSON TWELVE

Bonus Theme Ideas

Bonus Theme Ideas can be used at any time during this session: as an additional activity center, to extend the session for a longer time or for added theme excitement.

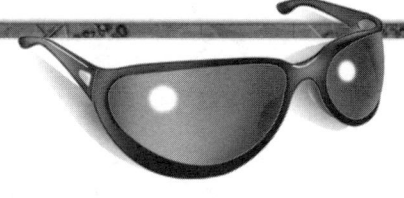

Agent Competition

Divide group into teams of special agents. Give a volunteer on each team (an older child, helper or leader) a sheet of paper. Ask volunteer to number paper from 1 to 10. While all agents close their eyes, ring a bell several times. (Optional: Stand behind a room divider while ringing bell, record sound ahead of time or play sounds from Internet site.) Agents open eyes, talk with team members to identify sound and write name of item next to number 1. Repeat activity for some or all of the following sounds (party noisemaker; jingling keys; rain stick; rhythm instruments such as triangle, tambourine or drum; music instruments such as flute, trumpet or guitar; clapping hands; ticking clock) or invent your own creative sounds!

Special Agent Information

Super Special Handshakes

Create a unique handshake (each person swipes index and middle fingers together before shaking hands, or each person taps knuckles before shaking hands, etc). At the start of a session of *Agents in Action*, secretly teach several children the handshake and ask them to teach the handshake to two or three others who teach the handshake to others and so on. See how fast everyone in *Agents in Action* can learn the handshake.

Special Agent Information

Sweet Words

Divide class into groups of two or three. Each group chooses the word "merciful" or "forgiveness." Give each group paper towels, graham crackers (or other crackers) and plastic knives. Place one or more colors of frosting and containers of small candies in a central location. Children spread thin layers of frosting on the graham crackers and use candy to form letters on graham crackers to spell out the word they chose. Children eat crackers they decorated. (Optional: Use icing in tubes or raisins to form letters. Use cream cheese or peanut butter instead of frosting.)

Special Agent Information

> **Post a note alerting parents to the use of food. Also, check registration forms for possible food allergies.**

Bible Story Center

for younger children
Philemon

LESSON TWELVE

Collect

Bible.

Introduction

Make an X with your arms if you can think of something wrong a kid your age might do. *Volunteers respond.* **Today in our Bible story we're going to hear what happened after a young man did something very wrong.**

Tell the Story

Onesimus was in trouble! He had done something very wrong! He had taken things that didn't belong to him. The things he had taken belonged to a man named Philemon. Onesimus knew he was in trouble, so he ran away from Philemon.

Special Agent Option

In a box labeled "Top Secret," place a sheet of paper and a marker. At the appropriate time in the story, remove paper and marker. Print Paul's letter (see below) on the paper to show children. As you print each letter of the words in the letter, children call out letters.

Onesimus ran until he was a long, long way from his home. But far from his home, Onesimus met Paul. Paul was a man who loved Jesus. Paul got to know Onesimus. He wanted to help Onesimus. So Paul told Onesimus about Jesus. Soon Onesimus loved Jesus, too.

Paul knew someone else, too. Even though Paul was far from the place where Onesimus had lived, Paul knew Philemon. Philemon was the man Onesimus had run away from! Philemon loved Jesus.

Onesimus knew it had been wrong to take things that belonged to Philemon. So Onesimus knew he needed to go back to Philemon and say that he was sorry.

Paul wanted to help Onesimus do what was right. So he wrote a letter to his friend Philemon. Paul wrote:

Dear Philemon,

I am sending Onesimus, whom I love, back to you.
Please welcome him as you would welcome me.
If he owes you anything, I will pay for it.

Your friend, Paul

Paul said to Onesimus, "You've been a good helper to me. But now it's time for you to go back to Philemon." That's just what Onesimus did!

God's Word & Me

Paul wanted Philemon to be kind to Onesimus, even though Onesimus had stolen things from Philemon. Being kind to others, even when they have done wrong, is called forgiving them or being merciful to them. In the Bible, Jesus said, "Be merciful." When we are merciful, it means we show God's love and kindness to others. When someone does something wrong, we can say "stop" and we can get a teacher or parent to help us. Then God will help us show His love and be kind.

Bible Story Center
for older children
Philemon

LESSON TWELVE

Collect

Bible, markers, classified ad sections of newspaper, tape.

Introduction

What's the best hiding place you've ever found? Volunteers respond. **Today we're going to hear about a man who hid in a big city. We'll find out why he didn't want anyone to find him!** As you tell the story, guide group to make up newspaper headlines describing the story action ("Slave Escapes!" "Slave Seen in Rome," "Paul and Onesimus Meet," "Onesimus Becomes a Christian," "Onesimus Returns to Colosse.") Volunteers use wide-tip markers to write headlines directly onto newspaper. Tape newspapers to classroom walls.

Special Agent Option

Before class, gather a white candle, scissors, newspaper, several sheets of white paper and several resealable baggies filled with dry coffee grounds. Trim the candlewick so that it is even with the wax. Using one end of the candle, write the daily mission "show mercy" on each sheet of paper, pressing firmly. Place all materials in a box labeled "Top Secret." At the end of the story, volunteers remove items, sprinkle coffee grounds on papers (placed on newspaper) and then shake off to make the daily mission appear.

Tell the Story

In the New Testament, we can read about a slave named Onesimus (oh-NEHS-uh-muhs). Onesimus was the slave of a man named Philemon (fi-LEE-muhn) who lived in the city of Colosse. But Onesimus escaped from Philemon—perhaps even stealing some of Philemon's money—and ran away to the big city of Rome! (Optional: Ask children to repeat unfamiliar names with you during the story.)

Rome was the biggest city in the empire; it was a place where a person could hide! And it was an exciting city—especially if you were a slave who was finally free to go where you wanted to go and do what you wanted to do.

But Onesimus must have felt scared. He probably didn't know anyone in the city. And if he DID see someone he knew, Onesimus would have hidden! If anyone who knew Onesimus saw him, that person might tell the soldiers that they'd seen a runaway slave! Then Onesimus would be captured and sent back to his master, Philemon. Onesimus would have been severely punished. He could be sent to work in a mine, beaten, tortured or even killed!

Somehow, Onesimus heard that Paul—the man who loved Jesus—was in Rome! No one knows exactly how Onesimus and Paul met. We only know that the two men became friends and that Onesimus became a great helper to Paul. Eventually, Onesimus told Paul what he had done.

Paul told Onesimus about Jesus. He probably told Onesimus that God loved him so much that He sent His Son, Jesus, to die to take the punishment for the wrong things he had done. Paul must have told Onesimus that if he believed in what Jesus did for him, he could trust God to forgive him. Onesimus asked God to forgive him, and Onesimus became a member of God's family.

The next days after Onesimus because a Christian must have been wonderful. Onesimus helped Paul by doing whatever Paul asked. And all the time, Onesimus was learning more and more about God and His Son, Jesus.

LESSON TWELVE

Then one day Paul called Onesimus to him. "Onesimus," Paul said, "I have an idea. My friend Tychicus (TIHK-ih-cuhs) is going on a trip. He's taking a letter from me to the Christians at Colosse. And I want you to go with him."

COLOSSE! Onesimus's heart jumped! A shiver of fear ran through him. Colosse was the town where Philemon, his master, lived. Paul wanted him to go back to his master!

It would be hard for Onesimus to go back to Philemon. Onesimus must have worried about how Philemon would treat him. Would Philemon want revenge because Onesimus had run away? But because Paul loved Onesimus as if he were his own son, Paul wanted to help Onesimus. So Paul wrote a letter to Philemon. "My friend, do me a favor," Paul wrote. "Welcome Onesimus back home the same way you would welcome me." Paul even said he was willing to pay back whatever money Onesimus might have owed Philemon!

When it was time to leave, Paul handed Onesimus the letter he had written. "Don't be frightened," Paul encouraged Onesimus. "In this letter I've asked Philemon to forgive you and treat you kindly as a brother in God's family."

God's Word & Me

Paul's words and actions made all the difference in Onesimus's life. He helped Onesimus learn that Jesus would forgive his sins, so he could become a member of God's family. And Paul's letter helped encourage Philemon to show mercy to Onesimus.

Read Luke 6:36. **Jesus said these words to help us know how to treat others who have treated us in wrong ways. Jesus said that because God is merciful and loving to us, we should show His mercy and love to others. When someone does something wrong to us, it's easy to first think about getting revenge. But Jesus' words remind us of showing God's love and mercy to others. We can ask God to help us be merciful and to know what to do when someone does something wrong to us.** (Talk with interested children about God's mercy and forgiveness that leads to our salvation. See "Leading a Child to Christ" on p. 12.)

>> **When might a kid your age want to get revenge?** (Someone hurts him or her on purpose. Someone tells a lie about him or her. Big brother never lets him or her choose which video game to play. A kid at school hogs the ball in a game.)

>> **What would it be like at (school) if kids never forgave each other? How would your (sports team) be different if kids showed mercy to each other?**

>> **Why is it good to show mercy and forgiveness?** (God tells us to. I might find out later that the person really didn't do something wrong to me. I can keep a friend when I forgive.)

>> **What has God done to show His mercy and forgiveness to us?** (Listens to our prayers and forgives us of the wrong things we do. Never gives up on us.)

>> **What are some good things you could do to show that you are merciful and showing God's love to others?** (Help someone even when he or she doesn't ask. Give someone more than is asked for.) Pray with children, thanking God for His mercy and forgiveness, and asking His help in showing mercy and forgiveness to others. Encourage children to pray aloud or silently, reminding them that God hears both spoken and unspoken prayers.

LESSON TWELVE

Game Center
for younger children
Philemon

Collect

Bible, Post-it Notes, markers in three or four colors, large sheet of paper, tape, blindfolds.

Prepare

Print each child's name on a Post-it Note. Draw three or four large hearts in different colors on a large sheet of paper. Tape paper onto wall at child's eye level.

Do

Children stand in a line. Give each child the note on which his or her name is written. Blindfold each child or ask child to close eyes while you gently spin the child around one or two times. Children walk up to the paper and attach their Post-it Notes. Child opens eyes or removes blindfold and looks to see if Post-it Note is attached to a heart. Repeat as time and interest permit.

God's Word

"Be merciful, just as your Father is merciful."
Luke 6:36

For Younger Children:
"Be merciful."

God's Word & Me

Because God forgives me, I can show mercy and forgive others who have treated me wrongly.

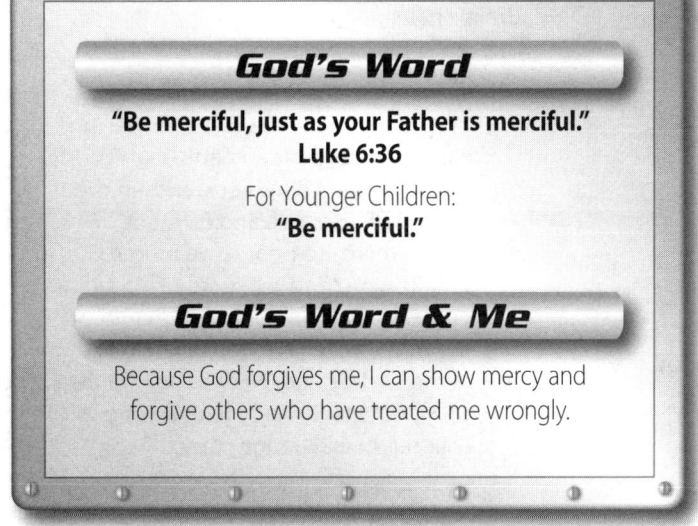

Talk About

>> When we see pictures of hearts, it reminds us of people who love and forgive us. When we forgive others, it means we are kind, even if they are unkind.

>> We can show love and forgiveness to our brothers and sisters. Tyler, what can you do to show your brother that you love him?

>> Jesus said, "Be merciful." When we are merciful, it means we show that we love and forgive others, even when they have been unkind to us. Kenna, who is in your family? You can show love and forgive your big sister. After someone says, "please forgive me," you can say, "I forgive you."

>> Madison, what do you and your brother like to do together? When you (play at the park), one of you might be unkind or mean. But you can forgive each other and be kind. Pray briefly, **Dear God, thank You for loving us. Please help us to show love and mercy to others. In Jesus' name, amen.**

For Older Children

Assign points to each heart, writing the highest number on the most difficult target. When a child places his or her Post-it Note on a heart, award the child double points if he or she can describe a situation in which someone his or her age can show mercy.

LESSON TWELVE

Game Center
for older children
Philemon

Collect
Bible, chairs.

Do

1. Children sit on chairs in a circle facing each other and play a game like Fruit Basket Upset. Volunteer stands in the middle of the circle and calls out, "Show mercy to people wearing red." Children wearing red jump up to trade places in the circle before the child in the middle can take one of the places in the circle. If the child in the middle calls out "Show mercy to everyone," all children must change places.

2. The child left without a place stands in the middle of the circle and begins the next round. Game continues as time allows or until all children have had a chance to be in the middle of the circle. Vary the criterion for who must trade places (children wearing tennis shoes, children wearing T-shirts, children wearing stripes, etc.).

God's Word
"Be merciful, just as your Father is merciful."
Luke 6:36

For Younger Children:
"Be merciful."

God's Word & Me
Because God forgives me, I can show mercy and forgive others who have treated me wrongly.

Talk About

>> Read Luke 6:36. **What does it mean to be merciful?** (It means to be kind, even when others are unkind and don't deserve kindness. It means to forgive them.)

>> **What are some of the hardest times to show mercy and forgive other people?** (When someone is mean more than once. When someone calls you names.)

>> **Why does forgiveness and mercy show God's love?** (God always forgives us when we ask. God's love includes forgiveness.)

>> **Showing mercy is not always easy. It's easy to think about getting revenge when someone has hurt us in some way. But what do you think might happen if people in a family, or kids on a soccer team, never showed mercy?** Lead children in prayer, thanking God for showing mercy and forgiveness to us and asking His help to show mercy to those who've treated us wrongly.

For Younger Children

Children sit in a circle. Stand in the middle of the circle and call out **Show mercy to everyone wearing red.** Instead of trading places, children wearing red jump up and clap hands. After several rounds, change the action (do jumping jacks, hop on one foot, swing arms in a circle, etc.).

LESSON TWELVE

Art Center
for younger children
Philemon

Collect

Bible, construction paper, scissors, crayons or markers, stickers, stapler or tape.

Prepare

Cut construction paper into 1½ x 6-in (4x15-cm) strips.

Do

1. Give each child several paper strips. Children write names on strips and decorate with drawings and/or stickers. (Be available to write names as needed.)

2. Show children how to form loops with their strips and link the loops together in a paper chain by stapling or taping. Make as many links as time and interest allow. (Optional: Hang chain in classroom. At the end of the session, cut apart and allow children to take home part of the chain.)

God's Word

"Be merciful, just as your Father is merciful."
Luke 6:36

For Younger Children:
"Be merciful."

God's Word & Me

Because God forgives me, I can show mercy and forgive others who have treated me wrongly.

Talk About

>> Kelsey, your name is on this purple loop. Quentin's name is on the green loop next to your loop. You and Quentin can show love to each other. You can forgive each other when someone has been unkind.

>> Madison, point to your name on our paper chain. Kaylee's name is next to your name. You and Kaylee can show love and forgive each other. When we forgive others, we are kind and treat them as friends.

>> Jesus said, "Be merciful." When we are merciful, it means that we can love and forgive others, even when others have made us angry. It's hard to show love and forgive when we feel mad, but God will help us. Pray briefly, **Dear God, thank You for loving us. Please help us show love and be merciful. In Jesus' name, amen.**

For Older Children

Before making the paper chain, children write on their paper strips ways they can show mercy to others.

LESSON TWELVE

Art Center
for older children
Philemon

Collect

Bible, Lesson 12 Pattern Page (p. 210), construction paper in a variety of colors, scissors, markers, glue, (decorating supplies such as stickers, glitter, etc.).

Prepare

Make a copy of the Pattern Page for each child.

Do

1. Give each child a Pattern Page. Child chooses color of construction paper on which to make a Mercy Poster as a reminder to show mercy.
2. Child colors and cuts out words from the Pattern Page. Children arrange and glue words on construction paper, and add drawings and/or other words. Display completed posters in classroom.

God's Word
"Be merciful, just as your Father is merciful."
Luke 6:36

For Younger Children:
"Be merciful."

God's Word & Me
Because God forgives me, I can show mercy and forgive others who have treated me wrongly.

Talk About

>> Read Luke 6:36. **How might someone act who is merciful? When have you seen a kid your age be merciful? Why does this verse say that we can show mercy?**

>> **Why might kids your age find it hard to be merciful?** (Because when someone hurts us it makes us mad. We don't want to trust others who have done wrong to us.)

>> **According to Luke 6:36, why can we show mercy and forgiveness?** (We can show mercy to those who have treated us wrongly, because that's what God has done for us.) **We have all done wrong things, and we've all needed to be forgiven. God loves us by forgiving us. When we forgive others, we share that love.**

>> **God understands why it can be hard to show mercy, and He will help us be forgiving, instead of getting revenge.** Pray, thanking God for His mercy and forgiveness and asking His help to show mercy.

For Younger Children

Before class, cut out the word "love" from the Pattern Pages. Children glue words to paper and then decorate with drawings and stickers.

© 2007 Gospel Light. Permission to photocopy granted. *Agents in Action*

LESSON TWELVE

Worship Center
for younger and older children
Philemon

Collect

Bibles, *Agent* Music CD and player, song charts (pp. 246, 252), at least two inflated and tied balloons, several beanbags.

Team Game

Divide group into two or more teams. Ask several volunteers from each team to line up in front of the group. Give first volunteer from each team a balloon. At your signal, volunteers run around the perimeter of the group tapping the balloons to keep them in the air. Continue with all volunteers to see which team's volunteers can finish first. Team members cheer for their team.

God's Word

"Be merciful, just as your Father is merciful."
Luke 6:36

For Younger Children:
"Be merciful."

God's Word & Me

Because God forgives me, I can show mercy and forgive others who have treated me wrongly.

Bible Verse Game

Repeat Luke 6:36 aloud with children. Then invite several volunteers to stand in front of group with their backs to the group. Give each volunteer a beanbag. Call out the Bible verse reference as a signal to volunteers to toss beanbags over their shoulders. Students who catch beanbags repeat the words of Luke 6:36 in unison. Repeat as time permits.

Song

Lead children in singing "Smart Choices." Add motions and/or clapping if desired.

Prayer

God understands when we feel like getting even with someone who has been mean to us. That's why He wants us to pray to Him and ask for His help in showing His love and mercy. Lead children in prayer, thanking God for His mercy and forgiveness and asking His help in being merciful to others.

Song

Lead children in singing "God's Kids." Add motions and/or clapping if desired.

LESSON TWELVE · Pattern Page

LESSON THIRTEEN

Trash Talk

Bible Story:
Word Power
James 3:2-12

Teacher's Devotional

In our current culture, many people believe that they have a governmentally protected right to say whatever comes into their heads. But as Christians, this freedom doesn't mean we have biblical approval to just pop off about any subject without considering the consequences.

Our words do matter. Proverbs tells us that the power of life and death are in the tongue. We've all seen that power at work when an adult verbally browbeats a child. The child appears to wither physically under the cruel and critical words! And sadly, the effect of those words doesn't stop on that day: Their power can be seen in damaged lives and felt in wounded hearts many years later.

James tells us that our tongues are very powerful. A wise word can change the outcome of a situation the way a small bit turns an enormous horse or a tiny rudder turns a large ship. But just as a small flame can ignite a huge fire, so an unwise word from an unguarded tongue can cause such widespread damage that recovery may require years.

Jesus told us that our mouths speak out of the abundance of our hearts. Take time this week to ask the Holy Spirit to show you the truth about your own heart. Ask Him to reveal to you times and situations where His control of your tongue can make a positive difference in others' lives. Become intentional about speaking words of blessing and gratitude every day. Our most effective teaching will be through the positive power of godly words. Our words can not only bless and comfort the kids we teach but can also give them the chance to learn a whole set of new words to replace the ones they might hear in our "say anything" society!

God's Word

"By this all men will know that you are my disciples, if you love one another."
John 13:35

For Younger Children:
"Love Jesus and show His love to others."

God's Word & Me

Remembering my love for Jesus helps me talk to others in ways that show His love to them.

LESSON THIRTEEN

Planning Page

Choose which centers you will provide and the order in which children will participate in them (see pp. 14-18 for schedule tips and pp. 24-25 for guidelines in combining older and younger children). Also plan who will lead each center (for staffing tips see pp. 19-21). Use the reproducible planning sheet (p. 238) to record your plans.

Bible Story Center

Bible Story
Word Power • James 3:2-12

Younger Child Option
Show items to illustrate story action

Older Child Option
Write letters on fingertips to read the daily mission "say good words"

Game Center

Younger Child Option
Find and sort hidden cards, and talk about saying kind words to show Jesus' love

Materials
Bible, Lesson 13 Pattern Page (p. 224), scissors

Older Child Option
Write examples of wrong ways to talk and toss them into the trash, and discuss ways of remembering to show Jesus' love by saying good words

Materials
Bible, paper, pens, trash can

Art Center

Younger Child Option
Paint mouths on drawings of faces, and talk about kind and good words that show Jesus' love

Materials
Bible, red gelatin, large bowl, hot water, mixing spoon, several shallow containers, newspaper, paper, crayons or markers, cotton swabs

Older Child Option
Create sculptures of items James compared to our words, and talk about using words to show Jesus' love

Materials
Bible, play dough, chenille wire, paper plates, scissors

Worship Center

For the Younger and Older Child
Participate in large-group activities to review Bible verse and to worship God together

Materials
Bibles, *Agent* Music CD and player, song charts (pp. 251, 254), four large sheets of construction paper, marker, several resealable plastic bags filled with individually wrapped candies or stickers

Coloring/Puzzle Center

Younger Child Option
Review the Bible story while completing coloring page

Materials
Lesson 13 Coloring Page (p. 225) for each student, crayons

Older Child Option
Review the Bible verse while completing puzzle page

Materials
Lesson 13 Puzzle Page (p. 226) for each student, pencils

214

© 2007 Gospel Light. Permission to photocopy granted. *Agents in Action*

LESSON THIRTEEN

Bonus Theme Ideas

Bonus Theme Ideas can be used at any time during this session: as an additional activity center, to extend the session for a longer time or for added theme excitement.

Family Photo Day

No. 1149

Create lasting memories at Family Photo Day! Send flyers home ahead of time, inviting families to bring their cameras and smiles for the last session of *Agents in Action!* Set up fun photo backdrops in several areas outdoors or in a large gathering area indoors. Use the following suggestions to create backdrops: (1) Hang a black or dark blue bed sheet as a backdrop. Attach neon circles of varying colors and sizes to the bed sheet. (2) Paint or draw on a length of butcher paper a giant manila folder. Letter "Top Secret" at the top of the folder. Families pose in front of the folder. For patterns and additional backdrop ideas, refer to the decorating ideas on pages 29-32, 234-237.

Special Agent Information

Mission Accomplished Award Ceremony

Use the certificate (see p. 229) to create a Mission Accomplished award for each child who attended *Agents in Action*. (Optional: To each award, attach an inflated balloon in which you have inserted a slip of paper on which is printed one of the daily missions. Also create thank-you awards for leaders and helpers.) Present the awards to children as part of a large-group gathering. Show video or display pictures of children participating in the activities of *Agents in Action*. If time permits, play one or more of children's favorite Team Games (see each lesson's Worship Center).

Special Agent Information

Cereal Mix-Up

No. 1149

Set up on one or more tables (depending on the number of children) at least three bowls of breakfast cereal, including at least one kid-favorite. Place several large spoons in each bowl. Give each child a disposable cup or bowl. Children use spoons to place cereal in cups or bowls. Limit the number of spoonfuls of each cereal to one. Serve juice or milk to drink.

Special Agent Information

> **Post a note alerting parents to the use of food. Also, check registration forms for possible food allergies.**

LESSON THIRTEEN

Bible Story Center
for younger children
James 3:2-12

Collect

Bible.

Introduction

Flex your arm like this to show your muscles. Demonstrate flexing arm and encourage children to imitate your action. **What is the strongest part of your body?** Volunteers answer. **Listen to find out how strong one part of your body can be. It may surprise you to find out!**

Special Agent Option

In a box labeled "Top Secret," place an envelope with a letter inside, a toy horse, a toy boat (showing the rudder if possible), red or orange construction paper cut in small and large flame shapes and a toy tree. At the appropriate times in the story, remove items from box. Show items to illustrate the story.

Tell the Story

James believed that Jesus was God's Son. James was one of Jesus' followers. James wanted to help other people learn how to love and obey God. So James wrote a letter to some people in God's family. We can read his letter in the Bible. One important thing James wrote about was how our words should show our love for God and others.

James said a person's words are like the bit in a horse's mouth. The bit is the small part of the halter that is put on a horse. Even a great BIG horse is moved one direction or another by moving the very small bit in the horse's mouth.

James also said our words are like the rudder of a boat. The rudder is a very little part of the boat. But when the rudder moves, it changes the direction of the whole boat. The bit and rudder are both small, but they make big changes in how the horse or boat move! Our words are a small part of what our bodies can do, but our words can make a big difference.

James also wrote that our words are like a small fire. A little fire can cause a whole forest to burn! Just a few little words can cause a lot of trouble, too. Sometimes just a few words can lead to anger, murder or even war! Our words can do good or bad things. That is why we have to be careful about what we say.

God's Word & Me

James wrote this letter so that we would know how important it is for our words to be good and kind. Talking in good and kind ways is a great way to show love. In the Bible Jesus told us that if we show love to each other, people will know how much we love Him. We talk to lots of people every day—our friends and the people we live with. Saying kind words instead of mean, unfriendly words will show how much we love Jesus.

LESSON THIRTEEN

Bible Story Center
for older children
James 3:2-12

Collect

Bible, paper, markers.

Introduction

When you hear the words "trash talk," what do you think of? Volunteers answer. **Some things that people say are so mean or disrespectful that we compare the words to garbage. Today we're going to hear what a man in the Bible said our tongues or words are like.** Before telling the Bible story, give each child paper and marker. Assign children these items to draw: horse, boat in water, tongue, small flame, large flame, forest, an animal, a bird, a reptile, a sea creature, a mouth. More than one child may draw the same picture. As you tell the story, invite children who drew pictures to show them or tape to classroom wall at the appropriate times.

Special Agent Option

Before class, print the following letters on separate sheets of paper: "sayg," "oodw" and "ords." Place papers and three ballpoint pens in a box labeled "Top Secret." At the end of the story, three volunteers remove papers and pens. Each volunteer writes the letters from one paper in order on the fingers of one hand. Then volunteers hold up their fingers and arrange themselves in order so that the daily mission "say good words" can be read.

Tell the Story

James was one of the first church leaders, and many people who study the Bible believe he was a younger brother of Jesus. He wrote the book of James in the Bible. This book was written as a letter to Jewish people who believed that Jesus is God's Son.

These believers lived in many different countries and were often treated unkindly by people who did not love Jesus. They needed lots of help in knowing how to love and obey God in everyday life. James's letter can help us know how God wants us to live, too.

James tried to help the readers of his letter understand how important it is to control the things we say. He wrote about some things the people were familiar with. The first was a horse's bit. A bit is a small piece of metal about as thick as two pencils. The bit is put into a horse's mouth and attached to the horse's reins. The direction the horse travels is controlled by the way the rider moves the reins and the bit.

Next, James compares the tongue to the rudder of a ship. A ship moves through the water like a knife slicing the water. The rudder is at the back of the boat. When the rudder is held straight, the boat pushes through the water in a straight line. But when the rudder is turned to one side or the other, the boat moves in a different direction. A very small rudder can change the direction of a very big boat.

The bit and rudder are very small, but the ways in which they are used make a BIG difference! The tongue is just a small part of our bodies, but the things we say with it can make BIG differences, too.

The tongue has so much power that the words we say with it affect the whole body. James compares the tongue to a small spark that can set an entire forest on fire. Just as a little spark can cause a huge, uncontrollable fire, just a few words can cause a lot of trouble! Words can be used to persuade others to do good or bad things. There have been times when people have done some extremely bad things because someone convinced them those things were okay to do. What people have said has led to anger, unfairness, prejudice, murder and even war.

LESSON THIRTEEN

James tells us that even though all kinds of animals, birds, reptiles and sea creatures can be tamed and controlled by people, we still can't control our own tongues! In fact, James says that we even use the same mouth to praise God and to say bad things to other people.

"This should not be!" says James. "We should use our tongues only to say good things." James wanted us to realize that we need God's power and love to help us control what we say.

God's Word & Me

It's surprising to think about how something as small as a tongue can make such a big difference in our lives and the lives of the people we talk to. But that's why James wrote almost a whole chapter in his letter about the power of the words we say. Talking to others in ways that show goodness and kindness is one of the best ways we can show how much we love others.

Jesus talked about showing love to others. Listen to what He said. Read John 13:35 aloud. **Jesus was saying that showing love to others shows how much we love and obey Him. You might hear kids around you saying mean things, gossiping, making fun of others or saying bad words. With God's help and remembering your love for Jesus, you can choose to make your words help others, instead of hurting them.**

>> **What are some times when kids your age might feel mad or sad because of what others say?** (Others tease them or tell them they aren't good enough.)

>> **When do kids your age have opportunities to choose to talk in good ways?** (When younger brothers or sisters keep bothering you. When others on a sports team make mistakes.)

>> **Why do you think it might be hard not to say bad words or talk in ways that hurt others' feelings?** (It's easy to talk before you think. Someone makes you mad. You hear others say bad words.) Pray with children, asking God's help in showing love for Jesus by talking in ways that help others instead of hurt them.

LESSON THIRTEEN

Game Center
for younger children
James 3:2-12

Collect
Bible, Lesson 13 Pattern Page (p. 224), scissors.

Prepare
Copy Pattern Page onto card stock, making one copy for every two children. Cut apart pages. Hide the cards around the classroom.

Do
1. Children look for hidden cards, with each child finding no more than three cards.
2. After children have found cards, help children sort cards into matching stacks. If time permits, play again, letting children hide the cards. (Variation: Some children may want to play a game like Memory, matching cards as they are turned over two at a time.)

God's Word
"By this all men will know that you are my disciples, if you love one another."
John 13:35

For Younger Children:
"Love Jesus and show His love to others."

God's Word & Me
Remembering my love for Jesus helps me talk to others in ways that show His love to them.

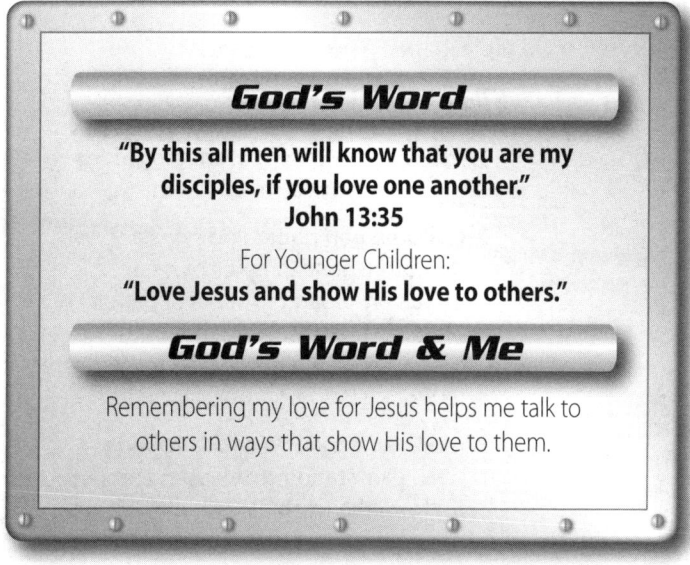

Talk About

>> Which of the mouths on these cards do you think is the silliest? Which mouth looks angry? Which mouth looks sad? Happy? When we talk to people, we can say words that are angry, sad or happy. When we say happy or kind words, it shows that we love Jesus.

>> The Bible says, "Love Jesus and show His love to others." One of the best ways to show Jesus' love to others is by saying kind words. **Ben, I heard you say "thank-you" when Zoey helped you pick up one of the cards. Saying thank-you is a way to show Jesus' love. When are some other times you can say thank-you to someone?**

>> **Nicky, who is someone in your family? You can say kind words to your (big brother).**

>> Every day we can say good words instead of bad words. We can ask God to help us say good and kind words. Pray briefly, **Dear God, we love You. We want to show Your love to others. Help us to say good and kind words. In Jesus' name, amen.**

For Older Children
Set out six disposable cups in two rows to make a grid. Use masking tape to attach cups to each other. Put several cards into every cup. Children take turns tossing coins into cups and collecting cards. In order to keep a card, child either says the words of John 13:35 or tells a situation in which kids can say words that help others, instead of hurt them.

LESSON THIRTEEN

Game Center
for older children
James 3:2-12

Collect
Bible, paper, pens, trash can.

Do

1. Ask children to tell mean things kids their age may say to each other.

2. Give children paper and pens and ask them to write examples of mean things on separate sheets of paper. Children may also write mean things others have said to them. Ask children to write on at least four papers.

3. Children stand in a circle around a trash can, standing at least 5 feet (1.5 m) from the trash can. Children crumple up their papers to make balls. At your signal, children begin tossing balls into trash can. Retrieve all balls, and repeat tossing them into the trash can. For each round, vary the manner in which children toss the balls: underhand; overhand; with back to trash can, toss ball over shoulder or between legs.

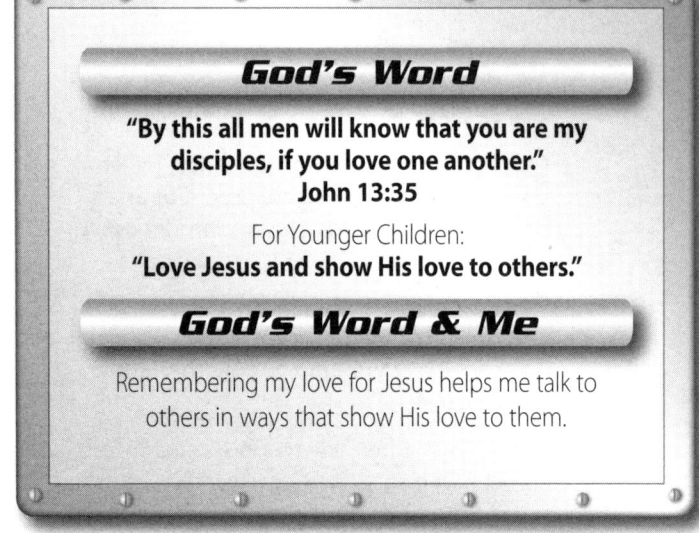

God's Word
"By this all men will know that you are my disciples, if you love one another."
John 13:35

For Younger Children:
"Love Jesus and show His love to others."

God's Word & Me
Remembering my love for Jesus helps me talk to others in ways that show His love to them.

Talk About

>> **The words we say can make a big difference in how people feel and act. Sometimes when a person says bad words or words that hurt others, we describe the words as "trash talk." What are some examples of things kids your age say that hurt others instead of help them?**

>> Read John 13:35. **How can our love for Jesus help us say words that help others instead of hurt them?** (It helps us to remember that Jesus loves everyone and that He wants us to love everyone, too.)

>> **How can we remember to say things that help others instead of hurt them? How can we remember to say good words instead of bad words?** (Pray and ask God for help. Remember that Jesus wants us to show His love to others.)

>> **When we love Jesus, our words will show our love for Him and for others. Let's pray and ask God to help us say good words, and to use our words to help others instead of hurt them.** Lead children in prayer.

For Younger Children

Children crumple up blank paper and take turns tossing paper balls into the trash can. Lead other children in saying kind words to each other ("You can do it!" "Good throw").

LESSON THIRTEEN

Art Center
for younger children
James 3:2-12

Collect

Bible, red gelatin, large bowl, hot water, mixing spoon, several shallow containers, newspaper, paper, crayons or markers, cotton swabs.

Prepare

Place gelatin into a bowl. Slowly pour a small amount of hot water into gelatin, mixing until it resembles tempera paint. Mixture will be grainy and thick. Place mixture into several containers. Cover tables with newspaper.

Do

1. Children use crayons or markers to draw faces without mouths.

2. **God wants the words we say with our mouths to be good and kind. Let's paint some sweet, smiling mouths!** Children use cotton swabs to paint red smiles on the faces they drew. As time permits, children may make more than one face or paint other pictures of their own choosing.

God's Word

"By this all men will know that you are my disciples, if you love one another."
John 13:35

For Younger Children:
"Love Jesus and show His love to others."

God's Word & Me

Remembering my love for Jesus helps me talk to others in ways that show His love to them.

Talk About

>> Brendan, thank you for saying "please" when you asked for a new cotton swab. "Please" is a kind word to say. When are some other times you can say please?

>> The Bible tells us, "Love Jesus and show His love to others." When we say kind words with our mouths it shows how much we love Jesus. Charis, who is someone you can say kind words to?

>> Sometimes we might hear others say bad words, or say words that hurt others' feelings. We can ask God to help us remember to say good words that will help others. Pray briefly, **Dear God, we love You. Help us talk in ways that show love to others. In Jesus' name, amen.**

For Older Children

Children use gelatin paint to draw pictures of situations in which kids can remember to say words that help instead of hurt others.

© 2007 Gospel Light. Permission to photocopy granted. *Agents in Action*

LESSON THIRTEEN

Art Center
for older children
James 3:2-12

Collect

Bible, play dough, chenille wire, paper plates, scissors.

Prepare

Make a sample candle.

Do

1. **In our Bible story today, James says that our tongues are like these small items: the bit on a horse's bridle, the rudder on a ship and a small flame.**

2. Give each child a fist-size lump of play dough and several lengths of chenille wire. Children create sculptures representing the items about which James wrote. Children use scissors to cut chenille wire as desired.

God's Word

"By this all men will know that you are my disciples, if you love one another."
John 13:35

For Younger Children:
"Love Jesus and show His love to others."

God's Word & Me

Remembering my love for Jesus helps me talk to others in ways that show His love to them.

Talk About

>> **In our Bible story, James refers to our tongues, or our words, as BEING powerful as a horse's bit, a ship's rudder and the spark of a fire. Why are all these items so powerful?** (They turn the horse or the ship, and the spark turns into a fire.)

>> **Why are our words so powerful? How might the things we say make a difference in the lives of others?**

>> Read John 13:35. **How does Jesus say other people will be able to know that we are Christians, or followers of Jesus? How can kids your age use their words to show that they love others?** (We can say things to encourage others or compliment them. We can pray for others. We keep away from making fun of others or gossiping about them.)

>> **What's the hardest part for kids in remembering to talk to others in ways that don't hurt them?** (We get angry. We say something without thinking. Other kids often say bad words.) Lead children in a brief prayer, asking God's help in showing love for Jesus by saying good words that help others instead of hurt them.

For Younger Children

Provide only play dough for children to make their creations.

© 2007 Gospel Light. Permission to photocopy granted. *Agents in Action*

LESSON THIRTEEN

Worship Center
for younger and older children
James 3:2-12

Collect

Bibles, *Agent* Music CD and player, song charts (pp. 251, 254), four large sheets of construction paper, marker, several resealable plastic bags filled with individually wrapped candies or stickers.

Preparation

Divide words of John 13:35 into four phrases. Print each phrase on a separate sheet of construction paper.

Team Game

Play "Smart Choices" on CD. While music plays, students toss plastic bags around the room. After 10 seconds, stop the music. Student holding the bag takes out one piece of candy or one sticker and reseals the bag. Continue until all students have taken a piece of candy or sticker from the bag. (If group is large, student gives candy or sticker to him- or herself and several others.)

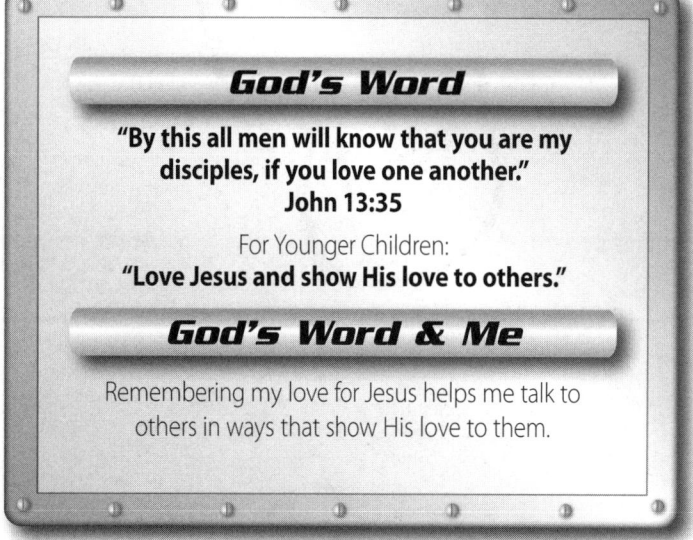

God's Word

"By this all men will know that you are my disciples, if you love one another."
John 13:35

For Younger Children:
"Love Jesus and show His love to others."

God's Word & Me

Remembering my love for Jesus helps me talk to others in ways that show His love to them.

Bible Verse Game

Repeat John 13:35 aloud with children. Then assign each child a number from one to four. Give each prepared verse paper to a child with one of the assigned numbers. Children holding papers stand facing group. Lead children in repeating verse with all children assigned number one saying the first phrase of the verse and so on. All children say the Bible reference. Repeat activity as time and interest permit, changing the phrases assigned to each group of children.

Song

Lead children in singing "Psalm 34:12-14." Add motions and/or clapping if desired.

Prayer

Because we have been talking today about the importance of the words we say, let's use our words in a good way by saying a prayer together. Lead children in prayer, saying one phrase at a time and asking children to repeat the phrase. Ask God's help in showing our love for Jesus by talking to others in ways that help them instead of hurting them.

Song

Lead children in singing "Train Me Up." Add motions and/or clapping if desired.

© 2007 Gospel Light. Permission to photocopy granted. *Agents in Action*

LESSON THIRTEEN · Pattern Page

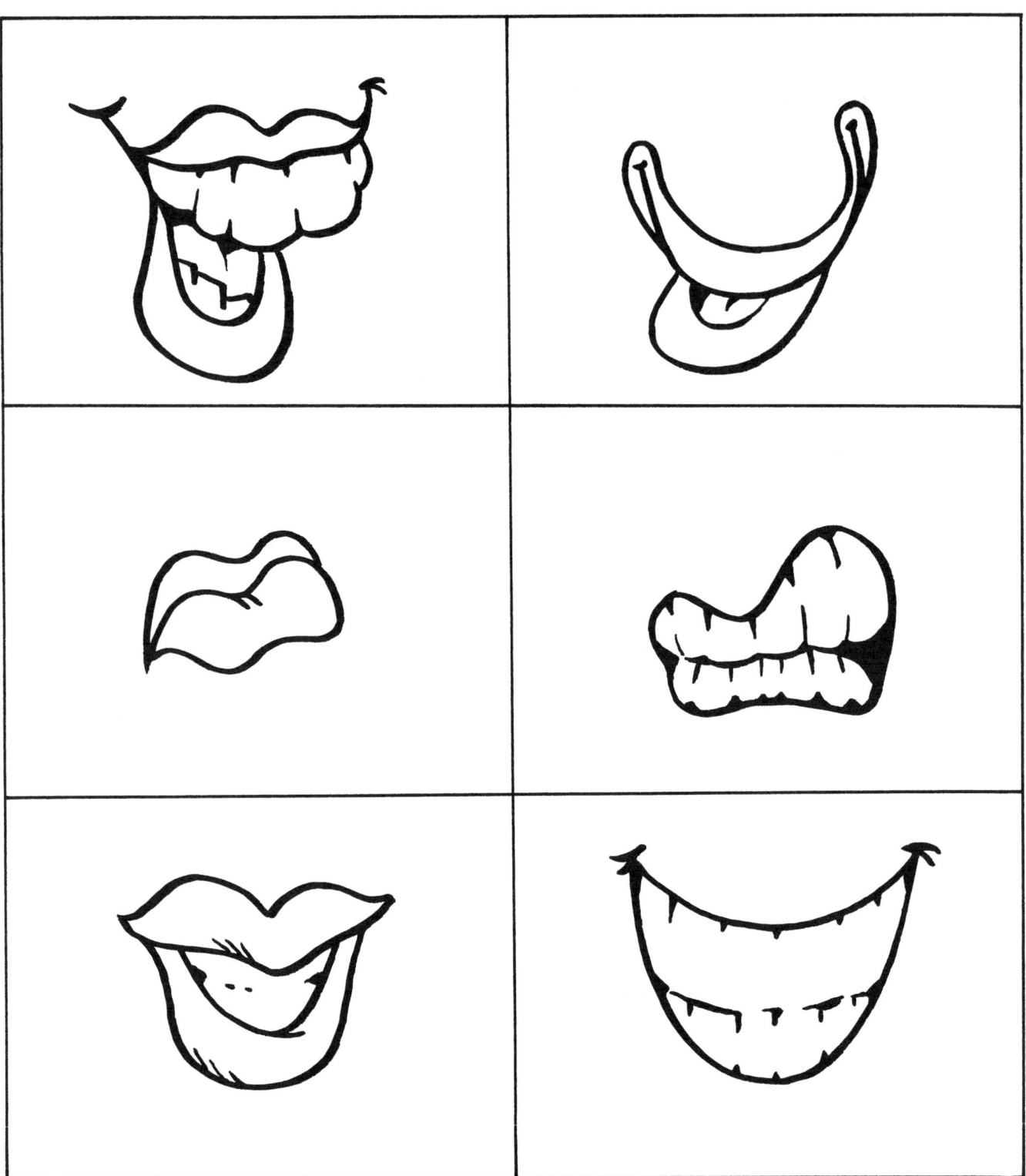

LESSON THIRTEEN • Coloring Page

Who is someone you can say good words to?

Be careful to say good words.
James 3:2-12

© 2007 Gospel Light. Permission to photocopy granted. *Agents in Action*

LESSON THIRTEEN • Puzzle Page

IT'S A DOG'S LIFE!

The Challenge

John 13:35
Uh-oh. The dog has torn up the Bible verse. Can you put the pieces together and then memorize the verse?

- will
- this
- John
- are
- "By
- if
- another."
- you
- that
- all
- you
- love
- my
- one
- 13:35
- disciples,
- men
- know

Resources

Look in this section to find helpful resources that you can customize for use in your church. You will find theme-related art, decorating patterns, a lesson-planning page, song charts, publicity flyers and more!

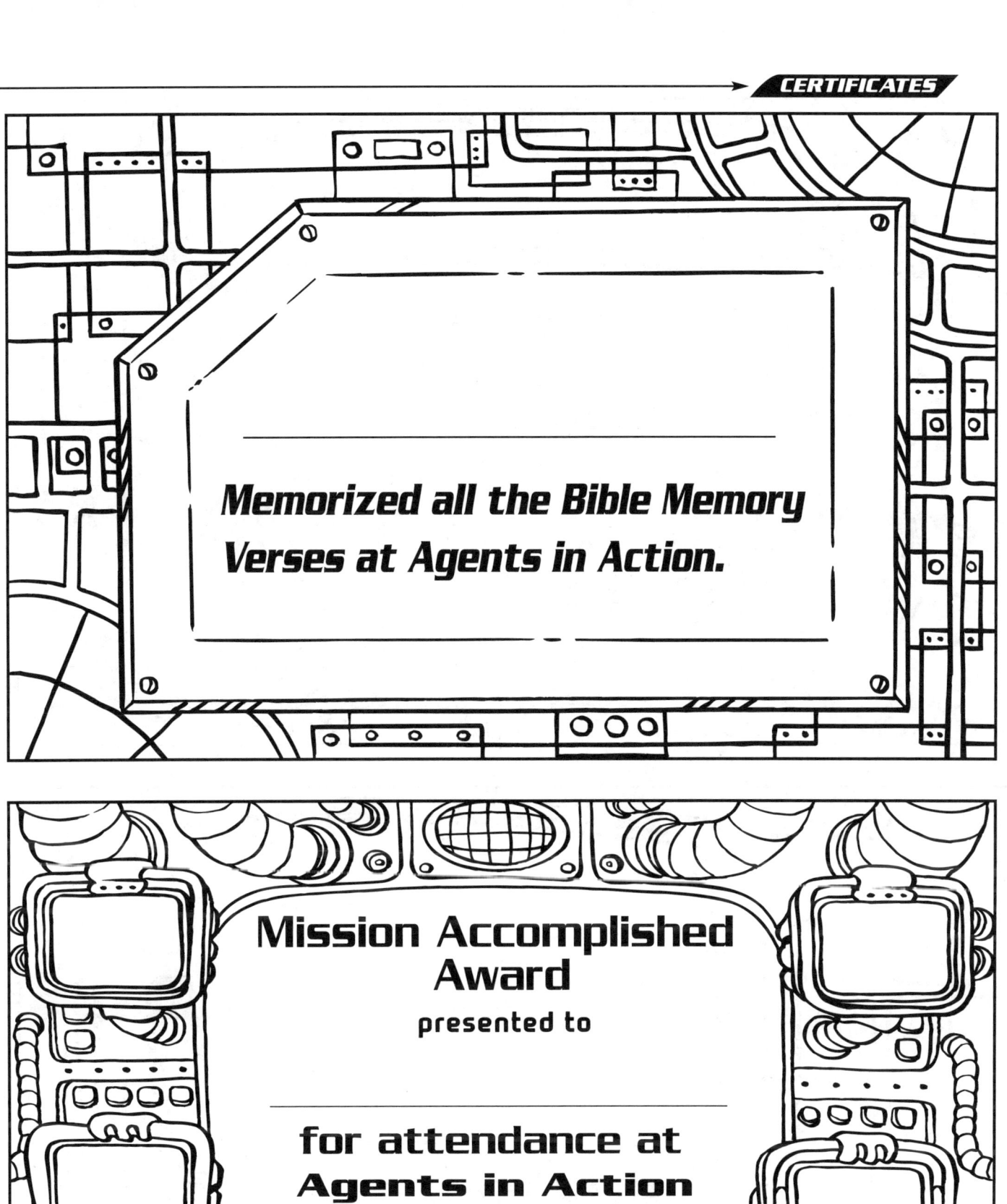

Thanks for being an Agent in Action!

Thank you for leading the way at Agents in Action.

FAMILY TALK

Today's date _____

What we read
_____
_____
_____
_____

One thing we already knew
_____
_____
_____

One thing we did not know
_____
_____
_____

One truth about God
_____
_____
_____
_____
_____

One thing to thank God for
_____
_____
_____
_____

One way we can live as God's disciples
_____
_____
_____
_____

One thing to ask God for
_____
_____
_____
_____
_____

© 2007 Gospel Light. Permission to photocopy granted. *Agents in Action*

PARENT LETTERS

Help parents become familiar with *Agents in Action* and encourage their child's attendance by sending a letter to each family several weeks before the program begins. Use this sample letter as inspiration to create your own letter. On page 233 you'll find two invitations you can modify to invite parents to join in on the fun at *Agents in Action*.

Dear Parents,

Plan now to have your child participate in unique special-agent excitement at *Agents in Action*—a 13-week adventure in discovering what it means to live courageously every day as God's disciple.

Each Sunday from 10:00 to 11:00 A.M. in the Children's Ministry Building your child is invited to a time of songs, games, Bible stories, creative art and more! Senior Agent guides are waiting to lead your child in the adventure of the summer.

Agents in Action begins Sunday, June 20th! Sign up today by calling the church office at 555-5555 or by e-mailing jean@yourchurch.org.

PATTERNS

Use these patterns to enhance bulletin announcements, forms and flyers. Pattern can also be used to decorate bulletin boards, classrooms, hallways and church buildings. Follow these three easy steps to enlarge patterns:

1. Make overhead transparencies of the patterns using a photocopier and project patterns onto butcher paper taped onto wall or onto portions of large appliance boxes.
2. Trace patterns with pencil.
3. Cut out patterns and then use markers or paint to color them. (Hint: To save time, you may also project patterns directly onto construction paper.)

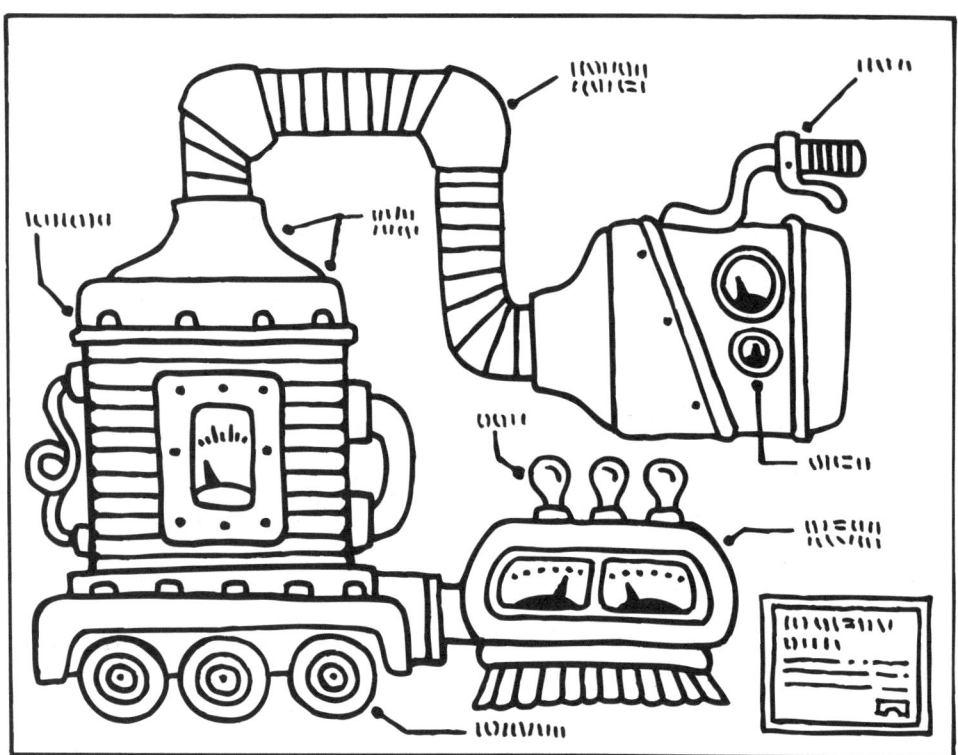

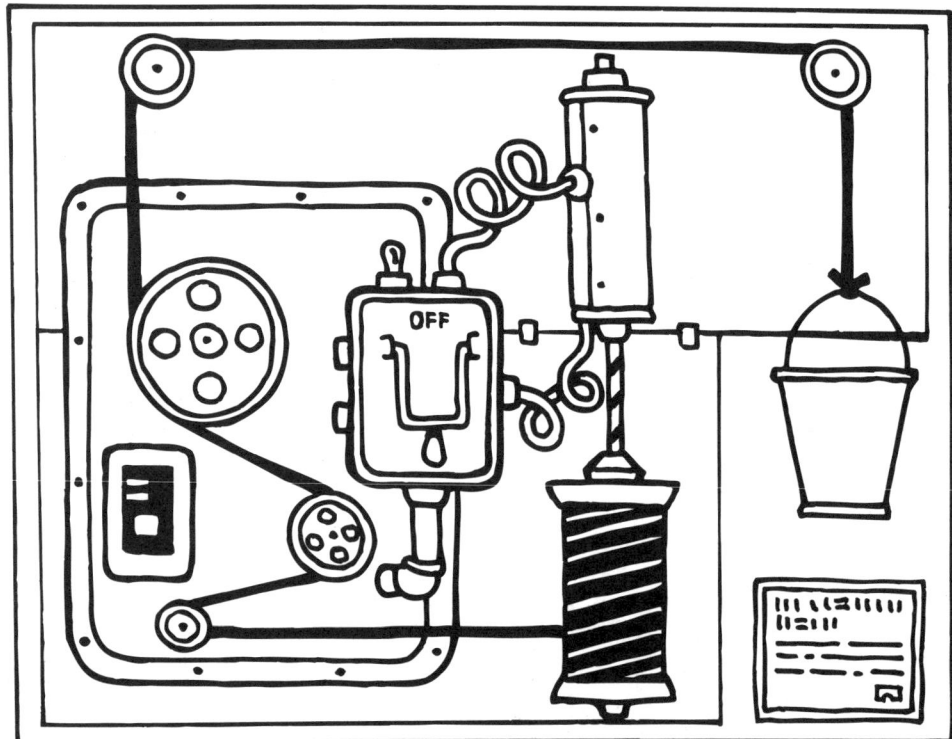

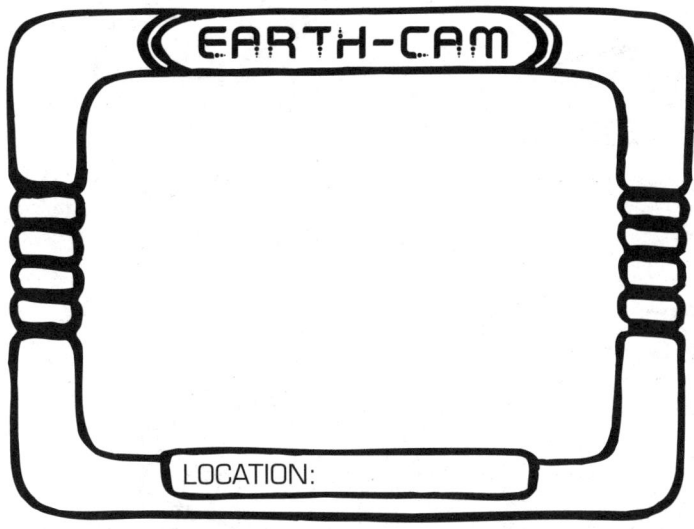

PLANNING PAGE

Agents in Action

Date(s) _____

Lesson # and Title _____

Teaching Team _____

Time

Center

Materials

Teachers

Helpers

Special Agent Adventure

Discover your Daily Mission at Agents in Action!

Date _____

Time _____

Place _____

TOP SECRET

NAME / NOM _____
No. _____

Sign up today!

Here's your mission!
Come to *Agents in Action* and meet the challenge of being a special agent for God!

Date _____

Time _____

Place _____

Sign up now!

Psst!
We're looking for you!
Don't miss out on a special-agent adventure!

Date _____

Time _____

Place _____

Sign up today!

PUZZLE ANSWERS

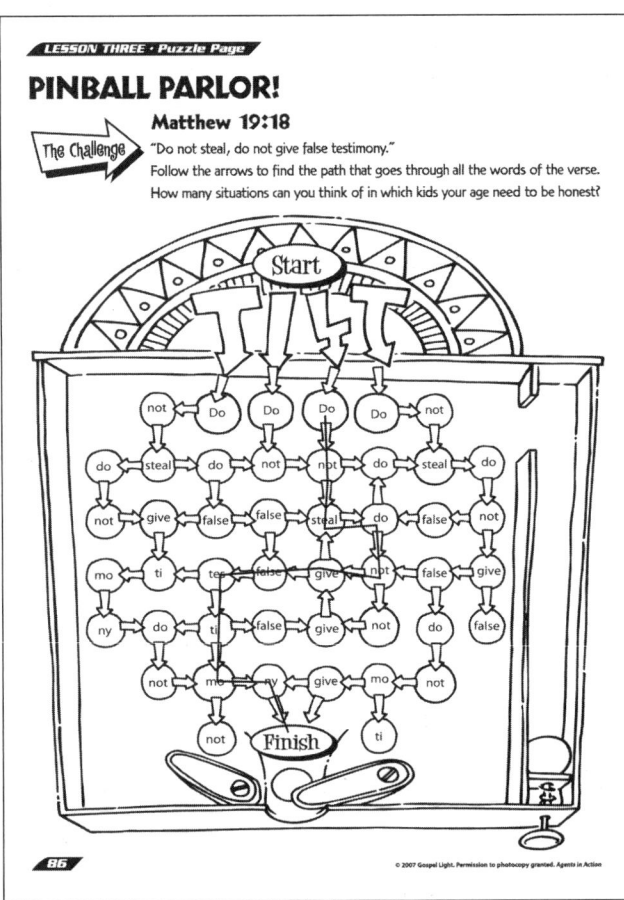

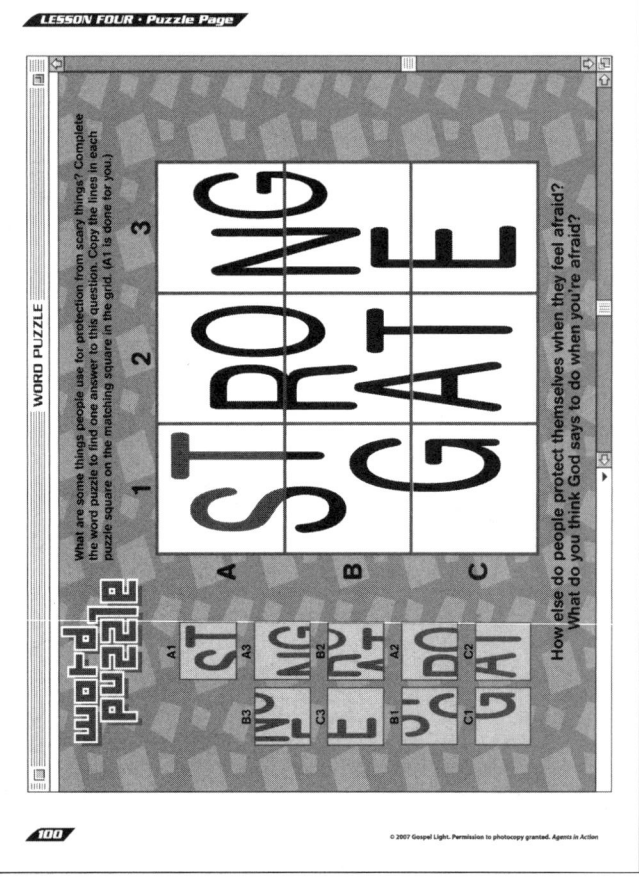

PUZZLE ANSWERS

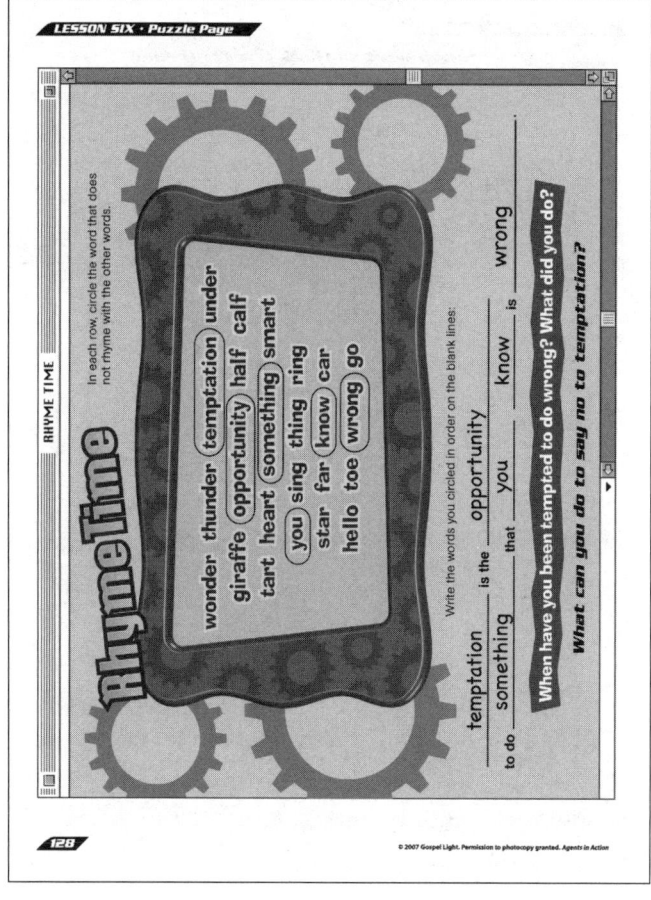

PUZZLE ANSWERS

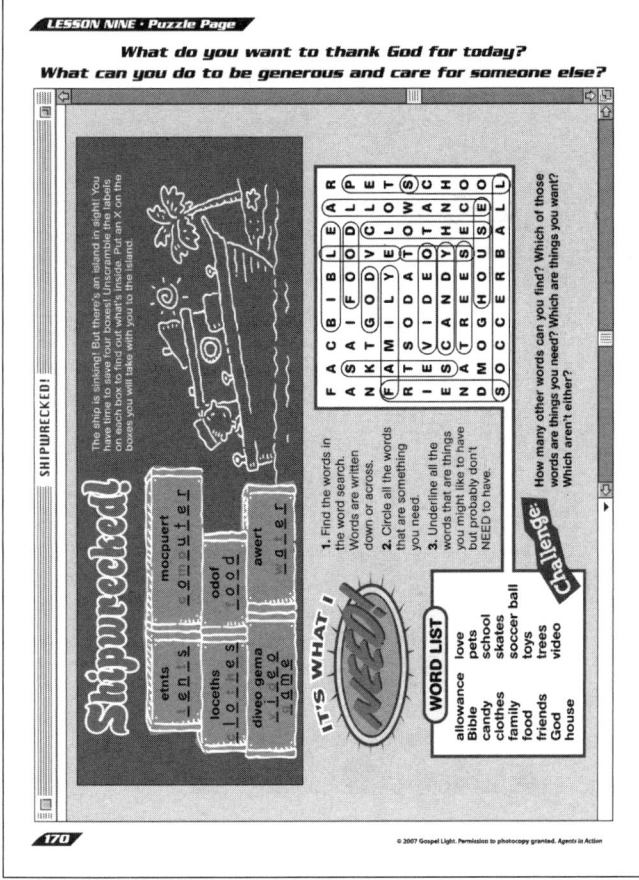

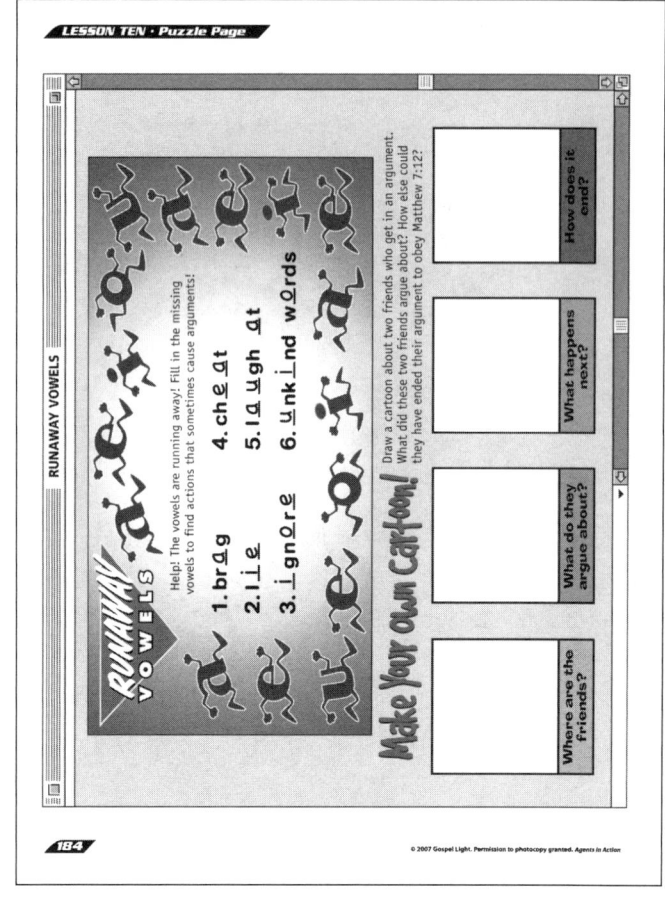

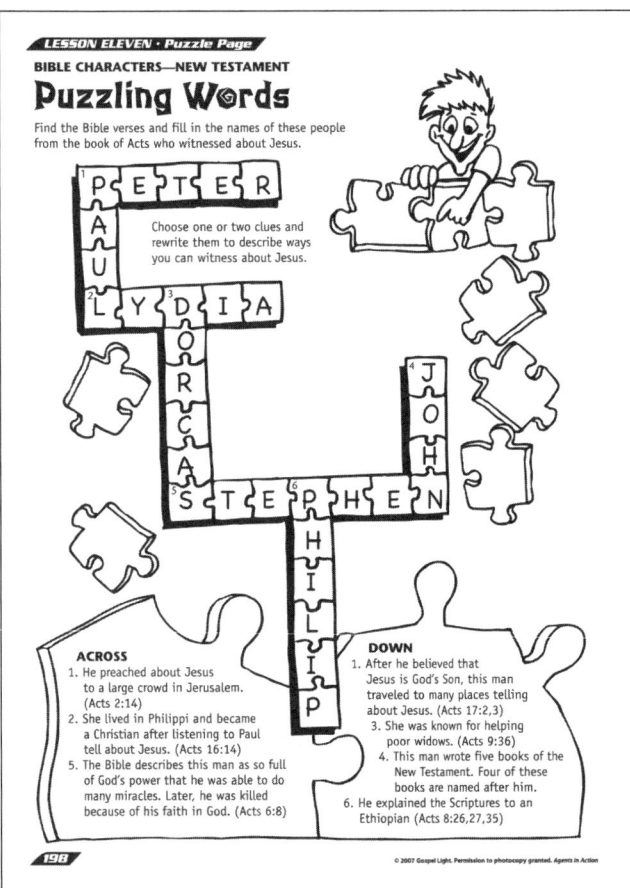

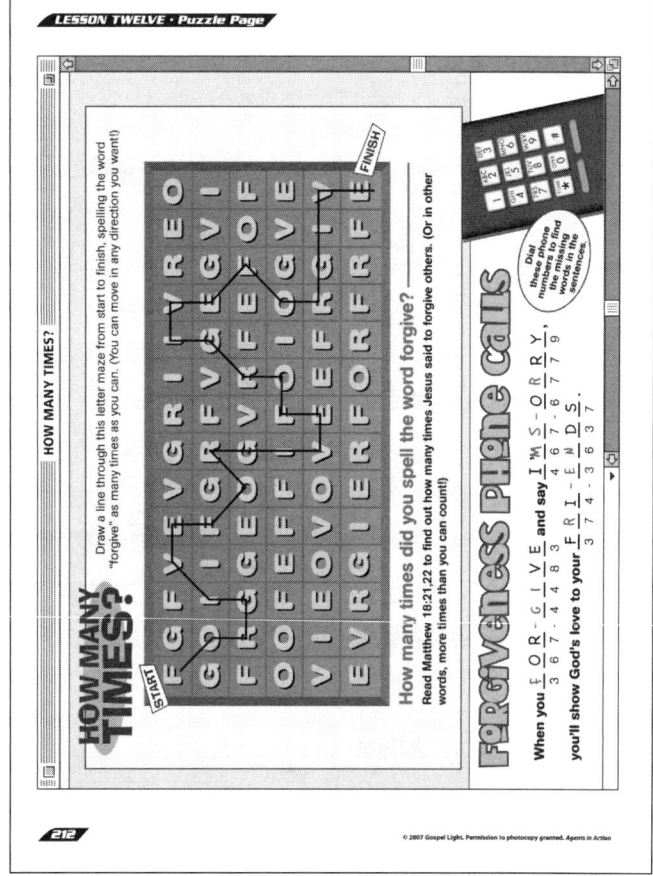

PUZZLE ANSWERS

Agents in Action Song Charts

God's Kids

by Jamie Owens Collins

We're a special team

Called to live extreme.

Strong and courageous,

Standing for the right.

We will all unite.

Love is contagious.

Even when it's hard,

We'll obey God's Word,

Following Jesus.

Won't you come along?

God will make us strong

To go where He leads us.

We're God's kids

Trusting in Jesus,

God's kids

Here to unite,

God's kids

Training for service.

We'll follow and lead
others to God's light.

All of the Time

You gotta trust (trust!), trust *(trust!)* in the Lord;

You gotta trust in the Lord with all of your heart.

You gotta trust (trust!), trust *(trust!)* in the Lord;

And obey God all of the time.

God knows how the world works;

God knows what's best for you.

God knows where you're goin'

And He will help you through!

You gotta trust *(trust!)*, trust *(trust!)* in the Lord;

You gotta trust in the Lord with all of your heart.

You gotta trust *(trust!)*, trust *(trust!)* in the Lord;

And obey God all of the time.

And obey God all of the time.

And obey God all of the time.

Words and Music by Judy and Marc Roth. © 2003 Gospel Light. Permission to photocopy granted. *Agents in Action*

Be Strong and Courageous

by Jamie Owens Collins

Chorus

Be strong *(be strong)* **and courageous.**

Be strong *(be strong)* **and courageous.**

Be strong *(be strong)* **and courageous.**

Be strong and courageous.

Do not be terrified.

Do not be discouraged.

For the Lord your God will be with you

Wherever you go.

Chorus

Do not be terrified.

Do not be discouraged.

For the Lord your God will be with you

Wherever you go.

Chorus

Bridge

Our God will make us strong,

Strong and courageous.

Our God will make us strong,

Strong and courageous.

Our God will make us strong,

Strong and courageous.

Chorus

Shout:

Be strong and courageous.

Gotta Give It Up!

Chorus

Gotta give it up, give it out, give it once again;

Gotta give generously.

Gotta give it up, give it out, give it once again;

'Cause the good goes around

And God gives it to you again.

God gives good gifts;

He's the greatest giver ever!

He gave Jesus to us!

If we're going to give like God gave to us,

Then we've gotta give good things—gotta be generous!

Chorus

Mission of Love

by Cathy Spurr

I'm a "not so secret" agent
Sent on a mission of love.
I'm here to tell the world around me
You are the Savior from above.
You came on a mission of mercy
To seek and to save the lost.
You left Your throne in heaven
To die upon the cross.

Chorus:
Mission of love—
I will follow where You lead me.
Mission of love—
In every word I say and do
I wanna be like You.

I'm a citizen of heaven,
but my mission's here on Earth.
I share Your promises with others
So they can have a second birth.
Jesus, dying was Your mission.
You saved the world from sin.
The grave—You left it empty
By rising up again.

Chorus

Bridge:
"Not so secret" agent
On a mission of love.
I'm a "not so secret" agent
On a mission of love.

You came on a
   mission of mercy
To seek and to save the lost.
You left Your throne in heaven
To die upon the cross.

Chorus:
Mission of love—
I will follow where You lead me.
Mission of love—
In every word I say and do

Repeat

I wanna be
like You.

Psalm 34:12-14

Whoever of you loves life

And desires to see many good days,

Keep your tongue from evil

And your lips from speaking lies.

Turn from evil and do good;

Seek peace and pursue it.

Repeat

Turn from evil and do good;

Seek peace and pursue it.

Smart Choices

It takes courage *(it takes courage)*

Every day *(every day)*

To make smart choices *(to make smart choices)*

And obey *(And obey!)*.

So be brave *(so be brave)*,

Don't be afraid *(don't be afraid!)*.

Choose to do things *(choose to do things)*

God's way *(God's way!)*.

Make smart choices! *(Smart choices!)*

Make up your mind to be kind;

When things get rough, don't stop *(Don't stop!)*.

Keep on doing what is right and don't give up!

Make smart choices! *(Smart choices!)*

It takes courage *(it takes courage)*

Every day *(every day)*

To make smart choices *(to make smart choices)*

And obey *(And obey!)*.

So be brave *(so be brave)*,

Don't be afraid *(don't be afraid!)*.

Choose to do things *(choose to do things)*

God's way *(God's way!)*.

Make smart choices! *(Smart choices!)*

Make smart choices! *(Smart choices!)*

Make smart choices!

Words and Music by Gary Pailer. © 2003 Gospel Light. Permission to photocopy granted. *Agents in Action*

That's What I'm Gonna Do

Jesus loves me and I love Him;

I talk to Him every day.

I want to be kind like Him;

Jesus, show me the way!

Chorus:

I can show the kind of kindness He showed to me;

I can give the kind of love that He gave.

I can help like He helped, and be patient, too.

Because I love You, Lord, that's what I'm gonna do.

Words and Music by Mary Gross Davis. © 2003 Gospel Light. Permission to photocopy granted. *Agents in Action*

Train Me Up

by Cathy Spurr

Train me up in His service.

Help me walk in the ways of the Lord.

Teach the words that give me power.

I am trusting in the plan of the Lord.

Chorus:

In His service, I will listen for direction.

In His service, I will fight the good fight.

In His service, I will follow where He leads me,

Singing, "Everybody in His name unite!"

Train me up in His service.

Help me stand, like a rock in the tide.

Courage comes when I trust Him.

I know my Savior's here by my side.

Chorus twice

Tag

Train me up to be

A servant to my King.

Train me up to know

The way that I should go.

Train me up!

THE ALL-PURPOSE CHILDREN'S MINISTRY SOLUTION!

For Grades 1 to 6

KidsTime is perfect for those times of the week when teachers need a **flexible, easy-to-use program**, or when there aren't enough teachers and children of different ages need to be combined into one group. These "year in a box" programs are an unbeatable value!

Use **KidsTime** for: Any number of kids • Any number of teachers • Limited budgets • Second hour on Sunday • Children's church • Midweek programs • Evening programs • Whenever you have a group of kids!

52-Lesson Kit
Grades 1 to 6
Reproducible
ISBN 08307.23455

Now teachers can make sure their kids get **God's Big Picture**—not just bits and pieces. With **KidsTime: God's Big Picture**, teachers can show them how the whole Bible fits together, the way God meant it. This course is packed with fun activities for kids and brings Scripture into focus as a beautiful portrait of God's love for His people and His interaction with them.

52-Lesson Kit
Grades 1 to 6
Reproducible
ISBN 08307.25415

KidsTime: God's People Celebrate gives kids the big picture of worship as they celebrate His gifts to us. Each lesson includes Bible stories, worship, music, games, art, puzzles and object talks. Includes Old Testament holiday celebrations, church calendar and seasonal holidays.

52-Lesson Kit
Grades 1 to 6
Reproducible
ISBN 08307.25792

KidsTime: God's Kids Grow Kit gives teachers a whole year's worth of fun-filled lessons that help kids explore the **fruit of the Spirit** through art, songs, games, Bible stories, service projects and more! Plus, kids can discover real-life stories of how Christians have shown the fruit of the Spirit. It's a great way to help kids grow the fruit of the Spirit in their own lives.

Available at your Gospel Light supplier or by calling 1-800-4-GOSPEL.

Gospel Light
God's Word for a Kid's World!
www.gospellight.com

Honor Your Sunday School Teachers

On Sunday School Teacher Appreciation Day the Third Sunday in October

Churches across America are invited to set aside the third Sunday in October as a day to honor Sunday School teachers for their dedication, hard work and life-changing impact on their students. That's why Gospel Light launched **Sunday School Teacher Appreciation Day** in 1993, with the goal of honoring the 15 million Sunday School teachers nationwide who dedicate themselves to teaching the Word of God to children, youth and adults.

Visit **www.mysundayschoolteacher.com** to learn great ways to honor your teachers on Sunday School Teacher Appreciation Day and throughout the year.

An integral part of Sunday School Teacher Appreciation Day is the national search for the **Sunday School Teacher of the Year.** This award was established in honor of Dr. Henrietta Mears— a famous Christian educator who influenced the lives of such well-known and respected Christian leaders as Dr. Billy Graham, Bill and Vonette Bright, Dr. Richard Halverson, and many more.

You can honor your Sunday School teachers by nominating them for this award. If one of your teachers is selected, he or she will receive **a dream vacation for two to Hawaii,** plus free curriculum, resources and more for your church!

Nominate your teachers online at **www.mysundayschoolteacher.com.**

Sponsored by

Gospel Light

Helping you honor Sunday School teachers, the unsung heroes of the faith.

In Partnership With